CU00669896

The Yogi's Joy

Also by Sangharakshita

Books on Buddhism
The Eternal Legacy
A Survey of Buddhism
The Ten Pillars of Buddhism
The Three Jewels

Edited Seminars and Lectures
The Bodhisattva Ideal
Buddha Mind
The Buddha's Victory
Buddhism for Today – and Tomorrow
Creative Symbols of Tantric Buddhism
The Drama of Cosmic Enlightenment
The Essence of Zen
A Guide to the Buddhist Path
Human Enlightenment
The Inconceivable Emancipation
Know Your Mind
Living with Awareness
Living with Kindness
The Meaning of Conversion in
    Buddhism
New Currents in Western Buddhism
Ritual and Devotion in Buddhism
The Taste of Freedom
Tibetan Buddhism: An Introduction
Vision and Transformation
What Is the Dharma?
What Is the Sangha?
Who Is the Buddha?
Wisdom Beyond Words

Essays
Alternative Traditions
Crossing the Stream
Forty-Three Years Ago
The FWBO and 'Protestant Buddhism'
Going for Refuge
The History of My Going for Refuge
The Priceless Jewel
Was the Buddha a Bhikkhu?

Memoirs and Letters
Facing Mount Kanchenjunga
In the Sign of the Golden Wheel
Moving Against the Stream
The Rainbow Road
Travel Letters
Through Buddhist Eyes
From Genesis to the Diamond Sutra

Art and Poetry
The Call of the Forest and Other Poems
Complete Poems 1941–1994
In the Realm of the Lotus
The Religion of Art

Miscellaneous
Ambedkar and Buddhism
A Stream of Stars

The Yogi's Joy

Songs of Milarepa

Sangharakshita

windhorse publications

Published by
Windhorse Publications Ltd
11 Park Road
Birmingham
B13 8AB
United Kingdom

© Sangharakshita 2006

Cover image: Angelo Cavalli / Getty Images
Cover design: Satyadarshin
Printed by Cromwell Press Ltd, Trowbridge, England
on Fineblade Extra, wood free / chlorine free paper
conforming to ISO 9706: 1994 (E) and ANSI / NISO Z39.48:1992

A catalogue record for this book is available from the British Library
ISBN-10: 1 899579 66 4
ISBN-13: 978 1 899579 66 2

The right of Sangharakshita to be identified as the author of this work
has been asserted by him in accordance with the Copyright, Designs and
Patents Act 1988

Every effort has been made to obtain permission to reprint selections
from *The Hundred Thousand Songs of Milarepa,* translation © Garma C.C.
Chang 1999, published by Shambhala Publications Inc. If any omission
has been made please let us know so that this may be rectified in a future
edition.

Contents

About the Author   vii
Foreword   ix
Preface   xiii

1 Milarepa's World and Philosophy   1

First Story – The Tale of Red Rock Jewel Valley
  2 Finding the Sangha   7

Second Story – The Song of a Yogi's Joy
  3 Beyond Fear   43

Third Story – The Meeting at Silver Spring
  4 A Man of the Beyond   63

  5 Free from Ego   83

  6 Pleasing the Guru   123

  7 Listening for the Teachings   143

  8 Laying Down Your Doubts   183

Notes and References   225
Further Reading   227
Index   229

About the Author

Sangharakshita was born Dennis Lingwood in South London, in 1925. Largely self-educated, he developed an interest in the cultures and philosophies of the East early on, and realized that he was a Buddhist at the age of sixteen.

The Second World War took him, as a conscript, to India, where he stayed on to become the Buddhist monk Sangharakshita. After studying for some years under leading teachers from the major Buddhist traditions, he went on to teach and write extensively. He also played a key part in the revival of Buddhism in India, particularly through his work among followers of Dr B.R. Ambedkar.

After twenty years in India, he returned to England to establish the Friends of the Western Buddhist Order in 1967, and the Western Buddhist Order (called Trailokya Bauddha Mahasangha in India) in 1968. A translator between East and West, between the traditional world and the modern, between principles and practices, Sangharakshita's depth of experience and clear thinking have been appreciated throughout the world. He has always particularly emphasized the decisive significance of commitment in the spiritual life, the paramount value of spiritual friendship and community, the link between religion and art, and the need for a 'new society' supportive of spiritual aspirations and ideals.

From his base in Birmingham, he is now focusing on personal contact with people, and on his writing.

Foreword

Milarepa lived in a cave. He was a hermit. He liked to meditate. Occasionally he would meet someone. He would sing songs to them. That's about it, really.

Oh yes, and this was in medieval Tibet, long before there was any Dalai Lama. Obscurity beckoned compellingly, but for one thing: Milarepa was a master of *mahāmudrā*, the direct realization of the nature of mind and reality, and he was able to communicate this realization to a visitor who would later be known as Gampopa and who would establish one of the leading schools of Tibetan Buddhism, the Kagyu, or 'Whispered Transmission'.

As a result, Milarepa is Tibet's best-loved historical Buddhist. He holds a similar place in the hearts of the Tibetan people to that of Ryōkan in the Japanese. Like Ryōkan, he was a hermit who left a legacy of poetry and kindness that has inspired the most ordinary people with the very highest teachings of Buddhism.

Obscurity also seemed to have marked Sangharakshita for its own when he was born plain Dennis Lingwood in an undistinguished London suburb in 1925, and even when, like Milarepa, he became a Buddhist and a poet. In the event, Sangharakshita's spiritual career has been anything but obscure, and the Buddhist movements he has led in India and in the West have been anything but reclusive. A number of his followers have become hermits, but most of them are engaged in making an impact on the world much more directly.

Sangharakshita has published standard books on Buddhism, several volumes of memoirs, a few collections of poetry and essays, and an occasional polemic. A whole extra layer of his literary output, however, consists of edited versions of his talks and seminars, of which this book is one.

So we have two quite distinct types of work that carry his name. One he has written himself in his own literary style; the other is closer to the style in which he speaks, especially the way he speaks in the context of a seminar. And it is not just a question of style. The origin of these books has an effect on their content too.

Clearly it involves some sleight of hand to turn a seminar into a book, but as his editors, we are disinclined to dress the material up as something it really isn't. It is not a thoroughly researched study of the text under examination, but more of a leisurely stroll around it in the company of someone with a profound experience of what the text is talking about and an extraordinarily well-stocked mind. For example, while he is evidently able to speak of the 'clear light of the void' from personal experience, he can also draw upon detailed knowledge of the eighteenth-century British imperial tradition in discussing its philosophical basis.

Sometimes one has to look for material from other sources to fill out a discussion that seems a bit truncated, but we try to include everything discussed on the seminar within the book, and to avoid more cutting and pasting between seminars than we have to. This is because there is usually a particular way of looking at the Dharma being put forward in any one seminar or series of seminars. You will get some occasionally slightly idiosyncratic angles of approach to the text under discussion, but there is a certain integrity to the seminar as a whole which we are keen to retain.

Sangharakshita has given more seminars on the songs of Milarepa than on any other teachings from a single individual. There are various reasons for this. There is the fact that Milarepa communicates in poetry. This chimes with Sangharakshita's view of the importance of refining our communication and our modes of experiencing the world. Then there is Milarepa's uncompromising rejection of the world's values. While he has always gone out to meet the world rather than exemplify complete renunciation like Milarepa, Sangharakshita has in his own way turned his back on mundane accommodations just as firmly. He has never traded his values or courted the world's approval.

Most significantly, perhaps, the songs express spiritual friendship. Like many of the Pali suttas or Zen koans, they usually express the Enlightened consciousness confronting a more or less worldly mind. More than this, they record an ongoing and developing relationship between them. In view of Milarepa's chosen lifestyle, they show what the spiritual life is essentially about. They illustrate one of Sangharakshita's constant themes, which is the fact that even if you go and live in a cave, your practice is essentially about human relationship.

Finally, the songs express a thorough delight in the Dharma. This again has been something Sangharakshita has insisted upon from the time he returned to England from India in the early 1960s, when he found people practising the Dharma as a form of grim masochism. Milarepa shows that however you choose to pursue your practice, even living in a cave and surviving on nettles, there is no excuse not to thoroughly enjoy it.

It is always a bit difficult to justify pursuing a solitary spiritual life. What possible good are you doing anyone apart from very possibly yourself? Milarepa embodies the answer to this. In the end it comes down to the Buddhist principle of interconnectedness or conditionality. In spite of Milarepa's devotion to seclusion and the solitary life – or should we say because of it? – here we are, nearly a thousand years later, and on the other side of the world, drawing inspiration from it.

Sangharakshita has led a much more obviously public life than Milarepa, firing the inspiration of perhaps hundreds of thousands of people over his years in India and in the West. But, like Milarepa, his concern has always been to connect with the individual, with what is truly individual and aware in his listener or reader. This book will, we hope, facilitate such a connection.

A lot of work goes into these books, and this is only possible thanks to the great generosity of individual donors and those who have over the years worked in shops and warehouses and vans to provide the Sangharakshita legacy fund with the means to support us. Special thanks are due to Vidyadevi, who very kindly checked the whole text herself and went through it with Sangharakshita, making amendments as necessary. Thanks also to the Windhorse Publications team, Shantavira in particular, who as usual shone the clear light of his editing professionalism on to all that was lazy and shoddy in our efforts.

Jinananda and Pabodhana
Spoken Word Project
October 2005

Preface

In Tibetan Buddhist art Milarepa (c.1040–1123) is depicted as an ascetic, naked except for a white loincloth and a red meditation band. He sits cross-legged in a cave in the snowy mountains. His cupped right hand is held to his ear to show that he is singing – joyfully singing songs of spiritual instruction. He sings to men and women of all sorts and conditions, as well as to demons and goddesses. His songs are rich in imagery, and laced with humour, and though adapted to the capacities of his hearers they frequently touch upon the deepest truths and sublimest realizations of Buddhism.

Although he has a special connection with the Kagyu school, Milarepa is revered by all Tibetan Buddhists, and the story of his life is known, and his songs are sung, throughout the Tibetan cultural area. For the last seventy or more years that life, and those songs, have also been known in the West, thanks initially to the joint labours of the American scholar Dr W.Y. Evans-Wentz and the Sikkimese lama Kazi Dawa-Samdup, whose pioneering work *Tibet's Great Yogi Milarepa* was published by the Oxford University Press in 1928 as the second volume of the famous Oxford Tibetan Series. Herein Milarepa, at the request of Rechung, one of his two chief disciples, tells how on the death of his father he was cheated out of his inheritance by his paternal uncle and aunt; how at the instigation of his mother he learned the Black Art and destroyed thirty-six of his family's enemies by magic; and how, repenting of the evil he had done, he finds his way to

Marpa the Translator (1012–1097) and becomes his disciple. Marpa is himself a disciple of the Indian tantric sage Naropa (1016–1100), a disciple of Tilopa (988–1069), who had received instruction directly from the Buddha Vajradhara. These gurus taught orally, and their lineage, of which Milarepa was to be the brightest ornament, thereafter became known in Tibet as the Kagyu school or School of the Oral Transmission.

The early Kagyu gurus were noted for the extreme severity with which they treated their disciples, and Marpa is no exception. In order to purify Milarepa of his sins and make him a fit candidate for tantric initiation, he subjects him to a series of strange trials and great tribulations both bodily and mental. At last his probation is completed, he is initiated, and Marpa predicts that as a result of his patience and faith in his guru he will have many worthy disciples full of faith, energy, intelligence, and compassion. Marpa then leaves on his last journey to India, and Milarepa pays a visit to his own birthplace. There he finds his house in ruins, the sacred books soaked in rain and covered with dust, and a weed-grown heap of rags and earth proves to be his mother's bones. The experience so disillusions him that he resolves to spend the rest of his life meditating in solitude. This he does, dwelling year after year amid the snows of the Himalayas, ever deepening his insight into the Dharma, attracting disciples, and teaching through his spiritual songs whoever comes to him. The marvels that accompany his last illness, death, and cremation attest to his having attained Buddhahood.

In 1962 our knowledge of Tibet's poet-yogi was greatly enlarged by the publication of *The Hundred Thousand Songs of Milarepa*, an annotated translation of the *Mila Grubum* by Garma C.C. Chang. The songs – not literally a hundred thousand in number – are distributed among a total of sixty-one stories, as Chang calls them; and during the years 1976–80 I held seminars on eleven of these stories. *A Yogi's Joy* is based on an edited transcript of three of the seminars, two of which were held in 1976 and one in 1978. All three seminars took place in a retreat centre in Norfolk, England, and in the course of each one of them we were swept in imagination from the flat East Anglian country-side to the awe-inspiring scenery of Tibet, with its towering snow-capped peaks, its deep sunless ravines, and its pleasant, flower-carpeted upland valleys. There we heard the clear voice of Milarepa singing his timeless songs. He sang to us, as he had sung to the men and women of his own day, of the joy of living without possessions, the joy of meditating in solitude, the joy of uncompromising commitment to the realization of the highest spiritual ideal.

In these days of consumerism, the mass media, and materialistic values, the world needs more than ever to listen to the voice of Milarepa and take the message of his songs to heart. It is my sincere hope that *A Yogi's Joy* may be a means of making that message more widely known.

Chapter 1

Milarepa's World and Philosophy

A Singing Guru

The stories we are going to consider here are taken from a work known as *The Hundred Thousand Songs of Milarepa*, which records the inspired poetic utterances of the famous, revered, and much loved eleventh-century Tibetan yogi and poet. The figure of one hundred thousand is a considerable exaggeration, of course, but the episodes I want to discuss do each include a number of songs which convey the distinctive flavour of the work as a whole: they are very approachable and often quite light-hearted, even humorous, while at the same time they express the very essence of dedicated spiritual practice.

They were composed almost a thousand years ago. At the time Milarepa was alive, the Normans were conquering England, and in continental Europe the Holy Roman Emperors were quarrelling with the papacy. In the Americas the Mayas were establishing a new empire in Yucatan, while in China the Northern Sung dynasty was appeasing the Mongols by surrendering territory. And in India a 1,500-year period of Buddhist culture was coming dramatically to an end – for this was the time of the Muslim invasion. Buddhist monasteries were being destroyed, monks were being murdered, gurus were being scattered, and as a result the teachings were being speedily lost. In Tibet, by contrast, Buddhism was enjoying a long-awaited renaissance. The arrival from India of the master Atīśa had coincided with a period in which centralized political control had broken up. As a result local fiefdoms were flourishing, presided over by regional nobles, and this helped to bring about a corresponding diversity of cultural and religious custom.

It is generally thought that the songs of Milarepa were compiled and written down by a yogi of the Kagyu school of Tibetan Buddhism in the fourteenth century, but we cannot be sure how many of them were passed down from Milarepa himself and how many of them were composed by the inspired compiler. It may well be that having put together the songs that had come down to his time, the writer felt there were gaps that needed to be filled and wrote extra songs where they seemed to be required. Which of the songs were sung by Milarepa himself is therefore a matter for scholars to research and debate, and we cannot take them as records of actual meetings at specific times and places. At least some of them may be composites of a number of occasions, people, and locations, but they have the fresh and vivid sense of actual events, and also communicate spiritual teachings of a high standard. From a literary point of view, the fact that the compiler may have put some of his own verses into the mouth of Milarepa hardly seems to matter. If he did, he was a great poet himself, with a considerable gift for narrative. From a spiritual point of view, if he composed some of the songs, he must have been a person of advanced spiritual development.

In Tibetan scroll paintings (called *thangkas*), Milarepa is often depicted as green in colour. This is because for many years he lived a solitary mountain existence, subsisting only on nettles, and apparently this had the effect of turning his body green. He is usually shown naked except for a small cotton cloth, his only covering in the bitter snows of the Tibetan mountain ranges. But he is remembered chiefly for his songs – and they really are songs, not just lyrical poems. In fact, we can get a pretty good idea how Milarepa's songs would have sounded. Singing and chanting are still popular and widespread among Tibetan people. I lived in the Himalayan town of Kalimpong in the 1950s, when it was starting to fill up with Tibetan refugees, and I would often meet Tibetan beggars, whether ordinary people or monks, who used to sing. They would come to the door and chant verses of blessing on the house, accompanying themselves on a little drum and setting the verses to a distinctive and pleasant melody.

The songs are about not only the harshness
and remoteness of the Tibetan mountain ranges,
but also the peaks and valleys of an inner terrain –
the inner world of the Tantric yogi.

Most of us are familiar with the kind of sound produced by Tibetan monks chanting pujas, but it is not only monks who chant in this way. Wherever there is a group of Tibetans working together, perhaps in the fields or building a house, you will hear a traditional song with very similar cadences, though without the complex overtones to be heard in the monastery. These are not sophisticated melodies; Tibetan songs are rather like those of village India, or Christian hymns, with each verse sung to the same simple tune. In the Tibetan folk tradition you sometimes have not even a melody but a simple succession of notes to which each group of two or four lines is sung. Many Tibetans could come up with a song like this more or less spontaneously, making it up as they went along. This is fairly easy because of the structure of the Tibetan language: Tibetan is largely monosyllabic and it is therefore not difficult to string words together in lines of eight or twelve syllables and chant them to a simple tune picked out on a single-stringed instrument. Anyone with a dash of ingenuity and inspiration can keep this up for a long time.

The 'hundred thousand' songs have been translated into English by Garma C.C. Chang. Here is an example of the way his translation sometimes comes close to the original verse form, with its repeated rhythm of more or less eight syllables, taken from the verses called 'Complimentary Song to the Deities of Red Rock Jewel Valley'.

This lonely spot where stands my hut
Is a place pleasing to the Buddhas,

A place where accomplished beings dwell,
A refuge where I dwell alone.[1]

The Tantric song form – the *vajra-gīta* – can be traced back to the songs of the wandering musician yogis of medieval India, who practised yoga, meditation, and other forms of spiritual training while supporting themselves in a variety of ways. Many lived a solitary life in hermitages or even cremation grounds, while others lived as householders, but they all had something in common: their uncompromising dedication to spiritual practice.

Milarepa is associated above all with inspiration, both lyrical and spiritual, and this is reflected in the poetic form in which it is expressed. The same is true of the Buddha himself, many of whose more exalted utterances are gathered in a collection of discourses known as the *Udānas*, teachings expressed in verse form suggesting heightened inspiration, a communication from an even higher level than is normal for an enlightened one.

The songs of Milarepa have significance for us because they express the truths and experiences of authentic Buddhist practice. They have an immediacy that resonates even today, so many years after they were first uttered. The songs are about not only the harshness and remoteness of the Tibetan mountain ranges, but also the peaks and valleys of an inner terrain – the inner world of the Tantric yogi.

First Story

The Tale of
Red Rock Jewel Valley

Chapter 2

Finding the Sangha

Milarepa's Mindfulness

Once the great Yogi Milarepa was staying at the Eagle Castle of (Red Rock) Jewel Valley, absorbing himself in the practice of the Mahāmudrā meditation. Feeling hungry, he decided to prepare some food, but after looking about he found there was nothing left in the cave, neither water nor fuel, let alone salt, oil, or flour. 'It seems that I have neglected things too much!' he said, 'I must go out and collect some wood.'

He went out. But when he had gathered a handful of twigs, a sudden storm arose, and the wind was strong enough to blow away the wood and tear his ragged robe. When he tried to hold the robe together, the wood blew away. When he tried to clutch the wood, the robe blew apart. (Frustrated,) Milarepa thought, 'Although I have been practising the Dharma and living in solitude for such a long time, I am still not rid of ego-clinging! What is the use of practising Dharma if one cannot subdue ego-clinging? Let the wind blow my wood away if it likes. Let the wind blow my robe off if it wishes!' Thinking thus, he ceased resisting. But, due to weakness from lack of food, with the next gust of wind he could no longer withstand the storm, and fell down in a faint.

When he came to, the storm was over. High up on the branch of a tree he saw a shred of his clothing swaying in the gentle breeze.

> *The utter futility of this world and all its affairs struck Milarepa,*
> *and a strong feeling of renunciation overwhelmed him.*

In 'The Tale of Red Rock Jewel Valley' we encounter Milarepa at a comparatively early stage in his career, when his practice is still quite a struggle and he is still more or less clothed. As we shall see, he also still possesses some books. Even so, he has evidently been practising meditation in solitude, following the practice of *mahāmudrā* – the union of bliss and emptiness – according to his guru's instructions, for a long time. And in this episode his practice suddenly bears fruit through an unexpected, if apparently trivial, turn of events, of which Milarepa is able to take advantage by means of a very basic practice: mindfulness.

It is clear that his practice of mindfulness is very effective because he is so quick to observe his instinctive reaction when his robe blows apart, and to realize what that reaction implies with regard to his spiritual development. The incident is so trivial that most people, even most practising Buddhists, wouldn't think twice about it, beyond perhaps noticing their momentary frustration at trying to do the work of three hands with two. But Milarepa is keeping a close and unremitting watch over himself, and it is the brief conflict in his mind that draws his attention to the deeper issue. Seeing beyond his frustration to the fundamental delusion underlying it, he realizes that while he is literally clinging to his robe, he is clinging to his ego just as tightly. As the wind snatches his robe from him, he observes himself possessively clinging to his meagre property and says to himself, 'What is making me cling to my robe in this way? It is because I feel that it is *mine*, it is *my* robe, *my* body needs it for covering. *I* need it.' At once recognizing this as evidence of a still active ego, he gives up his robe to the importunate tugging of the wind.

One of the best known accounts of the Buddha's teaching of mindfulness is the *Satipaṭṭhāna Sutta*,[2] the discourse on the four foundations of mindfulness. As one of the most important of the Pali *suttas*, or discourses, this text is part of the bedrock of modern-day Theravadin practice, and its theme of mindfulness remains integral to all traditions of Buddhism. Of particular relevance here is the practice of recollecting what are known as mental objects, especially the six sense bases and their objects. This aspect of mindfulness involves maintaining a continuous awareness that, as objects impinge upon consciousness via the sense bases or sense organs, various unhealthy mental states arise to intrude on that simple awareness. These unhealthy states, known collectively as the hindrances, include moods and thoughts of lust, ill will, sloth and torpor, restlessness and anxiety, and doubt. Each in its own way clouds the essential lightness and clarity of perception.

These deep-seated states of mind are a product of our karma, our deluded actions, and they form the very fabric of our self-view, our sense of who we are and hence what the world is. They are consequently extremely subtle and hard to detect. Mindfulness of one's mental processes is, for this reason, a particularly demanding practice, one that calls for every bit of striving one can muster.

Just these two things are expected of us and encapsulate everything we need to do.

Milarepa's sustained awareness of these subtle mental processes has enabled him to detect the arising of the fetter of self-view, the delusion that he is a fixed, separate entity, even as he is grasping desperately at his few remaining possessions, his robe and a few sticks of firewood. Indeed, it is at such a moment of instinctive reaction that this fetter will force itself into view, even though it is also at just such a moment that mindfulness is most likely to be lost.

Milarepa's mindfulness consists in seeing how, when the senses come into contact with their objects, any one of the hindrances may arise. Once we are able to refine consciousness to the extent that we can be aware of these subtle mental comings and goings, we then have only to understand deeply enough the significance of what we see to take the appropriate action. This calls for vigilant and unremitting practice. The hindrances do not arise with any great fanfare; on the contrary, they are extremely subtle. It is the very small things that give them away, and it is these we have to look out for, in other people and in ourselves.

This is as much as can be asked of anybody. We cannot be expected to be perfect all the time, or even much of the time. All we are invited to do is to stay awake, to keep watch over ourselves, especially with respect to small, seemingly insignificant things that we do or say or think or feel – and to take in the implications of what we notice. The task is to recognize what your observation tells you about yourself, and then to do whatever you need to do to adjust your attitude and bring it more into line with the way things really are.

The importance of mindfulness is reflected in the fact that – at least according to one tradition – the Buddha's last words to his disciples were, 'With mindfulness, strive' (*appamādena sampādetha* in Pali). It is as though just these two things are expected of us and encapsulate everything we need to do. Know what you are doing – pay attention to every last detail of your existence as it occurs. Take note of every detail of your experience as it impinges upon your consciousness – especially those details that others will probably miss. And if you notice any vestige of anything unskilful, any attachment, any impulse that 'that is mine, this is due to me,' take immediate action to change your attitude. The whole procedure is less complicated than it may sound. Milarepa manages to do it in the moment between his brief tussle with the elements and his blackout. But though it is simple and quick, its effects are truly momentous.

Near the end of this story, Milarepa comes to the conclusion that a demon was behind the storm. But why does he infer this? It may be difficult for us to imagine the power a storm in the mountains of Tibet. When I lived in the Himalayan town of Kalimpong, there was once an earth tremor that made the two-storey house in front of which I was standing actually jump a couple of inches. It was as though the whole mountain jumped. When we are exposed to the elements in this way, we get a salutary reminder of the insignificance of human intentions as far as those powers – however we interpret them – are concerned. One has only to experience the full force of such elemental powers, whether of storm, volcano, or earthquake, to begin to see the traditional belief that demons are behind those natural phenomena in a different light. Unprotected by the paraphernalia of modern civilization, we realize that we are at the mercy of natural forces beyond our control.

But here the storm is not to be taken entirely literally. Demon-created and apparently out of control, its fury and clamour are metaphors for the raging whirlwind of ego-clinging that makes our progress through this brief life of ours so very difficult and painful. Yet unlike the storms of the physical world, this tempest can be stilled if we know how to go about it. By bringing the subtle, almost imperceptible practice of mindfulness to the storm of our ego-clinging, we can eventually tame this demonic force. In Milarepa's case, just one moment of insight into the true nature of mind has caused the storm to abate, the demon of worldly clinging to vanish.

In that single hair he saw everything: old age, disease, and death, the end of all his worldly possessions.

His practice of mindfulness and insight continues when he comes round and finds himself lying naked on the ground. He has evidently been unconscious for a while because the storm is over, but the first thing he sees is a shred of his robe in the branches of a tree, fluttering in the now gentle breeze. Again, he is able to see the situation with clarity and creativity.

What strikes him is its absurdity. It is as though that shred of clothing, the last thing he possessed, represents all worldly attachments. In a mere shred of cloth he sees all worldly things, everything that one could cling to – wealth, possessions and pleasures, friends, family and connections, appearance, status and achievements. He sees that they are all liable to be taken away from us at any time. They can all just blow away.

Milarepa's practice of mahāmudrā is quite closely related to Zen, and his moment of insight is a little reminiscent of some of the stories of the Zen masters in which a very simple, apparently insignificant incident sparks off a deep realization. A monk, say, is meditating in the middle of the forest when he sees a single yellow leaf fall, and in that one moment gains insight into the transitory nature of all conditioned things. There is even a *Jātaka* tale in a similar vein (the *Jātakas* are the traditional folk tales about the Buddha's previous lives). A king is having his hair and beard trimmed when he notices that the combing and snipping stops for a moment while the barber plucks out a hair. 'What are you doing?' he says, and the barber replies, 'It is your first grey hair, sir, look.' The king gazes at that one grey hair, and then he gets up from his comfortable chair, throws off his fine clothes and walks straight out of the palace into the forest to become a wandering monk. In that single hair he saw everything: old age, disease, and death, the end of all his worldly possessions.[3]

Song of Spiritual Friendship

Milarepa's response to this realization is to sit down and meditate. As he does so, a cluster of white clouds rises from the valley to the east, above the temple of his guru, Marpa, whom he imagines teaching there his other disciples, Milarepa's 'brothers'. There seems to be a suggestion here that with the appearance of the cluster of white clouds something is happening – whether in physical form or as a vision – as the fruit of Milarepa's practice of the guru yoga, the formal visualization and veneration of his teacher. The clouds certainly serve to connect Milarepa's thoughts to his guru.

Milarepa desperately misses his guru. The profound spiritual connection between them is not enough for him in his present mood. What follows is a song of devotion to Marpa, and of longing for human contact with him. Milarepa wants to see his guru, face to face, in the flesh. He also misses Marpa's wife and his fellow disciples.

Though limited in reverence, I wish to see you;
Though weak in faith, I wish to join you.
The more I meditate, the more I long for my Guru.

Does your wife, Dagmema, still dwell with you?
To her I am more grateful than to my mother....

How happy I would be could I join the gathering,
At which you may be teaching the Hevajra Tantra....

Though short my diligence, I have need for learning;
Though poor my perseverance, I wish to practise.
The more I contemplate, the more I think of you;
The more I meditate, the more I think of my Guru.

The brothers from Weu and Tsang may be there.
If so, I would be joyful and happy.
Though inferior my Experience and Realization,
I wish to compare mine with theirs.

Devotion to the guru is fundamental to Tantric practice. Indeed, this episode begins, as do all the episodes of the collected Songs of Milarepa, with an expression of devotion and worship – 'Obeisance to all gurus' – which is meant to remind us of the source of the teachings. This salutation asserts the primacy of personal, oral teaching over mere book learning within the school of Tibetan Buddhism that takes its name from this overriding emphasis, the Kagyu or 'whispered transmission', the lineage to which Milarepa belongs. In other words, we are being warned that a text – any text – is not enough for our practical spiritual purposes.

The 'brothers' for whom Milarepa longs are his 'vajra brothers', his fellow trainees who have received initiation from the same guru. The term signals the importance of the relationship between them. Having the same *vajrācārya* or Tantric path and the same *vajra-guru* or Tantric guru creates an especially close bond with special responsibilities. Harmony is of tremendous significance in such a close-knit spiritual community, and to

13

dispute with your vajra brother is very damaging, spiritually speaking. As each of you has dedicated yourself to the same ideal and the same path, if you quarrel with a Dharma brother, you are quarrelling with your own commitment.

Milarepa naturally entitles his song 'Thoughts of my Guru'. However, there is a suggestion that he feels his separation from his vajra brothers even more intensely. The language in the final verse is painfully strong. If he misses his vajra brothers more than his guru, it is not because of any lack of devotion to Marpa; it is because they are more on his level. They are able to offer a kind of straightforward human companionship that he cannot get from someone he reveres so much. As he says, he can compare his experience with theirs, measure himself against them.

He may be in some spiritual contact with his vajra brothers through keeping them in mind, but it is clearly not enough to overcome his sense of isolation. Milarepa can at least practise the guru visualization as a means of getting close to his teacher, but as far as I know there is no Tantric practice in which you visualize your vajra brothers. But even if there were such a practice, it still wouldn't be enough. You would still want to meet up with them, to talk with them, to have tangible, personal contact. And this is Milarepa's experience. He still feels the physical separation, the acute and pressing need for simple, straightforward human company, and he prays to his guru to relieve him of the pain this need gives him.

Loneliness in the Spiritual Community

It is easy to lose heart at a time like this, when you have put in a lot of work and get nothing but pain and loneliness in return. Having been sent into the mountains to meditate on his own, Milarepa misses a sense of the spiritual community's support of his individual endeavour. Marpa and his disciples no doubt do comprise a true spiritual community, but it seems that in his darker moments Milarepa cannot always see them in that light. For all his conscious aspiration to the contrary, at least for the time being he is seeing the spiritual community not as a spiritual community, but as a group from whose warmth and companionship he feels excluded; and he is seeing himself not as an individual, but as a member of that group.

Samuel Johnson, the great eighteenth-century English critic, lexicographer, and conversationalist, once said that the reason for his attachment to human company was his fear that the melancholy that descended upon him when he was alone would drive him mad. In this sort of state it isn't exactly a friend you seek – even if a friend will serve your purpose – but simply someone to distract you from your experience of separateness. Not that the presence of another person will necessarily do this. After all, it is not physical solitude that engenders loneliness, but mental isolation, which the mere physical proximity of others can never completely eradicate.

If you are sufficiently mindful you will notice that subtle sense of loneliness in your experience all the time

To some extent such loneliness is inherent in conditioned existence. The very fact of one's subjectivity – that one has a sense of ego, or separate self – means that one will always feel to some extent cut off from others. The mere fact that others are *others* means that you are isolated and therefore experience loneliness. If you are sufficiently mindful you will notice that subtle sense of loneliness in your experience all the time, even – perhaps particularly – when you are with a good friend. The better you know someone and the more time you spend with them, the more you realize they are fundamentally different and ultimately separate from you. They think differently from you: they don't really penetrate into your thoughts, nor do you ever quite succeed in seeing things from their point of view. In the end you don't understand how it feels to be them, and nor can they understand how it feels to be you.

So, although you may live for years side by side with someone who is very dear to you, your very closeness may help you to see that you are really on your own. This is the kind of insight that can emerge from being aware and mindful when you are with another person. There can be warmth and companionship, but no amount of good friendship can – or should – alleviate the existential loneliness of conditioned existence. If companionship does help you to forget it, that isn't really a good thing. We should not expect from others more than they are able to give.

True spiritual fellowship fosters communication in its most mature sense: mutual responsiveness across a chasm. Even though you share a heartfelt ideal, you are both aware that as long as there is a sense of separate selfhood, you will always feel an element of loneliness, when you are on your own and even when you are with a friend. Indeed, it is your shared ideal that reminds you of that chasm between you. The more that knowledge is implicit in your communication, the more effective the communication will be. If you are in a reasonably positive state of mind, such an insight will be exhilarating rather than depressing. A good friend is someone with whom you can be alone.

Competitiveness in the Spiritual Community

Though inferior my Experience and Realization,
I wish to compare mine with theirs.

In expressing a wish to compare his experience with that of his vajra brothers, Milarepa makes reference to an aspect of the spiritual community that might seem inimical to harmony: that of comparing one's progress with others. Competition, however, is not always a bad thing, even in the spiritual community. Measuring yourself against others, testing your strength of body or brain against theirs, is a healthy impulse. It is important not just for the individual but for the social group, and it is good for everyone, even those who come off worst in the contest.

Competitiveness drives you to strive for as high a place as possible within the hierarchy of the group to which you belong, and through that struggle you find not only your place in the hierarchy but also your natural level of competence. You need to compete in order to discover how to make the best use of your abilities. If you have the ability to be a leader, you will naturally work your way up the hierarchy to occupy that position. Indeed, it is essential for the survival of the group and the species as a whole that you do so. Power hierarchies seem to have arisen originally in hunter-gatherer societies, primarily among the males, and their survival value is obvious. If the group is to be organized to defend itself from attack by other groups, it is in everyone's interests that the strongest and cleverest members should take the lead.

A normal healthy male thus has a drive to find out where he stands in relation to other men, and when you get a lot of men together there is invariably a tendency for the young bulls to challenge the old bull. What you end up with is a power structure, and ideally, if this structure is established by open competition, it will reflect the comparative strength and skill – as well as the shrewdness and cunning – of the individuals within it.

This basic drive has little to do with the spiritual life, except that any spiritual development has to begin with a healthy human individual. Maintaining the hierarchy of power through competitiveness is useful for many practical purposes and in any situation where a clear objective needs to be achieved. In large projects in particular, it may be impractical to give everyone an equal voice in forming every decision. But a hierarchy of power should not be confused with the spiritual hierarchy. Someone who is physically weak, and not particularly bright or ambitious in an ordinary way, may still have the drive to keep going on the spiritual path when strong men fall by the wayside.

Confusion can easily arise because a hierarchy of power is readily apparent to everyone, whereas a spiritual hierarchy is not. Moreover, there are always practical, organizational goals to be achieved even within the context of the spiritual community. It may be that some people like to get things done through hierarchical structures, while others prefer working in close co-operation on a more or less equal basis. This may mean that certain people end up taking charge of large spiritual institutions while others tend to be involved in smaller situations. Such arrangements do not imply any spiritual superiority or inferiority on the part of the individuals concerned. Within the context of the spiritual community, the hierarchy of power is to be regarded as instrumental and provisional only. Someone who occupies a higher place within the structure is not thereby more integrated, more developed as a person, more of an individual.

For some people being first in line, or being the centre of things, is so important that they can be thrown into a very negative mental state when that petty ambition is thwarted, and the spiritual community is by no means exempt from this. This is why the usual Buddhist convention is that when a number of people are to be ordained or initiated they line up in order of natural seniority, the eldest or the longest-standing disciple going first. This avoids any dispute.

So long as there is genuine friendship, competitiveness within the spiritual community is generally harmless and even sometimes useful from a practical point of view. But it should be competitiveness of a playful kind. And the more spiritually developed you are, the less you will mind where you find yourself in the hierarchy. You will just step quietly and unobtrusively into the position that your qualities – or lack of them – warrant.

In Milarepa's case, his qualities have led him to this desolate spot, many miles away from his companions in the spiritual life, although he is not yet quite reconciled to this state of affairs. But that is about to change.

Trusting in One's Own Experience
Milarepa's sincere faith in his guru finally brings him the answer he seeks. Although they are physically separated, his guru reveals himself in a vision, riding a lion. Mañjuśrī, the archetypal Bodhisattva of wisdom, is usually depicted riding a lion, so the fact that Marpa appears in the same way suggests that he is a manifestation of the wisdom aspect of the Dharma. In any case, his message is entirely reasonable. Rather than reminding

Milarepa of what will happen if he doesn't pull himself together and of what rewards await him if he does, Marpa simply reminds him how far he has come.

> *Have you not continually offered service to the Guru and to the Three Precious Ones above? Have you not dedicated your merits to sentient beings in the Six Realms? Have not you yourself reached that state of grace in which you can purify your sins and achieve merits?*

He draws Milarepa's attention to the positive aspects of his own experience, to the progress he knows he has already made. If his practice has had any beneficial results, then Milarepa has the firm basis he needs for faith in his continuing path.

Marpa's appearance in this way is reminiscent of the earth goddess who, according to the traditional accounts, appeared at a similarly critical moment in the Buddha's life, when the Buddha-to-be (Siddhartha) is being assailed by Māra. Māra doubts Siddhartha's right to sit on the *vajrāsana*, the diamond throne that only a Buddha-to-be can occupy. But the earth goddess arises to bear witness to the depth of Siddhartha's practice, to remind him of the long road he has travelled over many lifetimes to arrive at this place.[4]

The Three Jewels will do their bit if you do yours. They are always there; that is why they are called refuges. When you go for refuge to them they will never fail.

Becoming conscious of the positive outcome of his dedicated practice of mindfulness and devotion, even though it appears to have led him only to this lonely and desolate mountain, Milarepa has the intelligence to see that on the basis of what he has already experienced, the practices will eventually bear fruit. They will support you if you will commit yourself to them. If you will only jump into the air, the force of gravity can be relied upon to work.

The Three Jewels will do their bit if you do yours. They are always there; that is why they are called refuges. When you go for refuge to them they will never fail.

Milarepa's Song of Resolve

My earnest song, called 'Thoughts of my Guru,'
Must surely have been heard by you, my teacher;
Yet I am still in darkness.
Pray, pity me and grant me your protection!

Indomitable perseverance
Is the highest offering to my Guru.
The best way to please Him
Is to endure the hardship of meditation!
Abiding in this cave, alone,
Is the noblest service to the Ḍākinīs!...

Guru mine, pray grant me your protection!
Help this mendicant to stay ever in his hermitage.

The song shows Milarepa's mettle even in his moment of weakness. He is effectively saying, 'What else have I got?' He is still, as he says, in darkness, but he does not entreat Marpa to be gentle with him, to indulge his simple and innocent human yearning for the company of like-minded people. Instead, he asks his guru to help him persevere on the path set out for him. He sees that he must seek inspiration in the very hardship that seems to be drying up his inspiration. There is no way back, and he does not ask for one. This resurgence of faith in the path is enough to lift his flagging spirits. His inspiration returns, and his energies are again aroused.

Spirits of Place

Exalted, Milarepa adjusted his robe and carried a handful of
wood back to his cave. Inside, he was startled to find five Indian

demons with eyes as large as saucers. One was sitting on his bed and preaching, two were listening to the sermon, another was preparing and offering food, and the last was studying Milarepa's books.

Following his initial shock, Milarepa thought, 'These must be magical apparitions of the local deities who dislike me. Although I have been living here a long time, I have never given them any offering or compliment.

From this passage it would seem that Milarepa has retrieved both his robe and the wood he has collected. But here is another shock, perhaps even more disconcerting than the storm. His cave has suddenly become a little crowded. Five demons have arrived, apparently for an extended visit. They are Indian demons, rather than the home-grown Tibetan variety, so they are all the more strange and terrifying.

Milarepa's initial thought is that these demons are the local gods or spirits, irritated at having been ignored and appearing in malevolent form in order to frighten him into offering them some respect. He has overlooked the need to pay homage to them, make them offerings, show appreciation of their prior claim on the place where he wants to practise. He needs to placate them so that they do not disturb his meditation.

A local deity is the power of a particular area – literally the spirit of the place in a personalized form. It isn't just a mental response to the place; it is a perceptible presence. This is the difference between a modern experience of place and a traditional view. It is a universal human trait even today to personalize inanimate objects like ships and cars. People often have a kind of relationship with such things, involving affection and respect. We can also find ourselves reacting with irritation to the apparent malevolence of a gust of wind that blows away a hat, or a chair that gets in the way, or a car that won't start. But for modern, urban, rationalistic people, that is as far as our personalizing tendencies go. We tend to see the environment as an arrangement of more or less inanimate objects, interrelated by various physical processes.

But we should not regard this modern attitude as in any sense normal. In a pre-modern culture one's surroundings were always straightforwardly alive. Local deities are the literal per-sonification of the psychic atmosphere of particular locations and natural objects like trees. In Pali texts, for example, one comes across tree divinities who start speaking to one or another of the monks, perhaps rebuking him or encouraging him in his meditation. Such spirits are common in the folklore of primitive cultures. It is as though primitive people (I don't mean to imply any disparagement by the use of the term 'primitive') have a great sensitivity to the psychic atmosphere of a particular spot and a tendency to experience it in personal terms, as a spirit or divinity of some kind.

Many primitive peoples establish their whole religious culture upon these perceptions. Wherever they are, whether in the mid-dle of a desert or forest, or by a stream or gully, they sense some-one there, and regard this being or entity as the local deity. If you want to refer to a particular local atmosphere, the general effect that a region or place has on the psyche, you speak of the god or goddess of that tract of land or forest or cave or shrine. A certain numinous atmosphere becomes concentrated into a particular form or figure, so that the atmosphere of a place is *someone* rather than *something*. Without necessarily seeing or hearing anything, you feel a kind of presence.

My friend and teacher Yogi Chen (a Ch'an and Vajrayāna prac-titioner who used to live in a little bungalow near the bazaar in Kalimpong) used to tell me endless stories of his own encounters with gods and goddesses and other such beings, including these local deities. When I went to see him he might say, for example, 'Just before you arrived, such-and-such a deity came and told me what I was to say to you.' This sort of remark used to give me food for thought. I knew him well enough not to doubt his sincerity, and it was not a decision on his part to express his experience in these terms. This was the truth of his experience, however one might try to evaluate it. These beings were completely real to him, as real as the people who came to see him, if not more so. His was perhaps the most extreme case of this way of seeing that I have been closely associated with, though I have known other people whose experience was similar. It is as though such people are psychically organized to experience things in this way. It's rather like the way children experience things. They literally see forms and figures – not physically, but with an inner eye – and they may even hear voices. This is how they experience what most of us would describe in more impersonal terms as the atmosphere of a place.

Modern Westerners who find themselves susceptible to this way of experiencing the influence of a place tend to get on well with meditation, especially meditation of a visionary or devotional kind. But there are some places in Britain – Glastonbury, for example – that retain such a strong atmosphere that most people can feel it. Explain it how you will, you can feel an unusual quality in the very air of the place, and to speak of the local deity is probably the simplest and most straightforward way of referring to this. If you are receptive enough you can pick up some unseen quality in many places, perhaps particularly in woods and ancient forests.

Nor is the psychic atmosphere of such places always benign. At a place in England where I used to go on retreat, I noticed a distinct atmosphere among the trees nearby. Other people noticed it too, and found the forest a frightening place to be. The trees seemed angry and resentful, perhaps because they were planted so close together. Like people stuck on a congested train, they didn't have enough space. A nearby airfield may also have contributed to their discomfort; the noise from planes flying low overhead cannot have been good for their nerves. But whatever the reason for this unpleasant atmosphere, it was not just a poetic fancy on my part. I felt it quite directly. Those trees didn't like human beings; they weren't pleased to see me. By contrast, the woods near our retreat centre in Norfolk, Padmaloka, seem very happy.

It must have made quite a psychological difference to the monks of the Buddha's time that they lived out their lives under trees. Northern India was one great forest at the time, and is referred to as such in the Pali texts (the Pali term is *mahāvana*). The monks slept in the forest, they walked along narrow tracks through it, and they begged for alms in villages surrounded by it. Of course, since the Buddha's time many forests have been cut down and humanity has lost the company of very many trees. One can only speculate as to the effect of this loss on the human psyche, but perhaps it is significant that even in the most industrial of cities, the city planners have felt the need to plant trees along the streets and in the parks.

> Where humans do not dominate, we perhaps
> become aware of different psychic forces than those
> we are used to, and aware of ourselves as belonging
> to just another species of animal.

One can imagine that the effect of living in an environment populated by large numbers of animals would be similarly noticeable. On the plains of Africa the presence of enormous flocks and herds must give one a strong sensation of being a member of a single species among many, many others, part of a whole complex of living beings, the vast majority of which are non-human. Where humans do not dominate, we perhaps become aware of different psychic forces than those we are used to, and aware of ourselves as belonging to just another species of animal. At the same time, we see the gulf between ourselves and these other forms of life, and the specific significance of human life, and we feel our need for the companionship of other human beings. In the end, the experience of other forms of life may bring us back to an appreciation of our own kind, of those with whom we can communicate most fully.

It is not, after all, as if there is an absence of nature in towns and cities; it is more that nature is present in a particular form, that of an overwhelming preponderance of human beings, producing an extraordinary range of psychic energies. Even towns and cities have their local deities. In the *Mahāparinibbāna Sutta*, for example, the Buddha is described as arriving at a certain spot (Pāṭaligāma, near the modern Patna) and prophesying that one day a great city would be built there.[5] Apparently he detected the kind of powerful deities that incite men's minds to build cities (rather than, say, meditate). Even today, at the feet of the high-rise apartment blocks of modern Hong Kong or Bangkok, you will find shrines to the local gods, with incense burning and perhaps a few flowers as offerings. Our usual experience of nature, the countryside as we call it in England, is another thing altogether. Domesticated and cultivated, the countryside is less intensely stimulating, less inhabited in this sense of psychic presences, than either the city or nature in the wild.

Subduing Demons

The significant point to be drawn from Milarepa's encounter with these demons, however, is that the Buddhist ideal is to adopt a friendly attitude towards all such deities, whether they appear as benign spirits or as malignant demons. It is true that the teacher who is credited with establishing Buddhism in Tibet, Padmasambhava, is commonly said to have achieved this by subduing the local demons. But this terminology may be a little misleading, suggesting as it does an aggressive suppression of malignant spirits. In fact, 'demon' in the sense of 'devil' is a purely Christian usage of the Greek *daimon*, meaning a presiding genius or tutelary deity. Far from suppressing these powerful forces, Padmasambhava harnessed their energies, putting them at the service of the Dharma.

The Buddha himself always insisted on respecting the local gods and religious traditions, and when the figure of the Buddha first became an object of worship, he was depicted with major gods from the Hindu pantheon waiting upon him. One image, for example, shows him descending from the devaloka or heaven realms attended by Indra and Brahma. The old gods are thus not excluded but given their place in a greater scheme. The ethnic is integrated with the universal, the lower religious ideal with the higher spiritual and transcendental ideal.

If this integration does not take place in some way, trouble will ensue, for these strange forces are not as alien as they seem. Their existence is to some extent bound up with our own. The energies that find their expression in the form of the spirits and demons that appear in the folklore of indigenous culture also emerge as aspects of ourselves, and these basic energies cannot just be put to one side and ignored. You could perhaps do so if you were enlightened – the Buddha's enlightened disciple Sāriputta famously managed to ignore the violent attentions of a malignant demon completely on one occasion (as observed by his friend Moggallāna and recorded in the Pali canon).[6] But if we are not enlightened, these energies have to be harnessed, directed, assimilated, absorbed, which may mean bringing local deities into line. In folkloric terms, the demons have to be subdued.

Why, after all, should a fervent devotee of the Buddha himself have anything to fear from mere demons?

So if you are going to build a Buddhist temple in England, it is probably a mistake to build a replica of a Tibetan or Japanese building. You would first need to find a location that already had a positive atmosphere. Then you could introduce into the construction of the temple certain motifs or decorative touches with an indigenous significance. In place of bodhi leaves carved into the wooden beams you could have oak leaves, with all the associations that they embody for the English – druids, mistletoe, the protective 'wooden walls' of the Royal Navy, hearts of oak, strength, stability, and so on – and in this way you would to some extent incorporate the energies of the local culture into your spiritual purposes. All those associations would contribute their energies to the ideals to which the temple was dedicated, and gradually more and more features of the local culture could be brought in to support your spiritual aims.

So Milarepa sings a complimentary song to the demons in an attempt to charm them into leaving him alone. He lets them know that he has taken a Bodhisattva vow, and that therefore he wishes them well.

Ye local demons, ghosts, and gods,
All friends of Milarepa,
Drink the nectar of kindness and compassion,
Then return to your abodes.

But the Indian demons did not vanish, and stared balefully at Milarepa. Two of them advanced, one grimacing and biting his lower lip, and the other grinding his teeth horribly. A third, coming up behind, gave a violent, malicious laugh and shouted loudly.

Clearly the demons are not inclined to avail themselves of Milarepa's offer of the nectar of kindness and compassion. They are certainly not at all charmed. Realizing that this attempt to appease them has failed, Milarepa tries a different tactic. Delivering a powerful incantation, he calls on his higher energies to confront these dark forces that have invaded his practice. In doing this he is flexing his spiritual muscles, as it were. Why, after all, should a fervent devotee of the Buddha himself have anything to fear from mere demons? The demons must surely acknowledge that they have been beaten in a straight fight. But no. They remain unmoved.

Seeing that he is on entirely the wrong tack with them, Milarepa tries to put things right with a 'compassionate' lesson in Buddhist doctrine. Nonetheless, the demons obstinately stay put. In hindsight it is obvious why this ploy fails. It fails because it is a ploy. His motive in preaching the Dharma is not the spiritual welfare of the demons. The Dharma may indeed involve great compassion, but in this case it is not his own. As he has recourse to great compassion only when the wrathful Buddha meditation fails, it is not even ordinary compassion. He tries to get rid of them by force, and when that fails he tries to get rid of them by kindness, but his attitude remains the same.

The demons seem to have made themselves quite cosy in Milarepa's cave. But why do they present a scene of such studied domesticity? It seems an odd way for Indian demons to behave. The answer is that they are a particular kind of demon, best described not as spirits of place but as *pretas*, 'hungry ghosts'. Pretas are embodiments of craving or neurotic desire – hence their eyes like saucers – and the scene they are enacting is a kind of ghastly parody of the spiritual community for which Milarepa has been yearning.

Suddenly Milarepa realizes what is going on. He has misread the nature of these demons, taking them to be unfriendly local spirits, the neighbourhood thugs of the spirit world, when they are in fact something much closer to home. They are a kind of emanation of Milarepa's state of mind, of his *preta*-like longing to be supported in his weakness, to be distracted and comforted by the warmth and companionship of his vajra brothers. His craving turns the spiritual community in his own mind into a collection of hungry ghosts gathered together out of neurotic craving. In his heart of hearts this is what Milarepa wants, perhaps what we all want, but until now he has not understood that this is the case, so the demons have remained.

There is nothing wrong with the positive human group. One needs the support and encouragement of like-minded companions. But the true spiritual community is more than that. It means more than sharing a psychologically healthy lifestyle, more than satisfying the simple human desire for contact and warmth under the guise of engagement in spiritual practice. The demons represent aspects of Milarepa's own unsubdued ego, which takes the form of a subtle clinging to his identity as a member of the religious group. And you cannot get rid of ego with ego, even if that egotism takes up a wrathful Buddha meditation or gives a teaching on compassion to do it. He has been trying to rid himself of these unpleasant manifestations by force of will, when all he had to do was see their true nature.

In Biblical language, it is like trying to cast out Satan with the fire of Satan. As long as you are wrestling with the devil you will not get rid of him. If you fight against the forces of evil as if they were really out there ranged against you, you will only magnify your egotism. But if you recognize the devil in Buddhist terms, as Māra, you just have to see through him, to see him as a state of your own mind. After all, Milarepa says to himself, I am supposed to have seen through to the essential reality common to all things. I am void, the demons are void. Who is trying to get rid of what? So he sings his 'Song of Realization'.

The Wisdom of Youth

Father Guru, who conquered the Four Demons,
I bow to you, Marpa the Translator.

I, whom you see, the man with a name,
Son of Darsen Gharmo,
Was nurtured in my mother's womb,
Completing the Three Veins.
A baby, I slept in my cradle;
A youth, I watched the door;
A man, I lived on the high mountain.

Though the storm on the snow peak is awesome,
I have no fear.
Though the precipice is steep and perilous,
I am not afraid!

I, whom you see, the man with a name,
Am a son of the Golden Eagle;
I grew wings and feathers in the egg.
A child, I slept in my cradle;
A youth, I watched the door;
A man, I flew in the sky.
Though the sky is high and wide, I do not fear;
Though the way is steep and narrow, I am not afraid.

I, whom you see, the man with a name,
Am a son of Nya Chen Yor Mo, the King of fishes.
In my mother's womb, I rolled my golden eyes;
A child, I slept in my cradle;
A youth, I learned to swim;
A man, I swam in the great ocean.
Though thundering waves are frightening,
    I do not fear;
Though fishing hooks abound, I am not afraid.

I, whom you see, the man with a name,
Am a son of Ghagyu Lamas.
Faith grew in my mother's womb.
A baby, I entered the door of Dharma;
A youth, I studied Buddha's teaching;
A man, I lived alone in caves.
Though demons, ghosts, and devils multiply,
    I am not afraid.

The snow-lion's paws are never frozen,
Or of what use would it be
To call the lion 'King' –
He who has the Three Perfect Powers.

The eagle never falls down from the sky;
If so, would that not be absurd?
An iron block cannot be cracked by a stone;
If so, why refine the iron ore?
I, Milarepa, fear neither demons nor evils;
If they frightened Milarepa, to what avail
Would be his Realization and Enlightenment?

Ye ghosts and demons, enemies of the Dharma,
    I welcome you today!
It is my pleasure to receive you!
I pray you, stay; do not hasten to leave;
We will discourse and play together.
Although you would be gone, stay the night;

We will pit the Black against the White Dharma,
And see who plays the best.

Before you came, you vowed to afflict me.
Shame and disgrace would follow
If you returned with this vow unfulfilled.

Distracted first by the storm, then by the demons, Milarepa comes each time to himself again, as he reconnects with his realization of the mahāmudrā teaching. On each occasion, as a result of remembering his practice, he recognizes himself, and sees that his frustrating experience and the demons are not separate from the process of integrating his energies. In introducing himself as 'the man with a name', Milarepa is effectively recollecting himself. By his name he is known, recognized, recollected.

The golden eagle, the snow lion, and the king of fishes are traditional images and they often appear in Milarepa's songs. Here they serve to elaborate a basic theme, ringing the changes on his original statement. The principle they illustrate is his embodiment of Enlightenment, the idea that he has taken on Enlightenment as his essential nature, allowing him to live and move in the transcendental realm as they do in their natural environments. He can no more be frightened of demons than the eagle can fall out of the sky.

Not only this. Just as the eagle is an eagle even in the egg, so Milarepa is who he is even in his mother's womb, surrounded by the 'Three Veins' around which, according to Tibetan tradition, the embryo develops. His faith is not some alien growth. His realization of the void emerges in the process of his natural development; it is integral to what he is, not grafted on later.

It seems that when we are quite young – before we get involved in the world socially, economically, and sexually, when we are still fairly innocent, still a spectator – we see the simple reality of things quite clearly. Then for a few years we are led away from that knowledge. We listen to other people and get entangled with them, and we lose touch with our own vision and insight. It may be only in our early twenties, or much later, that it all starts to come back to us, perhaps slowly and painfully. Indeed, for a long time we may not get far beyond the knowledge we had when we were much younger.

There is perhaps a connection between this kind of experience and the Tibetan teaching on the intermediate state or *bardo*. It is generally understood in Tibetan Buddhism that when we are in the bardo state following physical death (*bardo* means 'in between'), we have opportunities for spiritual attainment that we are not able to assimilate. We have no way of contextualizing them, so we go bouncing down from level to level until we find some experience with which we are familiar and to which we can respond. Thus we arrive at our next rebirth, back in this world again. However, we have had that vision of reality in between, and there may be some vestige of this, however vague and obscure, lingering on in the early years of our next life.

There is an example of this in the life-story of the Buddha himself. The traditional accounts describe how one day he went to rest in the shade of a rose-apple tree while his father, the king, conducted a ritual first ploughing of the fields in springtime. As the boy rested in the cool shade of the tree, his mind progressed quite naturally through states of increasing clarity and joy into the meditative state known as the first *dhyāna*. At that time he had no context in which to place his experience, and he forgot it. It was only much later in his life, having left his spiritual teachers and gone to seek Enlightenment at the foot of the bodhi tree, that he found himself recollecting that incident from his boyhood.[7] Regaining a flavour of the spontaneous bliss he had experienced then, he thought, 'Is this the way?' And the rest, as they say, is history.

One important aspect of this story is that it appears to show that meditative experience is not gained by the forcible application of a particular technique, but unfolds as a process of natural growth and development. Techniques and practices are necessary to assist and guide this process, but it is as though one has to proceed by letting things grow naturally and by encouraging and coaxing that growth, rather than forcing one's development by sheer effort of will.

The common-sense view of personal development is that we begin life in ignorance and gradually learn more about the nature of things through experience and various kinds of training. The Buddha's experience under the rose-apple tree, however, suggests that from a spiritual point of view, important knowledge goes hand-in-hand with innocence and is lost with experience, at least with experience of a certain kind. In going out into the world with the aim of gaining wisdom, we are liable to get tangled up in all kinds of things and end up not wiser but more deluded. Even in the pursuit of spiritual training it is possible to entrap oneself further in time and place and personality and in doing so move still further from true wisdom, the understanding that is altogether beyond time and place and free from personality.

Milarepa rushes at the demons and they shrink back in fear, then swirl together and vanish. He is successful in dealing with them this time because he has realized what they really are. He rushes at them not because he has decided to act aggressively, but as an expression of his spiritual power, which in turn expresses his realization that in the ultimate sense there are no demons. There is nothing to be afraid of and therefore no need to get rid of them. It is nothing to him if they choose to stay.

'This was the Demon King, Vināyaka the Obstacle-Maker, who came searching for evil opportunities,' thought Milarepa. 'The storm, too, was undoubtedly his creation. By the mercy of my Guru, he had no chance to harm me.'

It seems that Milarepa's mahāmudrā practice and his realization of the mind as a transparency of voidness momentarily deserted him under the shock of being haunted by these hungry ghosts. But the earlier vision of his guru is what eventually recalled him to his experience of the truth of things, enabling him to disarm his visitors. This is presumably what he means by 'the mercy of my Guru'.

In retrospect it seems significant that Marpa earlier addressed Milarepa in that vision as 'Great Sorcerer', reminding his disciple of the powers of which he had made use before his conversion. Was Marpa giving him an implicit warning, in anticipation of the demonic challenge to come, not to fall back into his old habits? Perhaps he was saying, 'You have been meditating all this time in that cave, but aren't you still just a sorcerer trying to gain your ends by forcible means? Are you going to carry on imposing yourself on your situation, applying the powers at your disposal, just as in the old days you worked your will by force of magic?'

In the early stages of any spiritual career there has to be a struggle, and Milarepa evidently struggled hard and well. But he has reached an advanced stage where will-power is not the most positive quality to develop. He did fall briefly into his old habits when he attempted to use the Dharma in a kind of power game with the demons in order to rid himself of them, but then, drawing on the depth of his accumulated mindfulness and understanding, he finally saw through them.

Guarding the Jewels of Buddhist Practice

How do we safeguard the essential wisdom of the Dharma? It may seem as though Milarepa's answer is to avoid human contact at all costs and hide himself away in the mountains to pursue a life of meditation and abstinence. But the example of his life is not quite what it seems. It appears extreme, outstandingly austere, and solitary, perhaps more so even than that of Gautama the Buddha. But he still manages to embody the Mahāyāna ideal of compassion, of practising for the sake of others, as conspicuously as any teacher of that tradition. His songs have produced a tremendous effect on many generations of Tibetans, and the joy those songs express, with never a care for his material needs, even for basic food and shelter, must have inspired countless hermits in their own practice.

Milarepa's practice and way of life – his solitary, comfortless, but joyful life – is his teaching. He has attained the goal, but that is no reason to abandon the path, because the goal is not in the end separate from that path. Milarepa benefits people by exemplification, by living out the teaching he espouses without any compromise at all. His strength as a practitioner is in his commitment to his chosen path. Even though in principle he could have continued to practise under other conditions, settled in a monastery or even out in the world, he would not have done so by choice.

Milarepa sets an inspiring example of transcendental faith and joy, determination and mindful vigilance, but he does not offer a realistically practical lifestyle for us to follow. He lived in a society in which the Buddhist tradition was well established and where its doctrines and practices were widely understood and appreciated. He may have completely disregarded mundane, material matters himself, but there were faithful people who would certainly have made his life a little easier, at least from time to time. They would get to hear about him and appreciate the value of what he was doing enough to trudge up the mountain to supply him with with food and drink.

Unfortunately, such supportive conditions for the life of a hermit are very hard to find in the world today. For one thing, even ostensibly inaccessible places are much busier than they used to be. If you tried to follow Milarepa's example and meditate in a cave in the mountains, or in some relatively uninhabited region, you would be unlikely to find yourself alone for long, given the presence of backpackers and hikers, mountaineers and skiers, explorers and scientists, fossil-hunters, naturalists, and all the rest. And would all those people, or the local people, appreciate the significance of what you were doing? It may be a weakness of faith on my part, but I'm afraid I would not personally want to rely on the ravens to feed me, or the locals for that matter. They wouldn't be likely to think, 'Here's a yogi doing something important,' and come trotting along with food and drink. Indeed, if they took any interest in you, they might well report you to the authorities and recommend your detention on the grounds of impaired mental health.

You cannot bring into existence the perfect Buddhist culture, or the mature individuals to nurture it, at a stroke.

So we cannot get away from the world in quite the way Milarepa did. Escape is no longer possible. Escapism, yes, but not escape. Modern societies are not prepared to leave anyone or anything alone. Through our practice of mindfulness we can go some way towards creating our own internal refuge, but we still have to deal, all the time, with surroundings that are not conducive to stillness, simplicity, and contentment.

For most of us, therefore, Milarepa's example presents not so much a lifestyle to follow as a warning against over-confidence, and the danger of abandoning the safeguard of positive conditions prematurely. When you have been on retreat, it can seem very tempting to throw yourself back into worldly life, because you feel so full of energy and positivity. You cannot see the threat to your practice from the world around you. You don't see it coming; it just smothers and seduces you until your retreat seems like a distant dream.

The message of Milarepa's solitary life is a little reminiscent of a parable in the Pali canon. The Buddha says that the deer are safe as long as they feed high in the mountains, but when they come down to the fields to nibble the crops, they are liable to be shot. In the same way, he goes on, if monks stray from their ancestral grazing grounds, the pastures of meditation and the solitary life – if they start nibbling at the fringes of worldly life – then Māra is likely to take a pot-shot at them.[8] As Buddhists, we need to stay on our own home ground, and that means moving decisively away from the lower pastures of the mountain, where our ideals and aspirations are continually curbed and compromised by the worldly values that surround us.

We need to try, even in the midst of the world, to carve out a specifically Buddhist way of life, a kind of miniature Pure Land where people can work together, live together, and practise together in ways that do justice to their spiritual aspirations. It might take the form of residential communities, or right-livelihood businesses, or Buddhist centres dedicated to practising, communicating, and celebrating the Dharma. They would be places in which spiritual values could be nurtured and allowed to grow, sheltered – at least to some extent – from the inhospitable winds of the mundane world.

We cannot expect the situations we set up to offer perfect conditions for practice, any more that those who set them up will be perfectly accomplished practitioners. You cannot bring into existence the perfect Buddhist culture, or the mature individuals to nurture it, at a stroke. Especially at the beginning, they will be working with the limitations of the group mentality they have inherited. But it will be a start, a necessary beginning. And as those who are able to enjoy such conditions grow and develop spiritually, the conditions will get better, providing greater opportunity for further progress.

> The spiritual community consists of ordinary men and women who are prepared to struggle with their demons – just as even Milarepa had to do.

The very presence of such spiritual oases will have an effect on the surrounding culture. Newcomers will be attracted and inspired and will want to join in, and in this way spiritual values will gain ground within worldly society and be able to sustain a presence there. So the process can go on indefinitely, both in a structural, social sense, and in the sense of new levels of individual progress.

However, the spiritual community is not just a structure in which to live and work. It is also concerned with the ways in which individuals associate with each other. Ideally, the social structures we create among ourselves will provide a basis upon which to develop individuality in the truest sense, and certainly not to hold it back. After all, as human beings we are social animals. The Buddhist path is all about overcoming ego, and collective situations are very good places in which to bring this about. The essential context for spiritual progress is thus the sangha or spiritual community. This is the companionship that helps you grow rather than the group with which you must conform. The sangha, if it is a real sangha, provides a collective situation in which you can be honest about your thoughts and feelings, even though sometimes you may need to restrain yourself from acting on them. The 'middle way' of individuality avoids both individualism in the sense of disregard of others and a timid, mindless social conformity.

Decision-making is the central issue in any collective situation. All too often in everyday life we are faced with decisions that have been made for us, and this is bound to create inner conflict. In the spiritual community, however, you will ideally feel that you can talk about your conflicted feelings. You don't have to pretend you are keen to do something when you are not. If it is a question of preference rather than moral principle, you can even say, 'Well, to be honest I'd prefer to do something else – though I don't mind going along with what you want if it's important to you.' The principle here is to refrain from insisting on your preference while feeling free to be honest about what you prefer. In that case you can go along with what others want in spite of your own feelings. There is no pretence in that conformity, especially in view of the fact that feelings are evanescent and can change swiftly and genuinely. In the end, you can honestly want to do what the others want to do, even though you originally wanted to do something different. But whatever happens, the collective context has not held you back from the honest expression of your thoughts, nor coerced you into behaving in a certain way in order to avoid condemnation.

In this way our incipient individuality – our willingness to take responsibility for ourselves in self-motivated spiritual endeavour – begins to grow deeper roots. We will be able to protect

Buddhist ethical and spiritual values from becoming institution-alized, from serving and perpetuating worldly values rather than dissolving and transforming them. In time, as the spiritual community develops, contact with wider society will not be as costly to the individual's progress. We will be in a stronger pos-ition to deal creatively with the wider world, on our own terms. Perhaps eventually genuine hermits will be able to follow Milarepa's inspiring example, supported by the wider sangha. At that point we will have achieved something closer to the sup-portive conditions enjoyed by the cotton-clad yogi Milarepa in old Tibet.

Traditionally, the going forth from worldly entanglements is an integral part of the 'Going for Refuge' to the Buddha, his teaching, and the spiritual community. In our own case, the question is not so much whether we can establish a certain pre-conceived way of life or work but whether we can surround our-selves with conditions that support our spiritual aspirations. When you step away from the conditions you have inherited, when you go forth, to use the traditional phrase, to pursue the spiritual life, this is not just a shift in your external circumstances. Renunciation as an external act is significant only to the extent that it reflects an inner experience. If you go forth, in whatever way, with a genuine spiritual motivation, into a more avowedly Buddhist context, you are moving in the direction of Enlightenment.

The reaching of this decisive point is a turning away from the group and a turning towards the spiritual community. In the highest sense the spiritual community is represented by the whole Buddhist tradition, a lineage of gurus and teachers lead-ing all the way up to the Bodhisattvas and the Buddhas. But in a more everyday sense, and this is where we begin to transform our lives, the spiritual community consists of ordinary men and women who are prepared to struggle with their demons – just as even Milarepa had to do.

Second Story

The Song of a Yogi's Joy

Chapter 3

Beyond Fear

Here I have used David Snellgrove's translation,[9] in which this episode is called 'Mila Repa and the Novices'. At the time I gave the seminar on which this chapter is based, this seemed to me the best version available. Chang's better-known version, in which this episode is called 'Song of a Yogi's Joy', had yet to appear.

Beauty and Fear

The opening section of 'Song of a Yogi's Joy' brings us immediately into a remote, often terrifying elemental world. Milarepa is in a high and isolated mountainous region on the sparsely inhabited border between Nepal and Tibet, and judging by the name given to his temporary residence, the tiger-cave of Singa-dzong, he has chosen to occupy a fearsome place of shelter. But it soon becomes apparent that this rather alarmingly named cave is not as unsuitable for meditation as it sounds. Milarepa finds its atmosphere peaceful and tranquil; and then he sees something – or someone. He is visited by the radiantly beautiful figure of the local deity of Yolmo. Consequently, his meditation is calm and full of energy and joy.

This visitation suggests that Milarepa has a vivid sense that the atmosphere of the place is fully in harmony with his meditative mood and spiritual aspirations. It's as though the atmosphere of the cave is entirely attuned to his purpose, and ready to co-operate with his aspirations. Milarepa's attitude is simply to make the best use he can of this beneficial environment. Of course, this is very much in contrast to the atmosphere created by the demons of the previous chapter, and we can conclude that Milarepa's own mental state is quite different.

As it happens, Milarepa is not to be allowed to continue to enjoy his meditative time in the tiger's cave undisturbed; some other visitors are on their way. News evidently travelled fast even in the remotest parts of medieval Tibet, and as a result, Milarepa is visited by a group of five novices who comment on the perilous and isolated nature of the place and speculate rather intelligently as to whether it will benefit his meditation.

Incidentally, these novices are referred to as nuns in Chang's translation. Certainly, Tibetan Buddhist nuns are always technically novices, because women were not given full ordination in the Indo-Tibetan tradition, the original Buddhist order of nuns having died out within about a millennium of its inception. However, in this context it seems more likely that the novices visiting Milarepa are male.

Milarepa responds with his own impressions of his habitation – which has been chosen for him, it seems, by his teacher – and his observations come as a bit of a surprise. If we have had any kind of mental picture of this remote place up to now, it has been bleak, barren, and inhospitable. The tiger's cave offers nothing in the way of comfort, and appears – even to the eye of medieval Tibetan trainee monks, who would be used to levels of hardship that we would not contemplate – eerie and dangerous.

> Negative emotions get in the way of
> our appreciation of things and reduce our ability
> to see the world around us.

But Milarepa himself is full of praise for it. He talks in terms of colour and light, flowers and birdsong. There is even a suggestion of some human presence, or at least flowering meadows, even if they are so far from habitation that they are visited only rarely.

The novices' impression of the place is an example of the way negative emotions get in the way of our appreciation of things and reduce our ability to see the world around us. They see the loneliness of the location and the almost unbroken solitude of Milarepa's existence, and this is what makes the place frightening to them. Being overpowered in this way by the sense of solitude, they don't see the beauty.

This is a common reaction, of course. Some people find even the ordinary English countryside terrifying, seemingly happier to congregate in places where any disconcerting encounter with terror or beauty can safely be avoided. In places like art galleries, too, we are used to going around in a crowd, and some people are perhaps more comfortable with that than being left alone with all that beauty. But someone who is sufficiently absorbed in the collection will hardly notice the absence of other people in the gallery – and if they do notice, they will be only too happy to enjoy the art undisturbed.

Milarepa's whole life is like this. He is not oppressed by solitude – he does not feel lonely – and he is therefore free to enjoy the natural beauty of his surroundings. He knows this place is lonely, but he is glad of it and doesn't experience the loneliness as a threat. One might say that Milarepa is in harmony with the local deities, in a way that the novices are not. Where others experience loneliness and fear, Milarepa sees only beauty and joy. This is due to his attainment of what he calls 'the clear light of realization of the void'. The 'void' is śūnyatā, the Mahāyāna and Vajrayāna term for ultimate reality. But why does he call it the 'clear light'?

The Clear Light of the Void

> It is in such a lonely place as this,
> That I, the yogin Milarepa,
> Am joyous in the Clear Light of Realization of the Void,
> Joyous exceedingly at its many ways of appearance,
> Joyous at its greatness of variety.

Milarepa's use of this expression, which is very common in the literature of the tradition, signals a clear parting of the ways between the Yogācāra school of Buddhism and the rationalistic philosophising of any tradition, referring as it does to the actual experience of the void, not to some abstract theoretical construct. But why 'clear light of the void'? What kind of light is it?

The voidness or emptiness of this realization is not null and void, but a state of utter freedom. It is intensely positive, beautiful, lucid, and bright – such that one can really compare it only to the purity and energy of brilliantly clear light. Of course, this is a metaphor. It is certainly not light as we commonly understand it. For one thing, ordinary light has a source, whereas the pure light of the void doesn't come from anywhere – and it doesn't go anywhere. Śūnyatā is free of any duality such as subject and object, time and space, or even light and dark.

When we think of something we think of it as being this or that, or that rather than this, and we naturally think of ultimate reality in the same way. Certainly the expression 'clear light of the void' suggests that we are to think of it as having the nature of light rather than darkness. But this is only a manner of speaking. In fact, reality cannot be fixed to, or in, any one thing, or tied down in any way. Not of course that it is itself any kind of 'thing'.

The followers of the Yogācāra were concerned to follow a progressive path: first reduce all phenomena, all appearances, to the One Mind, and then realize that the One Mind is perfectly void of any distinction between subject and object. For the Yogācāra, mind is no more real in an ultimate sense than anything else. It is not any kind of universal substance from which everything ultimately derives. It must be seen to be void. There is mind, consciousness, awareness – completely pure, completely illuminated and bright, but within it there is no absolutely existent subject and object, or even a notion of a self in the ordinary sense. Of course, it is almost impossible for us to see this, to leave behind the idea of duality without seeing in its place some kind of unity, however subtle. This is why reality is sometimes referred to as 'not-two' or 'non-dual', thus avoiding the risk of a return to a fixed and final conception of what reality is like.

To speak of the void is perhaps as near as we can come to a description of the yogi's state of complete openness and freedom. We cannot fix down a clear description of the void, because its nature is not to be a particular thing with a fixed identity. 'It' is mobile, constantly changing, flowing, forever assuming different forms. Knowing the true nature of the void, we should not be surprised if it demonstrates its void nature by changing into something else. The enlightened mind does not try to pin reality down to any particular manifestation and insist on experiencing it only in that way.

'What a silly Buddha I was!'

When you see things from this perspective, the very idea of the attainment of a goal becomes absurd, because the goal is ultimately to transcend the duality that is necessarily involved in the attainment of a goal. You let go of any sense that you are realizing some separable, distinguishable attainment that you didn't have before and that others do not have. On the contrary, you realize that you were unknowingly a Buddha from the very beginning – like the beggar in a parable from the *Lotus Sūtra* (*Saddharma-puṇḍarīka*) who didn't realize that a priceless jewel had been sewn into the corner of his robe. You have not left the world of impurity behind or come into possession of the pure realm of nirvāṇa. Your own ordinary thought is confirmed in the Buddha state. The 'attainment' is outside time, and when you come to it, you realize that you have been there all the time. So when you gain Enlightenment you realize that you always were enlightened. Your original possession has simply been confirmed. The absurdity of the situation is often, apparently, what first strikes the newly enlightened person – hence the laughter that is so often reported in the Zen tradition as the natural reaction to the event. How ridiculous to think that one had ever been anything but enlightened! How silly to have suffered so much and so unnecessarily!

Free from saṁsāra, the round of mundane existence, you become free within saṁsāra. You are able to return to the world of suffering without taking that world of distinctions for absolute reality. The laughter therefore also arises from intense relief. It is as though, having spent your whole life deeply anxious about something, you suddenly see the truth of the situation, which is that there was never anything to worry about. 'How absurd all that anxiety and struggle was!' you say to yourself, 'What a fool I've been, thinking I was this and thinking I was that! I was just barking up the wrong tree.' And at that point you can afford to laugh. 'What a silly Buddha I was!'

Fear and Confusion in the Clear Light of the Void

Joyous with a body free from harmful karma,
Joyous in confusion of diversity,
Joyous midst fearful appearances,

Even that which appears confusing and fearful cannot extinguish Milarepa's joy. His assurance and confidence are not subject to external conditions. He feels no compulsion to impose any kind of logical order on the true nature of things. He doesn't insist on understanding the ultimate reality of things. He doesn't try to fit reality to any idea – even the idea of its variety. If its variety were suddenly to resolve itself back into a unity, he would be joyous in that too. Let reality be as it wishes. He doesn't hold on to it in any form. Let it be one, let it be many, let it be empty, let it be full – he doesn't mind, he remains joyous. He has no fixed ideas about reality to which he insists that his experience of it should conform. He is 'joyous in the Clear Light of Realization of the Void'.

In his meditations, too, though he may be visited by fearful apparitions of deities of various kinds, he sees them as just that – apparitions. All fear is ultimately fear of annihilation, and you gain courage by accepting that possibility, transcending the threatened self and going beyond it to a new self – at which point the process starts again. Milarepa can no longer be fooled by any sense of annihilation, and now he experiences only a deep fulfilment where fear used to be.

Milarepa's experience is not abstract or theoretical. His joy is rooted in bodily experience – the precious human body that Tibetan Buddhism traditionally prizes as the ideal vehicle for the attainment of Enlightenment. So he takes joy in the blessing of 'a body free from harmful karma', of being able to meditate without hindrance in the form of bodily pain or weakness. Not being dependent on the positive conditions he enjoys makes it easier for him not to take them for granted.

Distraction and Pain in the Enlightened Mind

Joyous in my freedom from that state where distractions rise and pass away.

The implication of this line is that with regard to distractions in meditation there are three distinct states of mind. There is, first, the state of mind in which distractions are experienced as arising and just hanging around. They may be recognized as distractions or hindrances, but they are not considered impermanent, and they are therefore difficult to deal with decisively or effectively.

Secondly, there is the state of mind in which a certain degree of understanding has arisen with regard to the impermanence of things. Distractions are experienced as transient, passing through the mind like clouds. Knowing that there is no need to turn an itch into a studied interest, you don't allow yourself to get involved in it, and the same goes for all distractions. Just because you feel an occasional hankering for certain worldly pleasures when you are on retreat, or for things in your day-to-day life that you have forsworn for a certain period or even for life, you don't have to take such yearnings seriously.

They are just momentary hindrances of craving or restlessness arising from previous conditioning.

> An enlightened person will be able to see potential distractions for what they are even as they arise, without falling under their spell.

Both these states of mind call for vigilance and effort. But being enlightened, Milarepa does not need to deliberately redirect his mental and emotional energies towards Enlightenment. It is at least questionable whether the fully enlightened mind will encounter distractions in the usual sense at all, because an enlightened person will be able to see potential distractions for what they are even as they arise, without falling under their spell.

Joyous exceedingly where hardship is great,
Joyous in freedom from sickness,
Joyous that suffering has turned to be joy,

Milarepa clearly endures extreme physical hardship – cold, hunger, and so on – but note that he is joyous *exceedingly* in these circumstances. This is because it is in such adverse conditions that his joy shines out as not being dependent on his circumstances. For Milarepa, even misfortune is a source of delight. He still experiences painful feelings of body and mind, but he finds joy in them, because every misfortune becomes another opportunity to experience the unconditioned nature of his joy. Note also that he is joyous not that suffering has turned *into* joy, but that suffering has turned to *be* joy. That is, suffering and joy are not experienced as separate. He continues to experience the suffering, but the suffering is now joy. He's hungry: it's a joyful experience to be hungry; he's cold: it's a joyful experience to be cold. For Milarepa every setback is a reminder of the impermanent, unpredictable nature of saṃsāra and the sheer pointlessness of holding on to things and experiences as though the world were anything other than a product of mind.

This is an aspect of the enlightened mind that it is important to get right. As long as it is associated with the physical body, there must always be the possibility at least of physical suffering, and even of the emotional suffering associated with life as a human being. But even though you suffer – whether the suffering is bodily pain or the emotional pain of losing someone close to you – your reaction to that pain, and your experience of it, will be entirely different from that of the unenlightened person.

The Creative Expression of the Enlightened Mind

Joyous in the treasure of triumphant songs now uttered,
Joyous exceedingly at the sounds and signs of multitudinous syllables,
Joyous at their turning into groups of words,

As an enlightened being, Milarepa enjoys the complete equanimity of his mind in all circumstances. He enjoys the pure creativity of its response: whatever he experiences, his mind does not react by clinging to the experience or cutting off from it; his response is always one of further positivity, further skilful activity. Whether in songs or in other kinds of spontaneous expression, he enjoys the playful and inexhaustible manifestation of the enlightened mind.

Like any hermit, Milarepa obviously relishes silence, but here he announces his enjoyment of singing and speaking. He enjoys watching the syllables coming out of his mouth and forming themselves into words and sentences. We can take it that his speech is not the expression of his ego, not 'self-expression' as we understand it, but more like the chanting of mantras and puja recitation. It is the spontaneous expression of the non-dual state.

Transcending Fear

After his initial paean to the joys of the yogi's way of life, Milarepa gives his visitors various teachings before concluding their meeting with a song that returns to his original theme of fear and the spiritual life. He begins the song by calling down the blessing of his teacher to help them come to firm knowledge, i.e. irreversible insight,

> *In the divine fortress of your own body.*

Chang, in his translation, makes this a more modest prayer for firm knowledge but, either way, the emphasis on the body is significant. Of course, one is most naturally fearful on behalf of the body or, if one is at all religious, for the state of one's soul, or one's 'merit', which the body, far from protecting, is perceived to put at risk through sense cravings. The idea of the body as a fortress therefore challenges some deeply rooted assumptions. Milarepa is reminding us that firm knowledge can be attained only within the psychophysical organism, the precious human body. The body is indeed the citadel of awakening.

> *Frightened by fears, I built up a castle.*
> *The voidness of absolute being, this was that castle,*
> *And of its destruction I now have no fear.*

The protection afforded by the voidness of absolute being is clearly not against the vicissitudes of life, or even against feeling exposed to them. It will not replace the need to take appropriate steps to minimize the effects of life's misfortunes. But it does protect one's positive state from being affected by those misfortunes or dependent on the outcome of events. If in its non-duality Milarepa's joy is a transcendence of joy, it is also a transcendence of fear. There is no attachment to the experience of joy, and thus no fear of losing it.

Fearlessness or *abhaya* is one of the fruits of spiritual practice and its development is a particularly important aspect of Buddhism. It is linked to the traditional description of the ultimate objective as a refuge. A castle is the ultimate material refuge, the securest place possible. It is also the ultimate expression of fear, and of the distinction we draw between self and other, us and them. The 'voidness of absolute being' means the ultimate non-reality of the very distinction between subject and object, self and other, and it becomes a castle because it protects us against fear itself. Fear indicates attachment to the self, in whatever way we conceive of it, and that in turn implies duality. We, fear any threat to the self from what we perceive as not self, as the other. As long as that distinction is perceived as absolute, we can never protect ourselves absolutely, and we will always be subject to fear.

Milarepa goes on to consider the various kinds of ordinary human fear, making the way we assuage each of them into a symbol for some spiritual or transcendental quality or set of qualities. This quality, instead of temporarily assuaging the need that gives rise to fear, cuts across the whole cycle of dependency, and thus removes the fear.

For instance, Milarepa's protection against the cold is the 'warmth within', which is a reference to the practice of *tumo*, 'psychic heat', by which spiritual means you can generate actual bodily heat. Less literally, we could take the experience of cold as representing loneliness, the chill of emotional deprivation. The producing of warmth within then becomes contentment or emotional positivity, a radiance that comes not from some external source but from one's own spiritual resources. It is a glow of inwardly generated well-being.

As for the fear of poverty, this is overcome by means of the 'seven inexhaustible jewels'. Traditionally these are of gold, silver, crystal, ruby, coral, agate, and cornelian. Again, we can look for a symbolic meaning here. The Buddhist tradition has two well-known sets of seven 'jewels'. There are the seven jewels of the *cakravarti-rāja*, the righteous or wheel-turning king: the elephant, the horse, the councillor, the woman, the commander-in-chief, and so on, and there also is a list of seven positive mental events called the 'seven jewels'. Either of these could be meant here. Milarepa is saying that by virtue of the spiritual qualities over which he has attained mastery, he has all the wealth in the world at his disposal. Far from being the impoverished beggar he appears to be, he is like a wheel-turning king, the world-govern-ing monarch whose laws and decrees are based not on tradition or selfish ambition but on the Dharma. Material poverty holds no fear for him, because the wealth he values is not material but springs from a renunciation of material wealth. The seven jewels can never be taken away from him by circumstances. As positive mental events, they are inexhaustible and endless.

Meditative absorption can be so tangibly and immediately beneficial that it is experienced as a sort of sustenance.

Inexhaustible too is the rapture and bliss of the concentrated mind attained through meditation.

> *Fearful of hunger, I sought for some food,*
> *Absorption in the absolute, this was that food,*
> *And from hunger I now have no fear.*

One is reminded here of the aspiration of a verse from the *Dhammapada*: 'Feeders on rapture shall we be.'[10] This is some-thing that any regular meditator will be able to appreciate. Medi-tative absorption can be so tangibly and immediately beneficial that it is experienced as a sort of sustenance. Rapture (Sanskrit *prīti*, Pali *pīti*) is an inner nourishment that keeps the concen-trated mind in a self-sufficient state of spiritual well-being. More generally, positive mental states, especially the state of mindful awareness, nourish the whole psychophysical organism. When attachment and aversion to things and experiences are aban-doned, fear of hunger is nowhere to be found.

Next in Milarepa's list of fears comes fear of thirst. This is the most frequent and immediately pressing of the physical appe-tites, and a powerful and seamless practice is needed to relieve the burden of fear associated with it: the nectar of mindfulness, as Milarepa calls it.

Finally, Milarepa evokes the fear of losing one's way.

Fearful of straying, I sought for a way,
The practice of two-in-one, this was that way,
And of straying I now have no fear.

The 'practice of two-in-one', which translates the term *yuga-naddha*, is a specifically Tantric reference to the non-duality of wisdom and compassion at the highest level. Once you have accomplished this, you have at last achieved, or embodied, the Middle Way. Until that point you have to keep asking yourself whether or not what you are doing is really the most skilful thing to be doing at that moment. Are you on the straight and narrow, or have you strayed a little off the path? Are you on the path of nirvāṇa or the path of saṁsāra? Are you making progress or are you stuck in dry intellectual understanding, barren concentration of mind, or uninspired if apparently skilful activity?

With the practice of non-duality, there is no distinction to be made between path and non-path. There is no right path or wrong path, and therefore no possibility of going astray. You no longer have to wonder if you are still on the right path. There is no path. The 'path' is one of no longer following a path. There is no question of choosing between alternatives. By uniting wisdom and compassion in your own experience you have also gone beyond the archetypes of the right and wrong paths: saṁsāra and nirvāṇa, the conditioned and the unconditioned. Milarepa's conclusion is that he is happy under any conditions whatsoever – and the next verse reveals the kind of conditions he has in mind.

At Yolmo in the tiger-cave of Singa-dzong
One trembles with fear at the roar of the tigress
And this sends one involuntarily to strict seclusion.

Towards the end of the song Milarepa adopts a more obviously literary tone as he notes the sights and sounds of his solitary hermitage and the emotions that these evoke. Whether or not this elevated style is responsible for an element of ambiguity in the meaning is debatable, but Chang's translation transfers the trembling from Milarepa to the tigress, whose 'roar' becomes a 'howling', a 'trembling cry'. But it would seem quite possible that even Milarepa would tremble with fear, having placed himself in close proximity to a tigress and her cubs. It is important to remember that being fearless does not mean that you never feel fear. The point is that even while he doesn't suppress his natural human reactions, he is able to be happy in the experience of fear. It is as though he relishes the roar of the tigress. His fearlessness does not exclude the experience of fear; he actually enjoys the fear that, as an embodied being, he naturally feels.

There is a kind of terror that is so invigorating as to be strangely pleasing; the proximity of danger makes you feel stronger, more courageous and heroic. Thus, trembling with fear can put heart into your practice and positively drive you to practise harder, with the awareness that whatever fearful experiences arise are finally no more than that – appearances, not fixed realities. You are the one element in the equation that can open up and release your tight hold upon objects – whether you crave them or fear them.

Together with this seclusion from the world comes the arising of compassion, which Milarepa then – as he sings in the next verse – feels for the tiger-cubs. This combination of withdrawal and compassion is very important in the teaching of the great founder of the Gelug school, Tsongkhapa: the withdrawal from the conditioned, accompanied by the arising of the bodhicitta – the will to Enlightenment for the sake of all beings – produces Enlightenment. It is not enough to withdraw; you must go out to the world in kindness as well. And, conversely, it is not enough to be compassionate; the element of withdrawal is also needed.

Working with Reflection

The cries of the monkeys cling to one's mind,
And this causes involuntarily a feeling of sadness,
But at the chattering of their young one just wants to laugh,
And this produces involuntarily an elevation of spirit.

References to the cries of monkeys feature prominently in Chinese poetry, in which they are intended to convey an impression of touching melancholy, associated with evening shadows and soft rain. To hear a monkey calling through the mist seems naturally to produce a sort of pleasing mournfulness; the haunting sound clings to the mind.

Milarepa shares this common emotional reflex and, as with his natural reaction of fear, he does not suppress it. But he doesn't wallow in it either. He doesn't allow his mind to drift from this keen responsiveness to the sadness of the world around him into a self-regarding melancholia. His solitary situation is one in which loneliness can quite easily turn into depression, and here he shows us how to work creatively with the moods that we might experience on solitary retreat, directing this initial response of sadness towards a broader appreciation of the situation in which we find ourselves.

> He isn't trying to hang on to his joy;
> in fact, he is letting go of it.

Attending to the comical chattering of the young monkeys, his initial reflectiveness turns into happy laughter, bringing an access of energy and an elevation of spirit. This positive result of a simple but creative shift of attention suggests the beginning of the spiralling process outlined in the traditional formulation of the *bodhyaṅgas*, the seven factors of Enlightenment. The upward spiral begins with mindfulness, continues with investigation of mental states, energy, joy, and so on, and culminates in an exalted state of insight and equanimity.

> *Sweet to the ear is the sad song of the cuckoo with its*
> *tremulous note,*
> *And one is caused to hearken involuntarily,*
> *And the varied cries of the raven are cheering to his neighbour*
> *the yogin.*

Happy is the state of one who lives in such a spot as this,
Without the presence of a single companion, and even in this
one is happy.
And now by the song of this rejoicing yogin
May the sufferings of all beings be removed.

Milarepa's attitude is never self-referential in the narrow sense. His equanimity is a state of mind free from fixed views, from one-sided reactions both to external physical events and to emotional or mental events. He does not see or feel things from just his own point of view. He is always able to take in the whole situation. His awareness is thus essentially appreciative in tone. The colour and vibrancy of these verses illustrate the fact that Milarepa's poetic sensibility is attuned to beauty wherever and whenever it may be discerned. His freedom from partial, self-referential, fixed views means also that he is not ascetic in the traditional sense of refusing to take pleasure in things.

Nonetheless this is more than just aesthetic appreciation – it is a practice, even if in Milarepa's case it has been perfected and is second nature. Whatever emotions arise, he shifts effortlessly in a continually more positive direction. He turns to good account all those lonely sights and sounds that could be, if one allowed, distracting or even dispiriting.

The fact that this elevation of mind is involuntary is characteristic of Milarepa's sublime mental state. The perceiving mind is, after all, impermanent, and for Milarepa impermanence is a source of delight. If your experience of 'yourself' is not separateness but the blissful void, you have transcended the duality of self and other that is the ultimate basis for loneliness. You are no longer an ego and therefore no longer distinct from other egos. How can you feel lonely if you don't experience the ultimate reality of yourself – even when absolutely alone – as separate from others?

What this closing section conveys is a sense that the world around Milarepa supports him in his practice. It does so because his practice is intimately concerned with that world. He expects to be uplifted by the cries of the raven because he feels he is the raven's neighbour. He sees himself as sharing the place where he lives with the wild natural forms – both animals and spirits – that have always occupied it and will continue to do so when he has moved on.

So it is not that Milarepa is happy *despite* his isolation. He is happy *in* it. He isn't trying to hang on to his joy; in fact, he is letting go of it. He isn't doing his best to be positive in a challenging situation; he actually sees his situation in positive terms. He is happy that he is without a single companion even as he offers up his happiness to the welfare of all beings. In his remote mountain hermitage, Milarepa renounces attachment to human community, to property, to any sense of separate self. And he does this not for the sake of a miserable, deprived existence, but the more fully to enjoy the freedom of the blissfully clear light of the void.

Third Story

The Meeting at Silver Spring

Chapter 4

A Man of the Beyond

The Ultimate Relationship

If 'The Song of a Yogi's Joy' offers an account of the enlightened state in isolation, 'The Meeting at Silver Spring' shows what happens when that enlightened state comes into contact with unenlightened humanity; when this sublime, seemingly incommunicable realization of ultimate truth or reality encounters someone who, at least initially, has not the slightest inkling that any such truth exists, much less that it could be communicated to him.

This really is a problem, and one that even the Buddha Śākyamuni had to solve once supreme Enlightenment had been attained. The Buddha's resolve to teach the Dharma arose, the legends say, from his response to the pleading of the god Brahmā Sahampati, whose intervention helped the Buddha see that there were at least some beings who had 'but little dust' to obscure their vision and who might be receptive to the highest truth.[1] In Milarepa's case, a similar impetus would seem to require him to practise 'for the benefit of all beings', even while he lives out of easy reach of any of those beings.

The central issues upon which this group of songs focuses are broadly twofold. First, there is the problem of the vast gulf that separates the worldly mind from the enlightened mind. How can something that lies beyond the reach of language be communicated? As we shall see, effective communication relies in large part on the pre-existing familiarity of both parties with the thing being described. Yet, for the unenlightened being, the non-dual state is utterly unknown. The issue here is essentially one of perspective.

The second issue provides the solution to this problem, at least in the tradition in which Milarepa practises. Enlightenment never arises in isolation from beings. There is no such thing as Enlightenment; there are only enlightened beings. The question of communication has to be answered in the sphere of human receptivity, not in the abstract terms of philosophy. The issue here is one, therefore, of the personal relationship between guru and disciple, and every relationship must begin with a meeting.

The Yogi's Dream: Ḍākinīs

The story begins one day in early autumn, when Milarepa goes on his almsround. He has spent the summer months in solitary retreat at North Shri Ri, dedicating himself to meditation. But now it is harvest time, and he sets off through the mountains. On his way, the great yogi stops to take a rest, and falls asleep. On the face of it, it perhaps seems odd that an experienced yogi, practised in mindfulness, should just drop off, but there is, as it turns out, a deeper process is at work, to which he is sensitive enough to respond, for he not only sleeps; he dreams.

> In his dream Milarepa is visited by a
> mysterious and beautiful girl, green in colour,
> with shining golden hair.

He sleeps, that is to say, only to dream. It is as though he senses that something is ready to come through, and he is sufficiently highly developed to allow that dreaming state to come over him. He is able just to let it happen, in the confidence that by so doing he is opening a channel of expression for positive forces that can come through in no other way.

In his dream Milarepa is visited by a mysterious and beautiful girl, green in colour, with shining golden hair. She is leading a youth who is about twenty years old. Turning to Milarepa, she tells him that the lotus of his heart is destined to have eight petals, and that the youth is one of them. So saying, the girl disappears.

When he wakes, Milarepa is quick to identify this figure as a *ḍākinī*. The Sanskrit term is the feminine and more familiar form of the word *ḍāka* and means, basically, 'she of space'. The Tibetans translate it as *kadoma*, commonly translated into English as 'sky-dancer' or 'celestial maiden'. So a ḍākinī is one who dances or flies through space, and is therefore free and unimpeded. At the same time, space represents mind in its absolute aspect. She does not so much move within space as embody the vast untapped store of emotional energy that can arise, as if from nowhere, from the very depths of the mind. More specifically – the sky being a symbol of śūnyatā or emptiness – the ḍākinī or sky-dancer is one who dwells in the consciousness of the conditioned nature of all things – that is, in the knowledge of their ultimate emptiness. In everyday life, we rarely experience passionate energies that are also positive. It may be only in our dreams that we come in contact with them at all. What the ḍākinī represents is the irruption of such energies into consciousness.

The 'great ḍākinīs,' as they are called, are no less than Buddhas in female form. At the other end of the scale, a ḍākinī may be no more than the kind of very attractive woman who has a certain almost magical quality – not just sex appeal – about her. A ḍākinī can be a sort of siren, fascinating and stimulating. In psychological terms she may be recognized as the anima; for the artist, she appears as a muse; but at the very highest level she is the inspirational aspect of Enlightenment itself.

In Milarepa's dream, the ḍākinī appears as a force of spiritual inspiration, welling up from unconscious depths. Her appearance suggests emotional energies in a pure, intensely refined form: one might say that she is midway between the ḍākinī as simply an exceptionally fascinating woman and the Ḍākinī with a capital Ḍ, the Ḍākinī as Buddha, as the moving spirit of Enlightenment. Her green colour makes it clear straightaway that she is quite out of the ordinary – certainly non-human. Green is also naturally associated with the earth, and suggests something springing up with a fresh energy. It is the colour of nature in its most restful, tranquil, and harmonious aspect, but it is also the colour of action, growth, and even inspiration.

As for the gold of her hair, fair hair would have been quite extraordinary to medieval Tibetans, so it indicates something rare and precious, not materially but in the sense of spiritual riches. Gold is in any case the colour of richness and abundance, suggesting the inexhaustible wealth of the enlightened mind, overflowing to the delight and benefit of living beings.

Milarepa's Karma

Milarepa goes on to contemplate the ḍākinī's words and the image they have conjured up of his heart as a lotus with eight petals. He realizes that these must represent 'eight superlative, destined, heart-like disciples', that is, disciples who are very close to the heart of the guru, who are, one might say, the guru's very heart. Milarepa concludes that he will soon come across a disciple who is what he calls 'Karma-exhausted'. This, more than any aptitude for scholarship or Buddhist devotion, is what will mark him out as a prospective 'heart son'. Such a person may not even be interested, at least initially, in becoming any kind of disciple, but he will nonetheless be in an ideal state of readiness to set out on the path of higher spiritual training.

'Karma' literally means 'action', and it is axiomatic to Buddhism that actions have consequences. Clearly some of these consequences will be spiritually positive, but some of them will be negative. Some of our actions, particularly those that have become habits, whether of body, speech, or mind, will get in the way of our progress towards insight, throwing up obstacles to prevent our carrying out even our best intentions. We may have resolved to lead a thoroughly spiritual life, for example, but find that there is something that hinders us from carrying out that resolution. There may be external circumstances set up by our past actions which now stand in the way of our present aims and aspirations, or we may be subject to habits and tendencies that are the result of ways in which we have repeatedly acted in the past.

In all likelihood, our karmic obstacles will arise as a combination of factors, both external and internal. According to Buddhism, it is our karma that has caused us to be reborn in the human realm at all. For this reason alone, it is highly unusual to encounter someone without any karmic traces. However, in the case of this 'heart-like disciple', nothing will be left over from the past to get in the way if he decides to take up the spiritual life. He has no previous unskilful actions hanging over him in the form of a karmic debt; he is free of any such burden.

This was by no means the case for Milarepa himself. Milarepa came to the Dharma encumbered by some very weighty negative karma indeed, but he worked through it with the help of his teacher Marpa. Marpa was a tough character who reared his disciples the hard way, so he was exactly the guru Milarepa needed. Having committed a number of serious misdeeds, even atrocities, including the murder of a whole group of people using sorcery, Milarepa was in need of strong spiritual medicine.

If you offer yourself – body, speech, and mind –
to your guru, you cannot very well complain
about how he treats you, and if you feel upset,
that means you are still holding something back.

Milarepa's is in some ways the classic Vajrayāna career. When he was a young child his father died and his uncle not only stole Milarepa's inheritance, but proceeded to mistreat him and his sister in abominable fashion, beating them, starving them, and forcing them to carry out menial tasks night and day. To prepare himself to take his revenge, Milarepa apprenticed himself to a sorcerer and became an adept himself. Making use of his supernormal powers, he brought down a great storm on his uncle's house, killing a large number of those inside, including the wicked uncle himself.

According to Buddhist doctrine, the karmic consequences of this act threatened considerable and protracted future suffering for Milarepa, and when he realized this, he knew there was only one option open to him: he had to gain Enlightenment in his present lifetime. His situation was so urgent that only the most intense spiritual practice and the highest Tantric teaching would be of any use to him. If he was not to go straight to hell after death, there could be no halfway house.

With this single aim in view, Milarepa sought out Marpa as his teacher, and endured under him the harsh training that his lamentable karmic situation demanded. In accordance with Tantric custom, Milarepa submitted himself completely to Marpa's will. The Tantric teacher – or *vajra-guru* – has a single aim: to introduce the disciple to the direct experience of their own essential nature, in other words, to the true nature of mind. In bringing the disciple to experience authentic reality, the guru has to disentangle him from words and theories, from his own conceptions and ideas about what he is. Sometimes this involves uncompromising and dramatic, even harrowing, tests of patience and resolve. In Milarepa's case, Marpa pushed him to the limit and beyond. As Milarepa recalls in the first of the songs in this chapter, 'I reduced my body to powder in his service.'[12]

The story of their relationship is a story of frustration, disappointment, torment, and extreme physical and mental hardship. But as Marpa pointed out to his disciple, if you offer yourself – body, speech, and mind – to your guru, you cannot very well complain about how he treats you, and if you feel upset, that means you are still holding something back. Indeed, Marpa tested his faith in him by behaving in an outrageously unreasonable manner, telling him several times to build a tower, then telling him to pull it down again. All this was to purify Milarepa sufficiently to be able to practise the mahāmudrā – the union of bliss and emptiness – effectively, and of course in the end, he succeeded in doing so.

But the disciple whom Milarepa is about to meet is in a very different situation from that of the young Milarepa: he is already open and receptive to the Dharma, and in a position, karmically speaking, for him to begin to put the Dharma into practice immediately.

Milarepa's Dry Feet

After waking from his dream, Milarepa again sets out on his way. He labours up the steep track leading to Bong, and eventually comes to a river whose clear waters glisten like silver. For a second time, the yogi lays down his head to sleep. Some time goes by, and when he wakes up, he is confronted by a young nobleman mounted on a handsome black horse. The expected meeting, it seems, is about to happen.

The young man would perhaps not have paid him any attention if Milarepa had been doing what a yogi is expected to do on the road – just walking along or perhaps sitting in meditation. But as it is, he asks him why he has been sleeping there. Milarepa engages the young man in conversation, and asks him to give him a ride through the river, explaining that wading through water is difficult at his age. The young man does not want to trouble himself, however; all he can think of is the good time he is going to have with the friends he is on his way to meet, and he is also concerned not to put his horse under unnecessary strain.

The youth has none of the humility or piety one might associate with someone destined to be the heart disciple of an enlightened yogi. One would not immediately recognize him as religious material. Yet it is precisely this unaffected and straightforward quality that marks him as well suited to the Tantric training. Indeed, it is a quality shared by many of the Tibetans I knew during my years in Kalimpong. They were hardy people, fond of what luxury and pleasure they could find, and keenly curious – all in all, good material for the Dharma. Many of them had an unspoilt, sincere, slightly naive quality which very few Westerners, nowadays at least, seem to have. I am reminded particularly of one of my Tibetan students, one of five brothers who were minor aristocrats from Kham in eastern Tibet. They did quite well as merchants and were well-to-do, bluff, and hearty fellows. As was customary, they divided their income into three equal parts: one third went to business and household expenses, another third was laid out for pleasure – picnics, parties, gambling, and so on – and the remainder was for the Dharma, and was donated to the monks. I once saw these brothers encountering a steam engine for the first time. It was a tiny mountain train, but as the wheels began to turn and the whistle hooted they displayed the kind of unaffected astonishment, wonder, and interest that is in many ways the ideal response to the Dharma. This sort of healthy, full-blooded attitude is rarely to be encountered in the more sophisticated cultures of the West.

So the young man's response to Milarepa is the straight-forward answer of an ordinary, well-adjusted human being. There is no indecisiveness, no neurotic anxiety about what the yogi will think, no prevarication or shame. He might seem a little selfish, but it is the natural and even healthy selfishness of youth; he wants to enjoy life, not worry about decrepit old yogis. He is not unfriendly; he says quite candidly that he doesn't want to perform this small favour, and straightforwardly explains why. Then he rides on without looking back – without, that is, feeling any irrational, neurotic guilt.

> Understood symbolically, Milarepa's feat represents
> the manifestation of a different realm of being,
> a higher metaphysical plane of existence.

At this point, Milarepa enters the 'Samādhi of Guru-Union', uniting himself with the unbroken Kagyu lineage. Having entered that state of concentration, he does something even more remarkable. Holding his breath, he walks on the surface of the river, gently and mindfully moving across the stream to the far side, whence he looks back to observe the young man who is still only half way across. The young man sees Milarepa gliding past him and cannot believe his eyes.

What the youth has seen, after all, cannot be explained by ordinary means. Milarepa's walking on water would appear to be a display of supernormal ability, a miracle, in other words. But if its only function was to be a marker of Milarepa's psychic power, it would be no more than a highly accomplished magic trick. In the present context, we need to look more deeply. Just as with

Milarepa's dream of the ḍākinī, we need to understand what this miracle symbolizes, rather as we would a dream image. Milarepa has presented the young man with something impossible. He seems to be showing that, for the yogic adept, the normal order of physical reality can be turned upside down easily and effortlessly, that the heavy and solid can be made to rise above the apparently fluid and ungraspable and find a firm foundation there. Understood symbolically, Milarepa's feat represents the manifestation of a different realm of being, a higher metaphysical plane of existence.

The young man, we learn, has a fairly sceptical turn of mind, and he does not accept the evidence of his senses without testing it. When he arrives at the bank, he takes a careful look at Milarepa's feet and finds that not even his soles are wet. He considers the possibility that he has been hallucinating, and looks for clues as to how Milarepa might have crossed the river. Only when he has exhausted the naturalistic possibilities does he embrace the supernormal explanation. His reason having been allowed full rein, faith then arises very readily and spontaneously.

The first thing he does is apologize and express regret for not having given Milarepa a ride. In a way this is odd, because of all people Milarepa was evidently the least in need of help in this respect. But of course the boy's regret is largely for himself, having missed an opportunity to do what an accomplished lama has asked of him. He realizes that what appeared to be an appeal for help was actually Milarepa's desire to do him a good turn, and he has frustrated that compassionate impulse. He has let Milarepa down, and in so doing he has let himself down. But he does not berate himself or wallow in regrets, and once he has bowed down to Milarepa many times, his natural inquisitiveness asserts itself. He asks him a whole series of questions – where is he from, who is his teacher, what meditation does he practise, where did he come from that day, and where is he going – which Milarepa answers by way of a song.

Milarepa's Song of the Tantric Path

First of all, Milarepa announces that he has travelled far in his pursuit of higher knowledge, and then goes on to describe his spiritual path. This includes learning the 'fierce exorcism of the Black and Red Planets' – that is, the darker arts of the Tantra. However, his teacher in these arts, for all his expertise, was not able, as Milarepa puts it, to clear his doubts. These doubts are not simply intellectual, but arise from a more fundamental emotional and existential perplexity.

As he goes on to say, Milarepa's career culminated in his initiation under his root guru, Marpa the Translator, who 'had experienced the mother-like Essence of Mind'. In the Vajrayāna it is sometimes said that the aim of one's practice is the meeting of the mother-mind with the son-mind, the mother-mind being the original, primordial mind and the son-mind being the phenomenal but enlightened mind as it reunites with its original source. So Milarepa is declaring his faith in the depth of Marpa's realization.

Nor is he in any doubt about the need for this guru-disciple relationship. There is no question of making a choice of guru, or of weighing up one against another. Marpa was his guru even before he met him. 'Just to hear his name caused my skin to tingle and my hair to rise.' And when he finally did meet Marpa, his heart was changed – that is, his faith was deepened – 'just by glancing at his face'.

Marpa initiated Milarepa into the Hevajra Tantra and 'Nāropa's skilful path' – that is, the six yogas of Nāropa. These are (1) the cultivation of inner heat or *tumo* as a means of controlling the subtle energies of the psychophysical organism; (2) the visualization of the illusory or subtle body created out of the six perfections; (3) controlling dreams and becoming conscious in the dream state; (4) realizing the mind as the clear light of śūnyatā; (5) training in the after-death experience of the bardos; and (6) training in the transference of consciousness at the moment of death.

After this, Milarepa 'took the vows and won the Four Initiations of the blessed Dem Chog'. Dem Chog (Sanskrit *saṁvara*: 'great bliss') is a specifically Tantric deity, shown in *yab-yum* form at the centre of the mandala. The four initiations are: the initiation with the jar; the secret initiation; the wisdom initiation; and, finally, one simply known as the 'fourth initiation'. They are also called the initiations of body, speech, mind, and the unity of the three, and together they amount to full Tantric initiation. So Milarepa has been initiated into the full practice of the Tantric path.

> By calling concepts 'playwords', he means
> he no longer takes them as referring to
> fixed or absolute realities.

All this leads up to the realization of the 'essence of Mahāmudrā'. This is the highest teaching according to the Kagyu tradition, referred to here by Milarepa as the 'Whispered Succession', of which in a sense Milarepa is the founder in Tibet. 'Mahāmudrā' literally means great symbol, great attitude, or great seal, and its purpose is the realization of the true nature of mind as beyond subject and object, resulting in what Milarepa describes (in his next song) as 'illuminating Self-Awareness'.

The prefix *mahā* means great, and in any Mahāyāna context refers not to size or extent but to śūnyatā – that is, to Enlightenment as the realization of emptiness. The term 'mahāmudrā' thus suggests a unity of form (*mudrā*) and emptiness that is beyond conceptualization. As a practice, it is an expedient means of realizing this unity. For the Yogācāra, śūnyatā is the nature of reality, which may be described as the non-duality of self and other, subject and object. Its subjective counterpart, the wisdom that realizes the nature of reality, is called *prajñā*. The experience itself is of course neither subjective nor objective; whether śūnyatā or prajñā, it is the sky-like realm of the ḍākinī. When Milarepa sings, 'I am a yogi (who can) dwell in the sky,' he means that his life is spontaneous and free of obstruction.

He also puts it here in terms of a total transcendence of thought and language. He has, he sings, 'realized in full the ultimate "Beyond-all-Playwords"'. The term *playwords*, meaning 'concepts', is found again and again in Milarepa's songs. By calling concepts 'playwords', he means he no longer takes them as referring to fixed or absolute realities. He has realized the nature of reality as unmediated and unbound by concepts in a way that echoes the perfection of wisdom teachings of the Mahāyāna. We can now perhaps begin to see more clearly the significance of his miraculous walking on the surface of the water.

Milarepa explains to the boy:

> *Having united the Four Elements,*
> *I have no fear of water.*

He is able to walk on water because he is no longer threatened by the separateness of the elements, whether within or without. He has fully accepted that he himself is composed of elements, and that death will return those elements back to the world. By no longer resisting the separate qualities of the elements even within himself, he has integrated them into non-dual awareness.

At the same time, by taking the everyday world and radically rearranging its material elements before the young man's incredulous eyes, he is demonstrating the depth of his understanding. He knows that the very idea of an element – like that of a self – is an entirely fictitious mental construct. He knows it in his bones. He is fully integrated not just emotionally, not even just physically, but in the sky-like non-duality of the mahāmudrā. In this state, there is no here or there, no self or other, and therefore no reliance on the separate qualities of the elements.

Freed at last from the burden of dualistic thinking, Milarepa lives without the illusory security of imagining that he knows for sure where he is going to sleep that night.

> *Where I shall go this evening, I am not certain,*
> *For mine is the yogi's way of life.*

He ends his song by briefly suggesting the basis of the young man's own values, exposing their ludicrous poverty and narrowness by comparison with those extolled in the inspiring account of his own quest.

> *Have you heard what I have sung,*
> *My happy boy who seeks nought but pleasure?*

The Youth's Salutation and Offering

As a result of his contact with Milarepa, the boy begins to realize that he is quite a different person from who he thought he was. He has been thinking of himself as a young playboy, but his meeting with Milarepa has made him aware of something much more fundamental, much more real, in his nature. And this tremendous upheaval, this bursting through into consciousness of something that was unconscious, is accompanied by weeping. The boy experiences his true nature, or something near to it, in the form of an unshakeable faith, a faith that amounts to an experience of transcendental insight. There is a tremendous release, not just of emotion but of energy, expressed in freely flowing tears.

> The guru is the Buddha principle active within
> the field of our own experience.

This is the kind of overwhelming effect that meeting the Tantric guru can have. A guru is someone who activates your dormant energies by bringing his own more integrated and freed-up energies into contact with yours. In the Tantric sense, therefore, the guru performs the same function as a Buddha. The guru is the Buddha principle active within the field of our own experience.

For many of us, the Buddha himself may be no more than an idea, a distant figure. But through the guru – should we happen to be in contact with one – we are in a position to receive the spiritual influence of all the Buddhas, and in this sense he is our point of contact with them. This is not to say that the guru is necessarily enlightened, but simply that, through his personal knowledge of his disciples, he can present the teachings of the Buddha in the way that is most effective for each person.

The guru is an interpreter, a translator, rather than a Buddha or even a teacher. His primary role is to activate dormant energy, although he may teach as a secondary function of that role. The guru may be said to stimulate the disciple's energies in a highly positive way, but he may also be said to stir up those energies in such a way as to make it impossible to ignore or deny them. The energies having been aroused, the disciple must then learn to work with them.

The boy declares:

> *You are the Sage unrecognized, a man of the beyond!*
> *You are the Buddha whom one meets so rarely.*

The boy is saying that he had not realized who Milarepa really was, but what he says also suggests that it is in the nature of the sage to be unrecognized. A sage doesn't necessarily have the kind of characteristics that will impress an ordinary person. Indeed, whatever charisma or conceptual wisdom he may emanate or dispense is more or less incidental in comparison with the reality of his attainment. 'A man of the beyond' is the kind of ascription one might find in the Pali canon, placing the enlightened being as it does firmly outside all ascriptions. He doesn't belong to this world; he belongs to the beyond; he is a new kind of man – indeed, he is a Buddha.

> *Your instructions are the preaching of the Nirmāṇakāya.*

The *nirmāṇakāya* is the body of reality or truth as it manifests within the mundane world – that is, it is what we conventionally think of as a Buddha. We gather, then, that the boy knows enough Buddhism to be able to appreciate quite precisely who Milarepa really is – he has the technical terms at his fingertips. In fact, as we learn later in the text, he is a student interested in Buddhist scholarship, as well as a playboy.

The young man then discloses a strange sense of having heard Milarepa's name before, and even of having seen him before, though he knows that he hasn't done so in the historical sense.

It seems that I have heard your name before,
But yet I am not sure.
It seems that I may have seen you before,
But again, I am not sure.

That he recognizes Milarepa's *name* is very significant. 'Name' here is not a label attached in the memory to a particular set of characteristics. Milarepa's name signifies his unique nature as an individual, indeed, his unconditioned nature. The boy's recognition of it suggests that Milarepa has made a profound impression on him, in a way that echoes Milarepa's own account of hearing the name of *his* teacher for the first time.

This recognition is therefore not only of the teacher but also of something deep within the young man himself. The meeting with Milarepa has confronted him with something he hadn't known was there – except that, at some level, part of him must have known that it was there all along, which is why it is not totally unfamiliar.

It is a moment of insight, a recognition of his true nature. And inasmuch as it is contact with Milarepa that has put him in touch with that deeper level of himself, it is as though he has known Milarepa before too. The two recognitions are inextricably connected in the young man's experience – Milarepa in some sense *is* that deeper level of himself. But what does this mean? The only way to put it is to say that it is an encounter outside time – that it takes place without before and after, without past, present, and future – although the young man does not quite see this clearly. It is not a discovery of the new so much as a recognition of the very, very old. This is what you experience when you come into contact with someone who is outside time. The temporal mind is trying to make sense of non-temporal reality, in which there is no before or after or now. You have an intuitive knowledge of having seen or known that person before, but you are unable to say how or when. You feel that you have always known them – 'always' not in the sense of taking place from the beginning and going on within time, but in the sense of coming from a dimension in which there is no present, past, or future.

It is thus not surprising that the youth is confused. Milarepa has put him in contact with a level of his being that is still very obscure to him. He has sparked off a veiled realization, an intuition of something beyond the parameters of a world conditioned by time. The young man encounters Milarepa outside time – at least, he experiences what Milarepa *is* outside time – that being the only way Milarepa as he really is can be experienced. His realization consists in his contact with Milarepa's innate or intrinsic Buddha nature, and thus in a sense with his own Buddha nature. But he continues to question his grip on his experience. His security in the present has been shaken, opened up, and he is no longer quite so self-assured.

> *Whether the obeisance that I made you*
> *Was sincere enough, I do not know.*

A few minutes earlier, when he had made his obeisance to Milarepa, he would have been certain of this. But now he has been introduced to new levels of himself, and he doesn't know where he's coming from, what level he is speaking from. The continuity of his experience has been interrupted. Though before he bowed to Milarepa many times, and asked his questions 'with great sincerity and faith', he is no longer the person who bowed a few minutes before, nor, he now realizes, is Milarepa the man to whom he thought he was bowing.

A Man of the World

Any auspicious meeting in Tibet involves the offering of gifts, and the young man now proceeds to offer Milarepa a whole series of them. He begins by making an offering of his horse, which runs, he says, like the wind. The horse's features and accoutrements are described in loving detail.

> *On his neck hangs a wondrous bell;*
> *On his back of well-known pedigree*
> *Is a saddle cloth, most warm and smooth;*
> *On it rests a strong wooden saddle.*
> *The girth is fashioned of steel from Mon....*
> *His forelock curls like a tiger's smile,*
> *Shining brightly like a mirrored star.*

These things are valuable in a way that is perhaps difficult for us to understand today, because they are symbolic of an attitude to material things that is very unusual these days. All these objects have been individually made by individual craftsmen; they each have their own character, to be appreciated and cherished. We might wonder what could possibly be special about an ordinary thing like a saddle-cloth, but the boy has a good word even for a humble object like that.

We find the same respect for objects in Homer's epic accounts of the ancient Greek world. We read not of a wooden bowl, but of a well-carved wooden bowl; likewise, a cauldron is strongly forged, and a sword is smoothly and expertly fashioned. Everything in this world stands out, everything has a presence. Objects have a clear provenance: you know where they have come from, from whom they have been passed down to you, where and how they were made – and all this makes a difference to your attitude to them.

In our age of mass production, in sharp contrast, there is a confusion of objects in our lives that inevitably blunts awareness. The disposability of objects, our knowledge that most things can be replaced, means that we don't feel we need to care for them or attend to them. When we see a factory-made object, we might appreciate the design, but a single example of that design is never unique. We can hardly conceive of how things have been made, or even where they were made, apart from the ubiquitous label saying 'Made in China'.

The young man is thus offering far more than we can really imagine. As for the horse itself, it represented the only form of transport in Tibet. There can be little doubt that a beautiful horse with all its fine equipment is tremendously valuable. This is no ordinary gift. Moreover, as the young man reminds Milarepa, a horse signifies a certain social prestige: 'To a man of the world, a good horse is his pride.' He is therefore unambiguously sacrificing his worldly pride – at least, that is his intention, although as we shall see, worldly pride is not to be so easily disposed of. And it is interesting to see why he is prepared to be so generous. It is out of a very proper spiritual fear.

> *Praying that you may keep me from the hell*
> *Into which I else would fall.*

He does not know, of course, that he is 'Karma-exhausted'. He does not realize how hopeful his situation really is. But it is in his intense awareness of spiritual danger that his best hope lies. It seems, in fact, that the depth of insight that has produced his fear of hell has also given him the faith that will prevent him falling into hell. We can see in his prayer a plea to Milarepa to help him make use of the merit he has, so that he can avoid the inevitable reversal of his karmic situation that would ensue from allowing that merit to go to waste.

Milarepa's Song of Prāṇa

As well as being his most valuable possession – as a fast car might be for a young man today – a horse is also a powerful symbol. The young man is placing at Milarepa's disposal not simply his prized horse, but – on a symbolic level – all his energies. Milarepa certainly points the youth in the direction of this symbolic interpretation of his offering. He acknowledges the young man as his patron or lay supporter, but he says he has another, better horse, with better accoutrements. He then lists the teachings and attainments of his tradition as the accoutrements to the central Tantric goal of mobilizing the psychic energies of the whole being, and directing them towards the experience of non-duality.

A horse of Prāṇa-Mind have I;
I adorn him with the silk scarf of Dhyāna,
His skin is the magic Ensuing Dhyāna Stage,

If dhyāna is meditation in the sense of the experience of higher, superconscious states, the 'Ensuing Dhyāna Stage' is the after-effect of the successful practice of meditation, the very positive state that continues even when you are engaged in ordinary activities afterwards. The same kind of thing happens after a retreat: you continue to experience the positive effects of that experience for weeks afterwards.

His headstall is the Prāṇa of Vital-force;
His forelock curl is Three-pointed Time,

Time is the devouring tiger of the boy's original image for his horse's forelock curl. But when past, present, and future are integrated, it becomes, as it were, a three-pointed star, reflecting the image the boy chose to describe his horse's forelock 'shining brightly like a mirrored star'. (The translator surmises that three-pointed time refers to the three favourable times for meditation.) But now there is a curious contradiction.

Tranquillity within is his adornment,
Bodily movement is his rein,
And ever-flowing inspiration is his bridle.
He gallops wildly along the Spine's Central Path.

The external and inessential nature of adornment is in direct contrast to the contained and self-sufficient nature of inner tranquillity – yet here they are set out as equivalent to each other, just as, paradoxically, bodily movement is given the function of holding back bodily movement, and untrammelled inspiration the function of constraining and controlling the head.

Nothing holds Milarepa back because there is nobody to be held back.

Milarepa is saying that he no longer needs any adornment, anything inessential, or any self-control. His action and non-action combine to create a perfectly balanced – yet dynamically energetic – practice. If ever-flowing inspiration is his bridle, this suggests that in the enlightened state, even though there is no holding back, everything is in its place. This is not chaos, but the dynamism of unfettered energy perfectly attuned to reality, in harmony with all that is positive, all that is free. Nothing holds Milarepa back because there is nobody to be held back. It is the bridle of no bridle, the restraint of no restraint. His energy enables him to gallop at full pelt even along the most obscure of routes and within the narrowest of confines – that is, the 'Spine's Central Path' (the median nerve through which the yogi trains himself to contain and channel his physical and psychic energies). All aspects of his being – body, mind, feelings, emotions – are engaged in this wild and beautiful release of energy.

In recognizing Milarepa as the 'Buddha whom one meets so rarely', and in renouncing his pride, the young man has already come a long way. But he still has much to learn. So, having proclaimed his mastery of his own energies, and his freedom from dependence on external sources of energy, Milarepa tells the young man that he doesn't need his horse. Refusing the gift, Milarepa concludes by throwing down a challenge: 'Go your way, young man, and look for pleasure!'

Chapter 5

Free from Ego

Energy and the Spiritual Life

The Tantra is concerned above all with energy, an emphasis which offsets in the most direct way possible the tendency to view the central concept of the Perfection of Wisdom teachings – 'voidness' or śūnyatā – as featureless, colourless, and without content. According to the Tantra, the void is alive with unleashed energy. It is attained not when the yogi has thought very hard about it, but when it illuminates the whole of his consciousness. The experience of the void is entirely bright and beautiful with fully experienced energy – a bright white light, containing within itself all the colours of the rainbow.

Philosophically, the counterbalance to the abstract teaching on śūnyatā is the Yogācāra view of 'Mind Only', which is shared by both Mahāyāna and Tantric schools of Buddhism, and open to being understood at a merely philosophical level. In the end, any philosophy can lose touch with its practical applications, and it is at the level of specific practices that we find the main difference, from the Vajrayāna point of view, between the Vajrayāna and the Mahāyāna teachings. The Vajrayāna is concerned with transforming the entire psychophysical organism, with refining, manipulating, and redirecting its mental and physical energies into increasingly subtle, concentrated, and refined states.

The Vajrayāna concretizes the highest teachings of the Dharma in a direct experience of the body, but its conception of the body does not stop with the material substratum of physical experience. The Tantric practitioner works with the subtle body, which resembles the physical body in every respect except that it is 'mind-formed' rather than simply an animated material form. Experienced at this level, the body manifests not as matter but as energy.

The avowed goal of the Vajrayāna is the direct experience of one's own essential nature, and the work of the Tantra is to bring this about through a radical transformation of energy. To begin this process, one's energies must be activated, indeed decisively stirred up, from their sleeping earthbound state. The significant moment at which these energies are roused is the point of initiation, or what is sometimes referred to as Tantric empowerment.

In all Buddhist traditions the spiritual has to be 'incorporated'.

My friend Yogi Chen, a Ch'an and Vajrayāna master whom I visited quite regularly when I lived in Kalimpong in the 1950s, used to make the point that although one might realize certain truths at a deeper than intellectual level by means of Mahāyāna meditation, such realization remained essentially mental and emotional. It did not involve the whole being, it did not incorporate all one's energies; according to him it was the specific function of the Tantra to bring even one's physical energies into that higher spiritual realization, to transform the body as well as the intellect and the emotions.

There is nothing really revolutionary about this Tantric perspective. Throughout the Buddhist tradition, including the Theravāda, it is emphasized that the experience of meditation is of the body as well as the mind. In the *Saṁyutta Nikāya* of the Pali canon, for example, we find the following account of the Buddha's meditative powers.

When, Ānanda, the Tathāgata immerses the body in the mind and the mind in the body, and when he dwells having entered upon a blissful perception and a buoyant perception in regard to

*the body, on that occasion the body of the Tathāgata rises up
without difficulty from the earth into the air. He wields the various kinds of spiritual power: having been one, he becomes many;
having been many, he becomes one.... he exercises mastery with
the body as far as the brahmā world.*[13]

The Pali texts are therefore no more in favour of a bloodless and
disembodied practice than are the Tantras. In all Buddhist traditions the spiritual has to be 'incorporated'. However, practitioners of the Vajrayāna placed particular emphasis on this aspect of
spiritual practice, primarily through teachings known as the
'inner yogas'. These are based on an understanding of the body
that differs radically from modern western notions of the physical. In the inner yogas, one works to transform the subtle energies of the illusory body, as it is called, which closely follows the
physical structure of the human organism. By means of a system
similar to that of the ancient Indian Tantra, the Vajrayāna maps
out the illusory body in a network of energy channels and energy
centres that correspond to certain areas of the 'gross' physical
body. This is what Milarepa is referring to when he sings (in the
first song of this episode) of his mastery of the practice of manipulating the *nāḍīs, prāṇa,* and *bindu.*

**The Tantra is designed to address this fundamental
problem of the spiritual life: that you can make
quite a lot of effort and get nowhere.**

Prāṇa, sometimes translated as 'breath', refers to these
psychophysical energies, while *bindu* refers specifically to mas-
culine sexual energy. *Nāḍī,* sometimes translated as 'vein', means
something more like 'nerve' – though not in the sense of the term
as it applies to the ordinary nervous system. The *nāḍīs* are something more like a subtle network of vital forces. Different texts
say different things about the subtle body, but the Tibetan tradition presents it as a subtle counterpart of the physical body, and
as coextensive with it.

According to the Tantra, the nerves of the subtle body correspond with the median nerve running down the physical spine.
On the left of the spinal column is the *lalanā*, coloured white and
corresponding to the moon and to water, while on the right is the
rasanā, which is red and corresponds to the sun and to fire.
Tantric practice consists in bringing the 'breath' (*prāṇa*) into what
is known as the central channel – the *avadhūtī* or subtle median
nerve. This involves mobilizing the various bodily and mental
forces and channelling them through one or other of the centres
of psycho-spiritual energy – known as chakras – that lie along
this subtle median nerve. The result is the liberation of these
forces as they are brought together into a consciously experienced single flow of subtle energy. There are said to be seven
chakras in all. The lowest chakra, the *mūlādhāra*, is at the peri-
neum. The second is a few fingers' breadth below the navel, the
third at the navel, the fourth at the heart, the fifth at the throat,
the sixth between the eyebrows, and the seventh at the crown of
the head. The Tantra symbolizes the chakras in the form of lotus
flowers of varying numbers of petals, the thousand-petalled
lotus being the topmost.

In this way the solar and lunar energies are brought together in
an ever more subtle yet increasingly concentrated synthesis.
Reason combines with emotion, meditation combines with
action in the world, and working on one's own development
combines with working for the welfare of others. Wisdom and
compassion are unified in the direct experience of reality, free
from any obstruction or delusion.

The method of the Tantra is based on the idea of correspond-
ence between higher and lower manifestations of energy, familiar in the West from the old axiom of European alchemy, 'As
above, so below.' The Tantric sage's engagement with the elemental nature of the material universe is intimately involved
with the transformation of consciousness – the inner world of the
mind. For example, certain of the chakras are associated with one
or another of the elements: earth, water, fire, air, and space. The
degree of refinement of the material elements relative to one

another corresponds to the varying degrees of integration and refinement of consciousness or psychophysical energy achieved through the opening of different chakras.

Enlightenment is dependent on energy being totally available on all levels, and within the Tantra this becomes the main focus of one's practice. Nor is this an exercise in abstract wish-fulfilment. It is worked out in the concrete details of everyday existence. If there are energies that are not going along with what you are essentially trying to do, even though they may not actively hold you back, they will nonetheless tend to sit like a dead weight on the energies that are actively trying to take you forward. The Tantra is designed to address this fundamental problem of the spiritual life: that you can make quite a lot of effort and still get nowhere.

> It is notable that people who could never be
> described as 'good' often have a lot of zest for life,
> which makes them a lot of fun to be with.

Liberation is essentially about liberating energies, which means experiencing them more fully. One of the ways we repress energy or lock it away is in habitual patterns of thought, feeling, and behaviour. If Buddhism is concerned with bringing about the direct experience of oneself in the very depths of one's being, it does so by bringing into consciousness this submerged energy of which we are usually unaware.

This is easier said than done. Ideally, you want to get rid of the negativity but retain the energy tied up within it. There is a lot of energy in anger, for example – you might even say that anger *is* raw, crude energy – and you can't afford to throw it away simply because it is tainted with ill will. Unfortunately, this is what often happens. The energy is thrown away with the negativity – which is perhaps why so many religious men and women, although they are good people, seem rather weak and bloodless and incapable of saying boo to a goose. It would seem that, in order to purge themselves of what they see as their human weakness and wickedness, they have also repressed their energy. This inevitably sets up further trouble later on. It is notable that people who could never be described as 'good' often have a lot of zest for life, which makes them a lot of fun to be with.

This is a major theme in the work of the poet and painter William Blake. His thesis is that we identify goodness with the faculty of reason that restrains energy, and the forces of evil with the energy that needs to be restrained. In *The Marriage of Heaven and Hell*, which is where this aspect of his ideas is most clearly to the fore, he asserts that 'The tigers of wrath are wiser than the horses of instruction' – that is, energy itself is good, and it is only the curbing of energy that is truly negative. In a note to this work he remarks, 'The reason Milton wrote in fetters when he wrote of Angels and God, and at liberty when of Devils and Hell, is because he was a true Poet, and of the Devil's party without knowing it.'

This is not to say that if you have lots of energy, you are bound to be wicked. Your energies should be accepted as essentially positive even if you may need to change how you express them. Energy can always be transformed. But if you clamp down on energy generally, positive energies like joy don't get the opportunity to arise at all, because they are locked in along with more negative energies, and the only outcome will be frustration. It's important to bear in mind that truly positive energy, whether one's own or someone else's, is often more difficult to deal with than negative energy. You know where you are with negative energy, whether you indulge it, clamp down on it, or react to it. But what do you do with joy, for example? It doesn't follow the comfortable cycle of unconscious reactivity that is the experience of negative emotions.

If we are to reclaim and integrate all our energies in the Tantric spirit, we have first to happily accept our cruder energies, however muddied they are with old, unhelpful karmic patterns, as the raw material of life. One good way of working with turbulent, difficult, and uncomfortable energies, and of keeping energy flowing while dissolving the negativity in it, is to chant mantras. You could do some mantra chanting to dissolve anger, for example, using the practice to coax energy out of the angry emotion and release it in the form of the chanting voice. However, one of the dangers of what could be called a pseudo-Tantric approach is that, on the pretext of transforming negativity, you end up, consciously or otherwise, using the practice to indulge negativity. In the case of chanting, you would need to be careful that you were truly transforming the energy and not simply transferring the negativity into the tone and quality of your chanting. You might find yourself chanting the mantra with an oppressive, constraining energy that not only reinforces your angry mood but communicates it to whoever else is present. One has to be receptive to the positive content of the mantra, putting the *energy* of one's negativity into the chanting, not the negativity itself, and always looking for a brighter, lighter, and more vital energy to come through.

For the Tantra, energy is primary, and one's ethical practice needs to be configured to take this into account. It is not enough simply to hold back from unskilful action. While unskilful action is always unskilful, holding back energy is unskilful too. From a Tantric perspective, if you don't put as much energy as you can into whatever you are doing, it isn't really worth bothering to do it. And according to Tantric ethics it is unskilful to block energy – whether your own or someone else's – and unskilful to mis-appropriate or exploit energy, misuse or abuse it, subvert or mis-direct it, pollute or muddy it.

Milarepa's Song of Protection
It is clearly difficult psychologically to offer something to someone who doesn't want or need the thing you're offering. Having turned down the horse, Milarepa is certainly not going to need spurs or boots. But the young man is not put off, and offers his boots anyway. They are evidently the best money can buy, made from elk, wild yak, and crocodile skin, embroidered with silk and decorated with brass spurs. He knows that the Tantra involves making offerings, and he is certainly doing the right thing in

making them. Moreover, he prefaces his offering by correctly observing that 'there is no attachment in your heart'.

Having made that observation, however, he seems to challenge Milarepa to prove it, suggesting that Milarepa may need boots to protect him from dogs with sharp teeth, brambles, and so on. It is as if he is trying to sell the boots to Milarepa, to tickle his fancy, to awaken in him a sense of dissatisfaction with a life without boots. Finally, however, he reverts to an attitude of personal sacrifice, of giving up something in which he invests his identity, and he concludes by asking for Milarepa's compassionate blessing. Even so, Milarepa refuses the offering.

> You need tough boots. They will hurt a bit to begin
> with, but they will last, and give you protection and
> a good grip in whatever terrain you encounter.

What Milarepa needs is what he already has: the inner boots of renunciation and mindfulness. The point he makes in the song is essentially the same as in the previous one. But what he says here is strangely reminiscent of an image from a work called the *Bodhicaryāvatāra*, by the eighth-century Indian Mahāyāna poet Śāntideva. In a verse from that work Śāntideva points out that in order to protect your feet you could try to cover the whole earth in leather or, more economically, you could fit two small pieces of leather to your feet and get the same protection.[14] He says that while most of us choose the sensible option in this respect by wearing shoes, we fail to protect ourselves against enemies by recourse to the same principle. You can gird yourself to kill your enemies whenever they try to prevent you from getting what you want; but this is a ridiculous policy when there is the alternative of practising the *mettā bhavānā*, the meditation through which one develops loving-kindness. In the cultivation of love for all that lives, you can protect yourself from thoughts of enmity arising in the first place.

If there is a need to weigh the concern to protect one's body from without against the concern to protect the mind from within, Milarepa is very clear about which he thinks is more important. Indeed, the kind of external situations in which a pair of stout boots provide protection have become so unimportant to him that they can be appropriated as metaphoric features of his inner landscape – Craving Meadow, Jealous Swamp, and the land of darkness and blind views. The dog of Hate and the steep hill of Pride are also to be avoided. All these names seem to anticipate in a curious way the language of John Bunyan's seventeenth-century classic of Nonconformist spirituality, *The Pilgrim's Progress*, with its Slough of Despond, Valley of Humiliation, and Doubting Castle. This song uses the same potent metaphor of the inner life as a journey towards a distant goal.

Obviously, the features of the spiritual landscape are produced by the mind of the individual negotiating them, and they keep reappearing, over and over again, so the journey is daunting to say the least. So what kind of footwear is required for such frustrating terrain? The answer is plain. There is no point in slipping your feet into something stylish and cosy. You need tough boots. They will hurt a bit to begin with, but they will last, and give you protection and a sure grip in whatever terrain you encounter.

I cut my boots from the hide of the renunciation of Saṁsāra
And with the leather of awakening from transiency and
    delusion.
I made my boots with the craftsmanship of deep faith in
    Karma,
With the dye of Non-clinging to the Myriad Forms,
And with the thread and rope of Devotion;[15]

To give up the untrustworthy protection offered by self-interest, to awaken to absolute insecurity, to accept that your unskilful actions of the past will have unforeseen consequences, these are the hard tasks of the spiritual life. But at some point one has to put these boots on. Devotion is of course the function of binding oneself to one's ideals with vows of dedication, so it is appropriately compared with bootlaces.

Buddhist practice is presented here as a source of protection which allows the practitioner to go unscathed through the world. It is quite a common conception, found also in the idea of the armour of śūnyatā and even in the image that traditionally illustrates the fourth level of meditative concentration or dhyāna, which is likened to a man who emerges from a pool on a hot day and wraps himself from head to foot in a white sheet.[16] (The Bible uses the same language in expressions such as the 'whole armour of God' and the 'shield of faith'.) Positive mental states are the best protection not only against the vicissitudes of material existence but, more importantly, against one's own tendency towards ego-centred thought and activity.

These are my boots, the boots of a yogi;

These boots are what enable Milarepa to navigate Craving Meadow, to scale the steep hill of Pride, and, one presumes, to resist the biting teeth of the dog of Hate. However, Milarepa's primary aim here, getting rid of ego-clinging, should not be confused with a kind of feeble self-effacement. It does not invite us to throw a wet blanket of self-admonishment over any feeling of pleasure at having done something well, with the thought, 'Oh dear, that's the ego.'

A friend of mine from my very early days back in England in the 1960s used to write me long letters every few months with lots of good advice, and she would constantly undercut any trace of self-assertion by apologizing for her ego. She would write, 'I was sorry not to hear from you for such a long time – but that's just my ego,' or 'I felt quite pleased when someone came to see me and said how nice my paintings were – but of course that's just my ego.' When one trips over oneself at every step in this way, I'm afraid it is just the ego saying, 'That's just my ego,' probably as an automatic ploy to forestall criticism. It is an inverted form of conceit, dressed up as non-ego. What one is apologizing for may well not be one's ego at all. One should not be too ego-conscious in this sense.

In fact, the Tantra, and the Mahāyāna generally, is careful to identify a positive form of pride which it calls Buddha-pride. It is unconnected with ego-clinging, and starts with an honest satisfaction with what one is doing. In traditional texts, the practitioner is encouraged to reflect, 'Having taken the Bodhisattva vow, I belong to the family of the Buddha which I must never disgrace. How can I consider committing an unskilful act that might bring shame to that name?'

We need not be thinking in terms of the Bodhisattva ideal to apply this to our own lives. If, for example, you are going to cook a meal for your friends and you want to do it to the best of your ability, your ego-centred motivation would be to prove that you are better than others, to win appreciation and acknowledgement of your efforts and skill. But a positive Buddha-pride attitude would be, 'How could I even think of neglecting to do this as skilfully as I can? Not to give of my best would be unworthy of the ideal to which I have committed myself, and of the regard I have for my friends. Indeed, it is a matter of pride to prepare the meal with mettā as well as skill. Otherwise, I would be letting myself down, letting my friends down, and letting the Buddha down.'

This is the kind of healthy self-respect of which the youth is eminently capable, given the straightforwardness of his general approach to life. But as yet he has not been able to transform his worldly self-respect into genuine Buddha-pride. He remains oblivious to the momentous shift in attitude that he will have to make if he is to become Milarepa's disciple.

Milarepa's Song of the Bardo

The young man addresses Milarepa now as a teacher.

> *Precious and accomplished Guru,*
> *Freed from Ego-clinging,*

Evoking the bleak hardship of Milarepa's wanderings, he offers his jacket against the cold – and again the offering is clearly of the highest quality. Being 'freed from ego-clinging', Milarepa is not likely to appreciate owning such a covetable garment, but this does not stop the young man from describing it in meticulous detail, from its lining and silk facings to its lynx fur trim and its collar and hem made of otter skin.

However, Milarepa refuses to acknowledge the claims to his attention of passing bodily discomfort when he has much more crucial matters to address. He puts up with material hardship to sharpen his concentration on the real issue: the teaching here is about ethical practice.

> *O'er the cities of the Six Realms in Saṁsāra,*
> *With fury blows the evil, Karmic wind.*
> *Driven by the senses and deprived of freedom,*
> *One wanders between life and death, roving in Bardo!...*
>
> *For my part, I aspire to the Realm of Reality,*
> *And adorn the cloth of pure mind and heart*
> *With the embroidery of immaculate discipline.*
> *Mindfulness is the tailor...*

In this powerful song Milarepa presents the essence of our predicament in any of the six realms of conditioned existence,[17] whether as gods or demons, animals, or human beings. In any mundane situation we are in some kind of bardo, that is, an intermediate state. The word 'bardo' is most often used to refer to the state between death and rebirth, but there are other bardos too, including the bardo of the dream state, the bardo of meditation, and the bardo of everyday life.

When we are in a dream, it seems entirely real. It is usually only when we wake up from it that we understand we have been dreaming. Similarly, to one who is enlightened and has woken up to the reality of things, everyday life will appear as it really is: transient and subject to ever-changing conditions. In other words, a bardo.

Seeing ordinary life as an intermediate state reminds us that we are involved in something we do not fully understand. We do not see the whole picture, although our worldly habits of mind conspire to hide this reality from us. Wandering the bardo in our confusion, we are buffeted, as Milarepa says, by the furious winds of evil karma – that is, by the effects of our past moral mistakes. We are usually not aware that our actions of body, speech, and mind will have ramifications in terms of our future experience. Hence the need to remember, to be mindful, and Milarepa produces a telling image of mindfulness as the tailor who puts the garment of our practice together.

> The practice of ethics becomes a matter of delicate
> and sensitive craftsmanship, the delightful flowering
> of one's practice rather than just its roots.

Milarepa also offers here a neat reversal of what may be our usual way of thinking. We might normally regard ethics as a worthy but dull base material which we can embroider with more colourful practices, but Milarepa adorns the cloth of *samādhi* or meditation with the embroidery of *śīla* or ethics. Seen as embroidery, the practice of ethics becomes a matter of delicate and sensitive craftsmanship, the delightful flowering of one's practice rather than just its roots.

Milarepa's is an advanced practice of ethical discipline, which in the Kagyu tradition is sometimes understood to follow three stages of development. At the first stage, you are able to work effectively at behaving skilfully and cultivating positive mental states, given the right supportive conditions around you, or at least regular contact with others who are practising in the same way. The second stage of ethical development is the maintenance of the purity of your practice even among people whose beliefs and habits are in opposition to your values and principles and way of life, perhaps even people living evil lives. To continue to practise effectively in a hostile environment represents a higher level of development. You are like a lotus flower growing from the mud.

With the third level, which Milarepa has reached, you are not only able to practise effectively under adverse conditions; you are unaffected by them. Saṁsāra and nirvāṇa – the state of worldly life and the state of enlightenment – are not separate, although they appear so to the unenlightened mind. With the realization of the true nature of mind, you understand that both are the products of human consciousness, and you are not personally attached to any one form of human consciousness over another. All forms are void. It is a fundamental Buddhist teaching that things have no *svabhāva*, no 'own being', no ultimate, individual, unchanging essence. Everything is fluid, unfixed, open.

So does Enlightenment take you beyond the working out of karma altogether?

So does Enlightenment take you beyond the working out of karma altogether? Having gone beyond conceptions of self and other, pleasure and pain, good and evil, do you no longer separate out cause and effect as absolute distinctions, and do you therefore no longer recognize and respect the operation of karma? The enlightened mind sees the conditioned and the unconditioned as non-dual – i.e. as an unreal distinction – but the distinction must be very real and clear for those of us who have not transcended it, if we are to have any chance of doing so. If we are going to think of changing our present state, if we have any notion of making progress, we have to discriminate between suffering and joy, confusion and clarity, fear and confidence, self and other, saṁsāra and nirvāṇa.

If you are enlightened and therefore 'above' duality, you still see that skilful actions on the mundane level produce happiness and unskilful actions produce pain. In other words, your realization of śūnyatā does not cancel out your respect for the law of conditionality as it operates on the mundane level. So an enlightened being does not ignore the law of cause and effect; in fact, one aspect of Enlightenment is the ability to see it with absolute clarity. Absolute truth does not negate relative truth on the level at which relative truth operates.

There is a famous Zen story that illustrates the danger of misunderstanding this aspect of Enlightenment. It concerns a 'spirit fox', a sort of haunted or spirit-possessed fox. A monk eventually exorcises this creature and then asks him how he came to be a spirit fox. It seems that the spirit fox was originally a Zen master, and that he became a spirit fox as a result of his wrong answer to an apparently simple question. The question was, 'What becomes of the law of karma when you become enlightened?' and the answer he gave was, 'When you become enlightened you go beyond the law of karma.' For that terrible mistake he had been reborn as a spirit fox for five hundred rebirths. So he asks the monk what he should have said. 'What you should have said', the monk replies, 'is that when you become enlightened, you do not get in the way of the law of karma.'[18]

I brighten the shoulder padding
With the Great Light (which shines at the time) of death.
I cut the hem of Bardo Enlightenment
To the 'measurement' of pure Magic-Bodies.

Finally, Milarepa introduces the theme of gaining Enlightenment in the bardo state between death and rebirth. When released from the physical body with which it has identified itself throughout life, the mind has a brief opportunity to realize its true nature. If you realize the Clear Light in the intermediate state after death, you become enlightened, and in doing so, you realize the 'pure Magic-Bodies'.

Here Milarepa is referring to a complex doctrine which was developed in the Buddhist tradition over many centuries. There is much that could be said about it, but in this context we will just try to get a basic sense of what he means by 'Magic-Bodies'.

The Trikāya Doctrine

The Tantric conception of Enlightenment is based on the perception that to be any kind of being, even an enlightened one, you always have to be embodied in some way. If there is no ultimate duality between conditioned and unconditioned, an enlightened mind must always come with an enlightened body. The question is: what kind of body?

The figure of the Buddha presents Buddhism with a paradox. The Buddha was a human being – albeit an enlightened one – who lived at a certain time and place. But he was much more than that. The Buddha is the manifestation in time and space of something that is beyond personality, beyond time and space, certainly beyond any conceptual designation on the part of the unenlightened, dualistic mind.

A distinction therefore emerged in the earliest days of Buddhism between the physical body of the historical Buddha and the non-dual enlightened state from which his teaching emanated. References in the Pali canon to the *dharmakāya* indicate that the early understanding of this 'body of truth' was that it was the totality of the truths taught by the Buddha. However, as the Buddhist tradition developed into the Mahāyāna, the conception of the *dharmakāya* began to be understood in metaphysical terms rather than simply in doctrinal terms, and the body of truth came to be regarded as identical with reality itself in all its non-dual formlessness.

> The sambhogakaya inhabits the vast reaches
> of time and space in a way that renders the
> Buddha ever present, always accessible.

It is in the later phases of the Mahāyāna, particularly in the Yogācāra, that we find a third conception of the Buddha – a third body – which is neither abstract and beyond thought nor concretely historical. This is the *sambhogakāya* (literally 'body of mutual enjoyment') – the archetypal Buddha or Bodhisattva, the ideal being. This, rather than the conception of the Buddha as a historical personality, came to be the focal point of the Mahāyāna sūtras. The sambhogakāya inhabits the vast reaches of time and space in a way that renders the Buddha ever present, always accessible. The physical body of the enlightened mind, meanwhile, came to be known as the *nirmāṇakāya*, or 'created body'.

These, then, are the three Buddha bodies. First there is the dharmakāya, the body of truth, of ultimate reality. Secondly there is what became known as the nirmāṇakāya, the historical, flesh-and-blood Buddha, a 'created body' or 'magic body', as Milarepa calls it. And thirdly, forming a bridge between the historical and the literally inconceivable, we find the sambhogakāya, the archetypal embodiment, which manifests in the forms of Buddha and Bodhisattva figures. These figures represent the ideal of the Buddha considered in the most elevated terms of myth and symbol, and are the basis of the visualization practices of the Vajrayāna.

It must be emphasized that the trikāya – the three Buddha bodies – are not to be understood as being separate from each other (although the translation of *kāya* as 'body', being somewhat over-literal, doesn't really help us to understand this). The three 'bodies' do not stand side by side or on top of each other; they are more like different dimensions of the Buddha-nature. Penetrate deeply into the historical Buddha and you encounter the sambhogakāya; penetrate more deeply still, and you reach the dharmakāya.

Another way of thinking of the trikāya doctrine is that it represents Enlightenment as the transformation of all aspects of being, the three kāyas of the Buddha corresponding on the transcendental level to body, speech, and mind on the mundane level. The task of the guru is to make the truth manifest in the disciple throughout his or her whole being by initiating and instructing him or her in a Tantric *sādhana*. The ensuing Enlightenment is said to consist in the transformation of one's body into nirmāṇakāya, one's speech into sambhogakāya, and one's mind or heart into dharmakāya. According to the Tantra, this transformation is a fuller, richer, and more complex realization than the kind of insight accessible to non-Tantric Buddhists.

For the Vajrayāna the route to the dharmakāya is through a direct encounter with the sambhogakāya, the archetypal realm. This is the basis of the visualization practices of the Tantric path; one goes for refuge to one's yidam, the archetypal Buddha or Bodhisattva to whom one is introduced at the moment of Tantric initiation. The visualization practices of the Vajrayāna are based on the pragmatic understanding that the sambhogakāya is as far ahead as we can see. Whatever lies beyond that must be left alone for the time being.

In any effort to understand the images, myths, and symbols of the Vajrayāna, we are inevitably held back by our natural tendency to literal-mindedness. The imagination is of far greater use in this context than the ordinary rational mind, because the reality represented by the sambhogakāya and manifested in the form of archetypal Buddhas and Bodhisattvas is accessible only by means of a visionary faculty. But what is required here is more than just imagination in the sense of an ability to build up images in the mind, or even a creative artistic faculty. Whatever mental images one creates must be infused with at least some sense of the Buddha's teaching that the true nature of conditioned things – including visionary experience – is impermanent and provisional. This meditative visionary faculty is not *above* the imagination; it is another dimension of imagination: Imagination with a capital I. It is essentially the same faculty.

From another point of view, one can also say that the formless is not necessarily closer to reality than that which has form. One could say that the dharmakāya is Buddhahood without form, the sambhogakāya is Buddhahood with form, and the two are non-different. In fact, Insight can be developed with regard to any conditioned object – even through contemplation of a matchbox if that matchbox is experienced as conditioned and empty of inherent existence. Realizing that because it came into existence it must therefore go out of existence, and that all apparent 'things' are like this, you can develop Insight. The reason we are not likely to develop Insight through contemplating a match-box is simply that we are not likely to have very strong feelings about that particular object, so it would be hard for us to concentrate on it very powerfully. However, if you have an experience of the sambhogakāya, a vision of a realm of archetypal forms, if you actually see a Bodhisattva, all your most refined emotional energies will be aroused and unified behind your contemplation of the aspect of reality that the figure symbolizes, and this may catapult you into Insight.

One could think of the nirmāṇakāya and the sambhogakāya as two veils hung before the dharmakāya, understood as reality in its pristine, unmediated form. The sambhogakāya veil is thinner, more diaphanous, and perhaps more brightly coloured than the nirmāṇakāya veil, but through both – whether through the personality of the historical Buddha or through the brilliant form of a visualized Buddha or Bodhisattva – the transcendental may be glimpsed.

Famously, some contemporaries of the historical Buddha, although they met and talked to him, had no idea of the transcendental reality he represented. Likewise, one can have a purely visual experience of a Buddha or Bodhisattva without any sense of that figure's true significance. In other words, it is quite possible to see either the nirmāṇakāya or sambhogakāya at face value, oblivious to the dharmakāya shining through. But to allow these forms to take us closer to an experience of the unconditioned nature of pure reality, we need not consciously strive to read significance in them or explain them in words. They can be left to speak for themselves, to have their own effect upon us. We just have to be receptive to them.

Milarepa's Song of Psychic Heat

Nothing if not persistent, the young man continues his guide to medieval Tibetan men's tailoring. Over his reddish-green jacket he is wearing a coat in grey-green wool hemmed with maroon fur, and this too he offers to Milarepa, who declares that, like all the other offerings, it is surplus to his requirements.

With the cloth of Ah Shea Vital Heat
Is the lapel of Four Cakras made.
My tailor is the inner Prāṇa-Mind
Who warms Tig Le and makes it flow;
The merged Bliss-Void experience
Is the needle used for sewing;

Milarepa's theme in the song with which he refuses this gift is tumo, psychic heat, a practice that assumed a great importance in the Vajrayāna traditions. Like the meditation on the bindu and the nāḍīs, the tumo practice works by means of special breathing practices and yogic postures designed to bring one's energies to an intense pitch of concentration. One then begins various visualizations of the inner fire, and these are said to have certain physical effects, in particular that of raising the body temperature regardless of external conditions. This is how Milarepa, the cotton-clad yogi, could withstand the bitter cold of his mountain hermitage.

Tumo is the 'cloth' that keeps him warm. This effect is a well-attested phenomenon associated with meditative concentration: you naturally generate physical heat when you meditate, heat that others can feel. It can sometimes even seem as though you have a feverishly high temperature – except that you feel not ill but happy and comfortable. Some yogis make a particular practice out of this experience of tumo.

The void is not just a clear mental experience, and tumo is not just a warm physical experience. They come together in an experience of intense bliss.

However, the idea of psychic heat should not be taken only on a literal level. The pleasurable experience of heat in the body is the psychophysical counterpart of the intense bliss which, according to the Tantra, has to be conjoined with a mental apprehension or intuition of voidness in the non-dual samādhi state. Bliss and emptiness are complementary aspects of what is actually a single experience. We find the same idea expressed in the traditional Mahāyāna notion of Enlightenment as the supreme union of samādhi and prajñā, of transcendental insight and supremely positive emotion. The Tantra simply emphasizes in more concrete terms that these two factors must always go together. The void is not just a clear mental experience, and tumo is not just a warm physical experience. They come together in an experience of intense bliss.

This idea that Enlightenment is blissful may seem to be in clear contrast to the cool, emotionally astringent nirvāṇa which Theravadin Buddhism is popularly supposed to envisage. In fact, though, the blissful element of nirvāṇa is emphasized throughout the Buddhist tradition; after all, the well-known expression *nibbānaṁ paramaṁ sukkhaṁ* ('nirvāṇa is the highest bliss') comes directly from the *Dhammapada* of the Pali canon.[19]

In deep states of meditation, the vital energies of the body become concentrated in an experience of profound stability. This process of the intensification of bodily energy and emotional and cognitive clarity can be traced in the formulation known as the seven factors of Enlightenment, or *bodhyaṅgas*, which is found throughout the Pali canon. As one's bodily energies become increasingly concentrated and refined, they are transformed – via the state of *prīti*, or rapture – into *sukha*, serene joy. The vital energy remains, but it is integrated into a succession of increasingly positive mental states, and consciousness becomes permeated with a blissful lightness and energy.

The producing of inner warmth then becomes contentment or emotional positivity, a radiance that is not stimulated by some external source but comes from your own spiritual resources. Wisdom's diamond-like clarity is utterly suffused with the blissful heat of inwardly generated well-being and contentment. The bliss gives content to the experience of voidness, while the voidness gives clarity to the experience of bliss. So you experience blissful inner heat and, at the same time, the illuminating void. Like fire and ice together.

The four higher chakras are 'made of' this vital heat; in other words, the tumo practice of chandali yoga involves heating the bindu or 'Tig Le'. This is a reference, literally speaking, to semen, but we can also take it to mean energy in its grosser form, which is gradually sublimated and made more and more subtle and refined. The 'inner Prāṇa-Mind' warms this energy and causes it to flow. In the course of being heated, the energy becomes sublimated and refined, and rises up, guided by the inner prāṇa mind, through the median nerve to awaken the four major psychic centres or chakras of the heart, the throat, the third eye, and the crown of the head.

This process is guided by cognitive insight into the clear void of śūnyatā, which engages all the vital energies in the form of a steadily intensifying bliss, finally to unite them with that clear experience of the void. To put it another way, the process of gathering one's energies is inherently and increasingly blissful, until that bliss is so intense that it unites with the clear void. And at this point the inborn vital heat manifests.

> *The cloth is Inborn Vital Heat.*
> *Now summer and winter are for me the same!*

When Milarepa says that summer and winter are the same for him, he means not only that he is impervious to extremes of climate, but that he has gone beyond all distinctions. This is the inborn vital heat, *sahajiya*, or inherent Buddha nature. It is a transcendental heat, which is conterminous with reality. It is not artificially produced; it needs only to be released. It is there from the beginning.

Milarepa's Song of the Guru

The young man's next song follows the usual pattern of salutation and praise of Milarepa's non-attachment, followed by solicitous but facile conjecture as to his material needs, and an offering of something that will supposedly meet them. He seems not to have heard what Milarepa has just been saying about his practice of tumo, because he surmises that 'you must sometimes feel the cold'. He therefore offers his hat, a heady confection of crocodile hide, vulture skin, and gaudy feathers around an intricate frame of precious metal. He recommends it to Milarepa not on aesthetic or practical grounds but on account of its exchange value, which is apparently that of a big yak. Rather than asking for some kind of blessing in return, he makes his first commitment.

In summer and in winter,
I will follow and pay homage to you!

Milarepa tells him not to be too rash; to keep his hat – and his head.

My dear young man,
Do not lose your head!

Milarepa is no longer at the mercy of the elements. Just as he has no fear of water,

I fear not the element of air within,
Nor do I depend on falcon's flesh.
I feel gay and joyous in a biting wind.

He has no need for wealth. Nor does he need a hat, as the crown of his head is already occupied – by his guru, Marpa, visualized above his head as part of the practice of guru yoga.

The guru yoga differs from lineage to lineage, but it usually begins with imagining your guru above your head. Then you go on to imagine your guru's guru above his head, and that guru's guru in turn above his head, and so on, through the whole lineage. Next you imagine the blessing of the gurus coming down through the lineage to you. And then you feel your mind united with your guru's mind, and his mind united with his own guru's mind, going back in this way to the Buddha, the original transcendental source of inspiration, usually visualized not as the historical Buddha Śākyamuni but in an archetypal or sambhoga-kāya form, perhaps Vajradhara or Amitābha.

As a devoted disciple you are supposed to be aware of your guru above your head all the time. This is because, according to the Vajrayāna, the guru does not just stand for the Buddha but *is* the Buddha, at least so far as the individual disciple is concerned. The guru is the master who helps you to transform your crude, mundane body, speech, and mind into the unconditioned body, speech, and mind of a Buddha. Consequently, you see your guru not only as the dharmakāya, the embodiment of the ultimate truth or ultimate reality, but also as the sambhogakāya, the manifestation of Buddhahood in time and space.

Gratitude opens us up to the fact of our interconnectedness with others.

The exercise is a simple matter of cultivating, experiencing, and expressing gratitude. Gratitude opens us up to the fact of our interconnectedness with others. Whenever we enjoy or achieve something, it is salutary to recognize and acknowledge the work and kindness of all the individuals who have contributed to it. But gratitude to the guru has an extra dimension, because what we are grateful for is beyond valuation. There is no hope of repaying the debt, except by passing the gift on to others. Another way of looking at this is to say that gratitude is a way of opening ourselves up to the merit accrued by the guru, which becomes inextricably linked with our own, as he passes it freely on to us.

The guru yoga is a formal version of something that should happen anyway in the spiritual life. We should all be grateful to whoever it was who first introduced us to the Dharma. There is a very famous example of this: the Buddha's most eminent disciple, Sāriputta, made a point of prostrating in gratitude every day of his life to Assaji, the disciple who gave him his first contact with the Dharma. Although Sāriputta quickly outstripped Assaji in spiritual attainment, Enlightened as he was, he continued to prostrate himself to the still unenlightened Assaji.[20]

> He is the Wish-Fulfilling Gem, Buddha's Transformation
>   Body.
> If you see him with the eye of veneration,
> You will find he is the Buddha Dorje-Chang!

The guru is the manifestation in the present time of the current of spiritual energy that has come down from the Buddha through the lineage of one's own tradition. The lineage, or line of transmission, is like a spiritual chain reaction. It is not the actual handing down of an object or thing. Even though the idea of transmission suggests that the disciple gains something which he or she did not previously have, the role of the guru is primarily to activate the disciple's energies. He (or sometimes she) enables the disciple to tap the vast source of inspiration and energy that lies hidden and unconscious in their own being.

Nor does transmission consist in a certificated process whereby a kind of spiritual management role is passed on from one generation to another. For one thing, a guru may have had many teachers and all the transmissions he has received through all of them are focused through him on the disciple. The lineage is not a sort of spiritual family tree that the interested disciple might like to trace back to the Buddha. It represents a direct experience of awakening, a living truth that has been stimulated again and again through the guru-disciple relationship.

Dorje-Chang is the Buddha Vajradhara, 'bearer of the vajra'. He is depicted with a vajra standing upright in his palm (the vajra being a symbol of ultimate reality), and sometimes a vajra bell as well, and he is considered to be the primordial originator of the whole Kagyu lineage, and thus their adi-guru or adi-Buddha. (The term *adi* means primordial, i.e. from the beginning.) But Vajradhara is the primordial guru or Buddha not in the sense of initiating the lineage in time, or even at the beginning of time. He symbolizes its origin as being outside time altogether, as being transcendental, and in that sense, without origin. Thus, adi really means 'without origin', and the adi-Buddha symbolizes the timeless nature of Enlightenment or Buddhahood. Buddhahood in its essence has no beginning. It cannot be said to arise, because it is always there. It represents a dimension beyond time, into which you break through on the attainment of Enlightenment, at which point you realize that you have always been there.

Milarepa's Song of the Treasure of Contentment
The youth next offers his most treasured possession:

> *This white translucent six-edged jade*

The youth is evidently quite well off. It should not be assumed, however, that these offerings are what he just happens to have about his person at the time. They almost certainly constitute most of his wealth. This is characteristic of traditional, pre-industrial societies, particularly nomadic cultures such as those of medieval Mongolia and Tibet. Your wealth is not kept in the bank, or in stocks and shares, or even in bars of gold under the bed. It is in your hat, your coat, your horse, your sword. You wear it – or your wife wears it in the form of gold ornaments. The womenfolk of nomadic tribal societies are like walking banks; in time of need they can sell a gold ring or a bangle. As the young man points out, 'With this jade you can never be poor.'

Of course, farmers and peasants hold their wealth in land and cattle, but the nobility traditionally carry their fortunes in the form of personal adornment. Even in England, as recently as the reign of Elizabeth I, young men would come to London from the country having sold large tracts of land in order to appear at court dressed in fabulously expensive clothes of silk and jewel-encrusted satin, hoping to catch the queen's eye and win preferment. They were, it was said, 'wearing their estates on their backs'. A sensible young man would invest a great deal of money in a gold hilt for his sword or a jewelled feather for his cap, in the hope of a good return in terms of advancement to fame and fortune, power, and prosperity. Tibetans who have not been urbanized and modernized still maintain this sort of attitude to anything they wear or carry. A nomad from the far-flung valleys of the Tibetan plateau would never think of wearing something fake or artificial if he could avoid it, especially on a trip to Lhasa or on pilgrimage. He would be sure to wear real gold, real jewels, quality leather and cloth.

We adorn whatever we value or love, whether it is ourselves or someone else, or the Three Jewels.

As usual, the young man prefaces his offering with a statement of faith in Milarepa, particularly in his non-attachment. He is able to acknowledge that there is no point in trying to seduce or buy Milarepa with his gift. But it is as if he has still not really taken in what he understands in theory. He cannot help pointing out that with this jade Milarepa can never be poor, so his lack of insight betrays itself.

Moreover, having offered his most precious possession, he can't help asking for a teaching instead of just a blessing. There is an unspoken assumption that the value of the offering calls for an equivalent spiritual reward. But Milarepa is still not prepared to accept the implication that he himself has any need or desire for anything. He replies according to the terms in which the offering has been made.

> *There is no end to human greed.*
> *Even with hoarded wealth head-high,*
> *One cannot reach contentment.*
> *I do not envy you your wealth and goods.*
>
> *The greatest treasure is contentment in my heart;*
> *The teaching of the Whispered Lineage is my wealth;*

Here Milarepa's teaching is completely continuous in principle with that of the historical Buddha. There is a verse in the *Dhammapada* that says just the same: *santuṭṭhiparamaṁ dhanaṁ* – 'Contentment is the greatest wealth.'[21]

> *My devotion to the Dharma is my ornament.*
> *I deck myself with Retaining Mindfulness;*

We adorn whatever we value or love, whether it is ourselves or someone else, or the Three Jewels. Milarepa prefers to adorn his breast only with the devotion of his heart to the Dharma. If he does wear any kind of decoration, it is what he calls 'retaining mindfulness', by which he means the recollection of meditative experience, especially dhyāna, through his daily life.

Milarepa is saying that by virtue of his spiritual attainments he has all the wealth in the world at his disposal. As a continuous stream of positive mental events, the spiritual qualities over which he has attained mastery are inexhaustible. They can never be taken away from him by circumstances. Material poverty consequently holds no fear for him. The wealth he values is not material – in fact it springs from a renunciation of material wealth. His wealth is the Dharma, and more specifically, the Dharma as expounded by his teachers. And this of course is very much the focus of the Kagyu tradition, the Whispered Lineage.

The lineage is whispered in the sense of being taught confidentially, that is to say, not in books or public talks, but in a very personal exchange. Other factors being equal, the greater the number of people one is speaking to, the more generalized, even approximate, is the teaching. When someone gives a teaching to many people at the same time, it is up to each listener to decide for themselves how it applies to them individually, which makes it much more difficult for genuine transformation to occur. The smaller the number of people, the more specific and therefore, in a sense, the more true the teaching can be. Even if you are addressing just two people, you have to direct what you say to what is common in them both, rather than what is individual and unique in each of them. The best situation for spiritual teaching is thus one-to-one communication, when what is truly individual in you makes contact with what is truly individual in the other person. When a guru does speak to just one person, he doesn't have to say much. One sentence may do. You can cut straight through all the general theory, the broad principles, and the full range of teachings designed to meet the needs of any conceivable kind of individual.

In the Tantric tradition generally, and in the Kagyu lineage in particular, it is usually said that any guru will find only a few disciples to whom he can communicate the teaching. In Milarepa's case, these are the eight 'heart disciples'. Each of them receives his own unique transmission of the Dharma, which is not necessarily a conceptual or verbalized teaching. The Zen tradition has a similar kind of transmission. It is this individual, unique teaching, 'whispered' into the ear of one person at a time, which makes the greatest impact.

The Youth's Song of Going for Refuge
Undeterred by Milarepa's refusal of his gifts, the young man now takes a new tack.

> It is natural for a supreme being like you not to want these illusory possessions. I now offer you my Three Companions. From now on I will never carry a weapon or kill sentient beings. I beg you to grant me the Ordination. I pray you to protect me with your compassionate grace!

As this offering makes especially clear, every time Milarepa turns him down the young man offers something more, and puts more of himself at stake. To begin with he was simply anxious to be saved from hell. Then he asked for Milarepa's compassionate blessing. Then he requested the teaching. And with this offering comes a glimmering of something not hinted at before: he realizes that the worldliness of his way of life is standing in the way of a deeper meeting with his teacher. He is no longer going to try to offer Milarepa material possessions in some expectation that he is going to find a use for them. Having acknowledged that the gifts he offers have no value for the cotton-clad yogi, he now takes a huge step forward. A far more profound ideal has begun to reveal itself to him and he is ready to reorganize his life in order to attain it. He is beginning, in other words, to take responsibility for his own spiritual life, a decision marked by his asking for ordination, presumably lay ordination as an upāsaka. Having done so, the youth throws himself under Milarepa's care, asking for the protection of his 'compassionate grace'.

All living beings emit an unseen and often unnoticed influence; we all generate an aura of some kind.

The concept of grace appears quite frequently in the Songs of Milarepa. The Tibetan term is *cheno* or *chinlap*, which in his translation of *Tibet's Great Yogī Milarepa* Lama Kazi Dawa-Samdup renders as 'grace-waves'.[22] The Pali term is *anubhāva – anu* meaning 'after', and *bhāva*, 'being', or 'becoming'. It's rather like an echo: somebody is in a certain state of mind, a certain mood, and an echo or reflection of that mood is produced in somebody else. It is a traditional Buddhist belief that all those of high spiritual attainment emit this kind of influence.

Of course, there is nothing special or exceptional about having an influence or impact on others. All living beings emit an unseen and often unnoticed influence; we all generate an aura of some kind, with varying degrees of power. But what is being spoken of here as grace is something exceptional. The more deeply your insight has penetrated, the more positive and powerful becomes your aura or influence, and in the case of the Buddhas and Bodhisattvas, it is without limit. They are always sending out these grace-waves, and we just have to open ourselves to them.

Contrary to popular belief, the strictly Buddhist understanding is that this anubhāva does not offer material protection from material misfortune. It is quite easy to slip into talking about the Buddhas and Bodhisattvas protecting beings in a literal sense, particularly in the context of popular Buddhism, but such notions are not in accordance with all aspects of the tradition. Some would say that you are helped, supported, and even protected by 'grave-waves' only in the sense that being more open to positive influences puts you in a more positive frame of mind, psychologically and spiritually. It is this that enables you to make progress. Exactly what the young man means by asking for protection we have no way of knowing. Perhaps he isn't quite sure himself; perhaps he is not clear in his own mind whether he is asking for mundane or spiritual protection, or some combination of the two.

What we may be sure of is that in renouncing the physical protection of his weapons for the spiritual protection of the guru, he is taking a huge step forward, especially given the time and place in which he lives. His weapons are part of his identity – hence his name for them: his Three Companions. They never leave his side, for without them he will feel powerless to respond to attack. Medieval Tibet was a dangerous place, with very little law and certainly no police to enforce it, and much depended upon your ability to defend yourself.

Warriors of Tibet

In trying to picture this young warrior and his attitude to life, I am again reminded of my Khamba student in Kalimpong. Khamba men are very distinctive, even among other Tibetans. There is something decidedly swashbuckling about them, with their big boots and cowboy hats, their swords tucked in their belts, and their jacket sleeves nonchalantly knotted around their waists. Looking at Khamba mule-drivers swaggering down the street in Kalimpong, you would think they owned the place, and people thought it best to get out of their way. I remember on one occasion going into a bank – a place of sober composure, even in India – and finding one of these Tibetans stretched out asleep on the floor. No one had dared to ask him to get up and move along; that would have been asking for trouble.

The Khambas' fondness for a good fight also influenced their choice of entertainment. Kalimpong had its own cinema, and you could count on a full house when the programme featured a western. Romantic films were just so much silly nonsense as far as the Khambas were concerned, but a cowboy film was a different matter, and the more shootings, fist-fights, and mayhem, the better they liked it. In short, they are a proud and defiant people, and a good deal less sophisticated than the city-dwellers of Lhasa, who tend to look down on them as rather barbaric and bellicose. But their bravery is legendary. The Khambas were the last Tibetans to surrender to the Chinese, continuing to harry them in guerrilla raids from the mountains even after the invaders had taken over their country.

At the same time the Khambas are very religious, and in the early days of the invasion, when they used to ambush caravans, they were careful to avoid robbing those of Buddhist lamas. My Khamba student once told me a story that epitomises the attitude of the Khamba warriors. It happened that a caravan belonging to one of the larger and more prestigious monasteries was passing though the land. It belonged to a tulku, an incarnate lama, for whom the Khamba are known to have tremendous respect. The usual custom with Tibetan caravans is for the leading horse to wear a special decoration, usually a red plume on its forehead, and to be trained not to allow any other horse or mule to get ahead of it. A caravan belonging to an incarnate lama would be made instantly recognizable by a distinctive variation of this form of decoration. However, in this case the manager of one of the big monasteries had decided that the leading horse should not wear its special insignia, so as not to advertise the caravan as being in any way unusual. If people knew that it belonged to an incarnate lama, the manager thought, it would be more likely to be attacked and robbed of the precious goods it could be expected to be carrying.

Unfortunately, this stratagem had the opposite effect to that intended. The Khamba men saw the unmarked caravan approaching in the distance and, considering it fair game, ambushed it and even killed a number of people in the process. When the guerrillas discovered in the course of their looting that it belonged to an incarnate lama, they were mortified and gave back all that they had taken, and begged the manager to convey their deepest apologies to the lama. They wished they could have restored the lives of those they had killed, but as for that, they said, it was the manager's fault for disguising the caravan.

This is very much the style and spirit of the Khambas, and we can be sure that the young nobleman whom Milarepa meets in 'The Meeting at Silver Spring' is more than a little like them. For him, life would have been a simple matter of protecting himself from real enemies who were in a position to do real and perhaps murderous harm. Your weapons and your willingness to use them would have had an important part to play your protection by instilling fear into others. With his weapons, the youth says, 'I was like a ruthless bandit.'

In giving up his weapons the youth places himself under the protection of spiritual rather than material power. He surrenders them because they are the means of taking care of his interests through violence, through breaking the precepts. So he is moving from the practice of *dāna*, generosity, the first of the six perfections of the Bodhisattva path, to the practice of *śīla* or morality, the second perfection. Having offered more and more of his possessions until he had nothing left to give, he is now ready to sacrifice his whole way of life in so far as it breaks the ethical precepts. He is ready to commit himself, to go for refuge to the Buddha, Dharma, and Sangha, and as part of this process he has to think about how he lives his life and make the changes necessary to bring it into line with the ethical ideals of the Dharma. So the meeting at Silver Spring has started to bite. He is beginning to think seriously about what being a disciple really entails. Now will Milarepa be satisfied?

Milarepa's Song of the Conqueror

No, is the answer. Milarepa is still unmoved, refusing to believe that the youth can keep his vow. He knows full well that there is a world of difference between intending to follow the ethical precepts and being able to put your noble aspirations into practice, especially when the going gets tough.

> *He who does not renounce the 'all-important' combat*
> *Will be imprisoned and lose his chance for freedom!*
> *Battles and armies are not for the yogi.*

'All-important' is in quotation marks here to signify that it refers to something that is accorded huge significance by social convention and popular assumptions but which just a little thought will reveal to be fairly trivial. For the young man, as for most males of any social standing in pre-industrial cultures, the all-important thing is combat. It used to be the same in Europe: to be a man of honour or, in England, a gentleman, involved being prepared to defend that honour when it was impugned. It may seem obviously absurd to have to wager your life on a duel because someone has insulted you, but it was all-important at the time.

Similar values persist in any culture where violence and aggressive competition prevail, such as urban gang culture. Membership of the group involves being prepared to defend the honour of being a member. In giving up his willingness to fight, the youth is giving up his allegiance to the collective values of his group. This is why his gift of weaponry represents a far more significant gesture than most of us can imagine.

Today, the false value that imprisons us is the importance we give to being a successful person.

In the industrial age, 'respectability' became all-important. Today, high status within one or another social grouping is dependent on a variety of signifiers that can be gathered under the general heading of 'success', usually linked to material prosperity. Today, the false value that imprisons us is the importance we give to being a successful person, by whatever criteria we judge success.

The world without is my quiver,
The Non-clinging Self-Illumination within
Is my sheath of leopard skin,
My weapon is the sword of Great Wisdom.

The Two-in-One Path is my rope,
My thumb-guard is the merit of meditation.

The two-in-one path is that of wisdom and compassion. The path of compassion or skilful means is pursued within the sphere of external activity, among other living beings, in saṁsāra. The path of wisdom, on the other hand, is followed, in a sense, in the world within. But there is no real distinction to be made between external and internal, mundane and transcendental, saṁsāra and nirvāṇa. To follow the two-in-one path is to integrate the outer world and the 'Non-clinging Self-Illumination within', seeing them as one, seeing saṁsāra and nirvāṇa as perfectly interwoven in a living vision of non-duality. The two-in-one path is the path of the Mahāyāna, which sees the non-duality of form and emptiness, rupa and śūnyatā.

Upon the bow-string of Ultimate Unborn Voidness
I set steady the notch of Bodhi-Heart;
I shoot the arrow of the Four Infinities
At the army of the Five Poisons.

In Mahāyāna and Vajrayāna Buddhism, Enlightenment is inseparable from the heartfelt desire to rescue all beings from the sufferings of saṁsāra. This is the bodhi-heart, the bodhicitta, the will to Enlightenment for the sake of all beings, which is the main spiritual faculty to be cultivated by the Mahāyānist. Withdrawal from the mundane, accompanied by the arising of the bodhicitta, produces Enlightenment. The traditional conclusion to any Mahāyāna practice is therefore to transfer any merit accruing to oneself through that practice to benefit all beings. (Of course, in doing so, one makes it possible for the practice to contribute to one's own liberation.)

As for the ultimate unborn voidness, this is the goal of Enlightenment itself. So why is it the bow-string and not the target? Well, as the verse reminds us, the ultimate voidness is unborn. As absolute reality, it is outside time, so it does not exist as a target in time and space. Nor should we forget that an arrow is a lethal weapon, and that one aims an arrow to destroy a target. It is therefore more appropriate that the target should be something we do seek to destroy through our spiritual practice: the 'army of the Five Poisons'.

> Greed, resentment, vanity, envy, and
> shallowness are like an occupying army,
> attacking our peace and happiness minute
> by minute, hour by hour, day by day.

The 'Four Infinities' of the arrow with which the poisons are to be pierced and brought down are the four meditation practices called the *brahma-vihāras*, the 'illimitables', or the 'divine abidings'. As this verse tells us, they are steadied and powered by their connection with ultimate reality through the bodhicitta. The brahma-vihāras are *mettā* or universal friendliness, *karuṇā* or compassion, *muditā* or sympathetic joy, and *upekkhā* or equanimity. The five poisons are usually listed as craving, hatred, pride or conceit, ignorance, and distraction – though sometimes jealousy is substituted for distraction. These are our states of mind most of the time. Greed, resentment, vanity, envy, and shallowness are like an occupying army, attacking our peace and happiness minute by minute, hour by hour, day by day.

Without taking the imagery too literally, it is perhaps noteworthy that the while usually each brahma-vihāra meditation is meant to target one poison in particular, they are here directed collectively at the poisons together. That is, the positive emotions are seen as different aspects of essentially one and the same emotional attitude or direction, just as the poisons are seen as inextricably tangled up in each other.

The song is unequivocally martial in tone and intent. Milarepa is saying, 'Be a warrior by all means, but use your warrior's strength to fight the inner, spiritual battle.' In this way he is trying to transpose the young man's energies, martial as they are – and thus in a sense the tough young man himself – from the worldly plane to the spiritual plane. He wants to make him a spiritual warrior.

A battle is a telling and perennial metaphor for the spiritual life, suggesting an intensity of focus, a sense of something all-important at stake, and the need to make a choice between values that are set in eternal opposition to one another. It is familiar enough in the Christian tradition, of course; one thinks of hymns like 'Onward Christian Soldiers', and Blake's 'Jerusalem':

> *Bring me my bow of burning gold:*
> *Bring me my arrows of desire:*
> *Bring me my spear: O clouds unfold!*
> *Bring me my chariot of fire.*
>
> *I will not cease from mental fight,*
> *Nor shall my sword sleep in my hand,*
> *Till we have built Jerusalem...*[23]

The tradition of the warrior persists in other ways too. Even today, the aristocratic ideal of the medieval knight or the samurai warrior is a potent one, with its challenges to honour that are not to be refused, and its tests of courage and generosity, loyalty and purity. For all its unequivocal commitment to the principle of causing no harm to living beings, Buddhism also makes use of military metaphors and images to denote the heroic warrior-like spirit that is a vital spiritual quality. Weapons of one kind or another are wielded by Bodhisattvas to signify certain transcendental qualities. For example, Mañjughoṣa, the Bodhisattva of wisdom, wields in his right hand a sword with which he is said to cut through ignorance.

The military metaphor has its dangers, most obviously in the tendency to turn an inward and spiritual struggle to realize one's highest ideals into a conflict with external forces that are seen to oppose those ideals. However appropriate or otherwise it may be to engage in some kind of external conflict, this should not be confused with the real spiritual struggle, which takes place within. The military analogy also suggests a high price will be paid for failure or defeat, but this does not apply to the spiritual battle. Those who do not commit themselves to the struggle cannot be said to have been defeated, while those who do so are guaranteed to triumph. As Milarepa sings in conclusion,

There is no doubt I shall win the battle;

Another risk associated with the idea of the spiritual warrior is that you become too ascetic, and under the pretext of 'fighting the good fight' force the pace of your practice, allaying your neurotic guilt by punishing yourself. And there is an even greater risk of being too hard on other people, of expressing hatred and ill will under the pretext of encouraging others to take on the heroic ideal. In view of this, it is especially significant that the practices mentioned in this context are those specifically concerned with the cultivation of positive emotion, of kindness towards all that lives, including oneself.

That battles and armies are perennially fascinating and awe-inspiring, even for monks, is illustrated by the presence in the *Vinaya*, the rules of monastic conduct, of a rule prohibiting bhikkhus from 'looking at armies'.[24] As Milarepa says, 'Battles and armies are not for the yogi.' Even today, people can develop quite an unhealthy interest in the progress of war as it unfolds in the news. But the energy of that interest can be harnessed in the service of the very different kind of battle that is the spiritual life.

The combative approach to the spiritual life is of course by no means the only way to describe the Buddhist path. It is not a literal description of the spiritual life but a metaphor, and another metaphor will do just as well, especially if it holds more appeal. Instead of the ideal of the knight-errant, you may just as fruitfully be inspired by the ideal of the gardener, or the healer, say, not destroying the poisons but nurturing positive qualities or alleviating suffering, engaging in a co-operative process rather than a counteractive one. If the warrior is basically a mas-culine ideal, the complementary ideal is more feminine – recep-tive and co-operative rather than confrontational. You might even be inspired by a childlike ideal of innocence and openness, like that exemplified by the much-loved Japanese poet, Ryōkan. Or you might prefer the image of the flower, imagining yourself growing in a garden, opening your leaves and blossoming in stillness and silence, just unfolding your petals, sending forth your perfume, and gazing up at the face of the sun. Again, there are well known Christian references to such models – one thinks of Mary, the 'handmaid of the Lord' and Jesus' tribute to the 'lilies of the field'.

In taking inspiration from these metaphors, you're not think-ing in terms of acting like a warrior, or a gardener, or a flower. Your aim is to transpose mundane qualities into spiritual ones, seeking to be a spiritual warrior, a spiritual healer, a spiritual flower, a spiritual handmaid, a spiritual gardener. However effective the healer, however beautiful the flower, however innocent the child, and however nurturing the gardener, such an ideal is a model of the spiritual life, not the spiritual life itself.

By the same token, calling one ideal masculine and another feminine is not to say that as spiritual ideals these have anything to do with how masculine or feminine you are in the ordinary sense. Warriors may almost always be men, but spiritual warriors can be of either sex, and so can spiritual flowers and even spirit-ual handmaids. As so often in the spiritual life, one has to be very careful not to be literalistic.

We may say that the warrior ideal represents *vīrya* – energy in pursuit of the good – while the flower represents the opposite or complementary spiritual faculty, *samādhi* – meditation and contemplation. As so often in the spiritual life, there is a paradox here. Milarepa speaks to the young man's real interests in order to harness and transform the energy engaged with them, and the effect should be to internalize the young man's combativeness, to turn it against itself, so that he is fighting his own aggression. The effect of the warrior ideal on this young man will thus be to turn him into more of a spiritual flower. The warrior type of person needs to be encouraged to sit still, to be quiet and patient, to be a warrior in meditation; he or she will still be intensely active, but in an entirely different way. Conversely, if you are inspired by the ideal of nurturing or healing or blossoming, you have to be encouraged to internalize these qualities so that they express themselves with the vigour and heroism that real growth requires.

The opposite way of looking at these ideals can also work. If you tend to be slack and sluggish, you might still be able to find inspiration in the warrior ideal, while if you are a restless, aggressive type, you may be able to cultivate a yearning to be more contemplative, to be a spiritual flower. Either way, it is important that we do not simply carry our ordinary habits over into the spiritual life. And for this, the warrior ideal is always needed – at the service of, or in the context of, the ideal of the flower.

Chapter 6

Pleasing the Guru

Judging the Guru

You Yogi, who are the living Buddha,
Although many know the Dharma,
Few can practise it.[25]

Aware of his great good fortune in finding Milarepa and of this tremendous opportunity, the young man is now even keener to place himself under Milarepa's instruction, if the master will only accept him. In the opening lines of his song, the would-be disciple puts his finger on a crucial – if apparently rather elementary – point: that while intellectual understanding is relatively common, actual practice and ultimate realization is very rare. But to dismiss this point as elementary would be to miss it altogether. It is easy to take the point; it is much more difficult to apply it to our own situation.

We tend not to realize how much we identify with what we think we know rather than what we actually know from our own experience. Entranced by theory and perhaps rather alienated from our experience, we find that trying to put spiritual principles into practice has none of the alluring charm of the play of ideas, but that, as the youth quite rightly observes, it is simply hard work. We almost inevitably imagine that if we know something in conceptual terms we really do know it. The amount of knowledge one can amass about Buddhism can become very impressive, without necessarily leaving any impression in terms of practice even at the most elementary level. Even the ability to write books about Buddhism can make a formidable contrast with what is put into daily practice. But the young man values Milarepa's teaching as arising from, he says, 'hard work'.

It is not only that very few people try to put the teachings into practice. The youth says that few people have the *capacity* to practise. The implication seems to be that in view of our knowledge of the clear benefits of practising the Dharma, the fact that we fail to do so must be acknowledged as a kind of disability. It is a disability that can be overcome, but it runs very deep.

> *One in hundreds is hard to find*
> *Who can give proof of his accomplishment.*

The young man goes on to say that it is hard to find one among hundreds (presumably hundreds of those who practise the spiritual life) 'who can give proof of his accomplishment'. This calls to mind Sri Krishna's famous observation in the *Bhagavad-Gita* that 'among a thousand people, perhaps only one searches for me; and out of a thousand who search for me, perhaps only one finds me'.[26]

But how is it possible to give 'proof of accomplishment'? There is no way to prove beyond doubt that someone has reached a given level of spiritual attainment. This is one of the themes of the *Diamond Sutra*: that even if you have the 32 major and 68 minor marks of a great man, this does not prove that you are a Buddha. A yogi may be leading a life of great simplicity and self-denial, but someone unsympathetic to what the yogi is trying to do will see only a destitute beggar. This is exactly the view taken by Milarepa's own sister: she is quite scathing on the subject of his status as a yogi. The only evidence she is prepared to recognize is what she can see: temples and numerous disciples, and the financial rewards that come with them. She remarks derisively that Milarepa is so wretched that he hasn't even a blanket with which to cover his nakedness. And even if one is disposed to be rather more impressed by outward signs of spiritual ability than Milarepa's materially-minded sister, one must bear in mind that even his ability to walk on water shows only either that he has supernormal powers or that he can provoke hallucinations. It doesn't prove transcendental insight. Yet the young man shows complete faith in Milarepa, due to his own readiness to follow the spiritual path. Come what may, he knows that Milarepa must be his guru.

> When you have been with a particular guru
> for a while and nothing much seems to have
> happened, it is often the guru whom you find
> wanting rather than your own efforts.

The only 'proof' of someone's transcendental attainment is one's own intuitive conviction. Clearly this is what has led the young man to make his decisive commitment to follow Milarepa. There is nothing provisional about his decision, no question of making do with Milarepa until the next guru comes along. From what he says, he isn't wondering whether, if this doesn't work out, he might find a guru who suits him better or who can work bigger miracles.

Flitting from guru to guru is a weakness that is not confined to the West. The closest friend I made in my time in Kalimpong, Dhardo Rimpoche, who was also my teacher, told me that the Tibetans are as prone to it as anyone else. When he arrived in Kalimpong in the late 1940s, as the only incarnate lama in the town he was the object of great respect and devotion. It was Rimpoche this and Rimpoche that, and he received offerings and invitations, and performed ceremonies and blessings for people morning, noon, and night. A few years later another incarnate lama arrived, and almost overnight Dhardo Rimpoche was dropped in favour of the new lama in town. As more and more lamas turned up – and by the time I settled there dozens of lamas had crossed over the mountains to Kalimpong as refugees – the townsfolk became quite dizzy with indecision. They were unable to resist the temptation to sample the latest spiritual sensation, be it a head lama or the chief abbot of a great monastery, or the incarnation of this bodhisattva or that siddha. And when they heard that the Dorje Lamo, the one and only female incarnation, was on her way, everyone naturally wanted to be among the first to get her blessing.

Of course, the eminent gurus didn't play along with this cupidity on the part of their disciples. For example, there were three great Nyingma gurus in Kalimpong who, because they were closely connected in terms of their common tradition and knew each other quite well, were the subject of considerable speculation with regard to their comparative status. Eventually, a disciple of all three summoned up the nerve to ask one of them, very politely, to satisfy everyone's curiosity. Was one of them greater than the other two, and if so, which of them was it? The guru thought for a moment, and then he said, 'Well, I'll tell you how things stand. As a matter of fact one of us is much more developed than the others, but as for which one it is, none of you will ever know.'

The type of teaching offered by a guru might not suit one's temperament, and this might be a good reason for seeking out another. A little shopping around might be appropriate at the initial stages of one's spiritual career. But there are people who spend their whole lives drifting from one teacher to another. Why? It often has to do with a half-conscious expectation that the guru can somehow do it all for you. When you have been with a particular guru for a while and nothing much seems to have happened, it is often the guru whom you find wanting rather than your own efforts, and if you find yourself in this position, the sheer novelty of a new guru, with a new set of teachings, new practices, even new jokes, all promising a new beginning and fresh hope, is very appealing. So instead of refreshing your spiritual practice by digging deeper into it, you trade in your stale old guru for an exciting new one.

Milarepa himself, as he says in the opening song of this episode, called off his search for a guru as soon as he heard Marpa's name. After that, his path was one of complete submission to his guru's wishes. Even though Marpa himself led a householder's life, with a wife and family, when he insisted that Milarepa should follow the solitary life of a hermit, Milarepa did not question his decision. This is not to say that Marpa could literally order Milarepa to do anything; that is not how a spiritual relationship works. There can be no desire on the part of any follower of the Dharma to exert power over anyone else. Power has no place in the spiritual community, and that includes the relationship between a Tantric guru and his disciple. But the nature of the guru-disciple relationship is such that a guru's quietest hints or gentlest recommendations have the force of commands for his heart disciples.

The guru's role is to knock the ego on the head – so to speak – not pat it on the back.

As it happens, Marpa is unlikely to have expressed himself with reticence. It was not his way. By all accounts he was a rather peppery character, and one can't imagine him saying, 'This is just a suggestion, but I think it would be a good idea for you to spend the rest of your life in solitude up a remote mountain.' He would just have barked at Milarepa, 'Off you go!' and Milarepa, being Milarepa, would have obeyed instantly – but not because he was under Marpa's thumb. It is the receptivity of the disciple that gives the force of a command to the guru's suggestions or orders. However loudly Marpa barked at him, Milarepa was free to do as he pleased; his obedience sprang entirely from his supreme receptivity to his guru.

Without this unquestioning attitude, the relationship between a guru and his disciple will not work, because any such relationship is naturally volatile, being based – in a sense – on a conflict of interests. For example, if you obey a guru in order to win his approval, he is more than likely to withhold that approval. You might appear to be doing all sorts of good and virtuous things when in fact you are just looking for recognition from the guru, and when he spots this he will not pat you on the back. After all, it is the ego in us that wants praise from the guru, but the guru's role is to knock the ego on the head – so to speak – not pat it on the back.

So if the guru is doing his job, your grasping after approval will not be satisfied but possibly give way to resentment and disappointment in your teacher. Feeling let down, thinking he doesn't appreciate you, you may become sullen and uncooperative. This is particularly unfortunate. Your relationship with the guru is, after all, more than just ordinary friendship. He embodies your highest aspiration, so if you reject him, you lose your connection with your own guiding ideals. He will of course remain open to you, but you might close off the channel of communication from your side, and even start to find fault with him.

Looking for faults in the teacher or guru can be a way of unconsciously evading one's spiritual responsibility. If one consciously accepts certain principles, one should feel a responsibility to put them into practice. If one then fails to do so, finding fault with the teacher is a convenient way of explaining away one's failure. One might find oneself blaming the teacher or even the whole sangha. To the extent that the spiritual community as a whole represents a sort of collective guru figure in relation to oneself, one may come to see it in an entirely negative light.

There is a broader principle here, which can be applied to the way we see anyone. We may well be aware of other people's behaviour as skilful or unskilful, but we must try not to pass narrow moral judgement on them. Never mind whether the judgement is negative or positive; the principle is that we shouldn't judge people simply in terms of virtues and faults.

So how should we see other people? We can't help seeing them in some way or another, and we will certainly see both their faults and their virtues. But we shouldn't see them exclusively in those terms; we shouldn't reduce them to good or bad or a combination of the two. The best way to see them is as living, growing, developing human beings. If we are to do justice to others, we must always consider what they do in the context of the person doing it; their deeds shouldn't be seen in isolation from the overall growth and development of the individual. In short, we should always try to see the person, not what he or she does.

The more carefully you try to look at someone, the more difficult it seems to be to know and judge them. Naturally their actions do express something of their character. But as well as understanding the person in the light of their actions, you have to understand their actions in the light of the person. The same goes for what they say: to understand someone's words fully, you have to relate them back to the person speaking them. Suppose someone repeats to you something that a friend of yours has said, or describes something your friend has done, without knowing your friend very well. As you know your friend better than they do, you will probably understand what they said or did rather better than them, and you may be able to explain that there has been a misunderstanding. Sometimes the person behind the action or words is bigger than the actions or the words, and sometimes of course he or she is smaller. But you cannot arrive at any real knowledge of a person simply through knowing what they have done or said, without reference to who they are as a whole.

Our tendency is to see faults rather than virtues.

Tibetans, and Tantric practitioners generally, make a great deal of the point that the disciple cannot really understand the actions of the guru. While this can be made the basis of a lot of humbug and even exploitation, in principle it is true. You cannot fully understand the words or the actions of someone more developed than yourself any more than a dog can fully understand the words or actions of its master. If this analogy seems brutal, it might help to reflect that while a dog can never become a human being, as a disciple you can equal, and surpass, the spiritual attainments of your guru – if you want to. Once we start passing moral judgement on people, our tendency is to see faults rather than virtues; at least, it is the faults that seem to stand out. But

there is a particular danger in passing judgement on the character of our teacher, as we will then lose faith in him and his advice,
and we will no longer be able to commit ourselves wholeheartedly to the ideals to which he has introduced us. Indeed, to the
extent that we are out of communication with him, we are cutting ourselves off from our inspiration and undermining our
practice.

Paying for the Teaching

Your teachings spring from much hard work,
And so I dare not ask without paying first....
I now offer you this knife and belt.
Later, I will ask you for the Teachings.

Milarepa had to perform all sorts of tasks for Marpa before he
was given Marpa's 'compassionate blessing' and the teachings
he needed. Marpa himself had to pay in gold for the teachings
that he gathered in India. But Milarepa is a different sort of guru.
He will not accept such offerings. So what can the young man do
to get the teachings?

Traditionally the Dharma cannot be bought. Any material support received is not linked to the teaching given, because to make
such a link suggests some kind of equivalence in value between
the teaching and whatever mundane wealth is offered in return
for it, which is crucially to misrepresent the nature of the
Dharma. At the same time, one has to be prepared to make an
offering of one's material wealth as a token of one's commitment
to spiritual values above mundane ones. The young man certainly has a robust understanding of this attitude. When he says,
'I dare not ask without paying first,' he means he would be
ashamed to do so. But he is not asking for the teachings there and
then; he is now prepared to leave a decent interval between the
offering and the request.

It is a question not of bargaining for the Dharma, but of putting
one's money where one's mouth is. For money is what we are

talking about here. Money is the easiest thing to give – it is specifically designed for ease of disbursement. All you have to do is put your hand in your pocket and take the stuff out, or sign a cheque and hand it over. Yet it is sometimes money that we find it most difficult to give. The teachings we want from the guru are the fruit of perhaps decades of determined application to meditation, of hardship and privation – and we want it all for nothing. Marpa said as much to Milarepa himself. According to *The Life of Milarepa*, when Milarepa first asked for the teachings, Marpa replied, 'Is it to reward your many crimes that I went to India at the risk of my life? You say you want these teachings which are the living breath of the dakinis and for which, disdaining riches, I offered gold without measure. I hope you are only joking! Anyone else would kill you for that!'[27]

Money is not sordid; it's just that we tend to become sordid where money is involved.

The difficulty we experience in parting with our money is a symbolic recognition of the much greater difficulty the teacher has experienced in the course of his own mastery of the teachings. Giving as generously as you can is thus what makes a meeting between teacher and disciple possible. The meeting is based on a mutual recognition of what is truly important: that the worldly value of the offering is as nothing when compared to the value of the teaching.

The Tantra therefore traditionally insists on a significant financial outlay to signify the full commitment of your energies and resources. Originally the disciple was meant to give his entire worldly wealth. At the time of Tantric initiation you brought along all your property – usually made portable in the form of a bag of gold – and you offered it all to the guru. Later this was changed, and you were asked instead to make a substantial cash payment, however much you could manage. If you think about it, this is not necessarily a watering down of the principle, because it still exposes any lack of commitment on your part.

When you are told you can give what you like, the struggle going on in your mind may be all too apparent. 'Shall I give a hundred or might I get away with fifty? Maybe I should give sixty to be on the safe side.' Someone in this position might find they were less concerned about how much they could give for the teaching than about how little they could get it for, or that they were tempted to hedge their bets in case the teachings proved not to transform their life as advertised. If you are betrayed by a loss of nerve, an unspoken admission that you are going to allow your spiritual life to be governed by mundane considerations, this is a sure sign of a lack of spiritual receptivity.

There is often a degree of misunderstanding with regard to money and the spiritual life. People think that if you are a holy person you shouldn't be concerned with anything as grubby as money; the whole subject of cash is regarded in spiritual circles as rather indecent. But money is not sordid; it's just that we tend to become sordid where money is involved. We associate money with the mean and grasping attitude that it can tend to arouse in us, rather than seeing it as a way of expressing generosity and open-handedness.

A guru's teaching is not a commodity.

A more significant misunderstanding in this context is the idea that teachings of this nature can be given external form and placed at our disposal in the way that information can be gained from a book or a seminar, a lecture or a conversation. A guru's teaching is not a commodity. You can't acquire it from books or special mantras. It is a meeting of minds, a communication in the sense of a mutual resonance between individuals, and it can take place only when both people are completely open and un-guarded, and have no expectations in terms of the content of the communication. Even if all the communication seems to be flow-ing one way, it is more than that one-way flow. It is not like a file being downloaded to one computer from another. It is always an exchange.

The teacher is by definition open to the disciple. His wisdom is compassionate in nature, and he is simply waiting for an opportunity to give it. But he can do so only if the disciple is receptive. Given that the disciple is – again by definition – more restricted in his or her view of reality and of what the teaching means, the teacher must sometimes simply hold back. To use a traditional metaphor, if your pot is upside down, the guru cannot pour anything into it.

If you are expecting the teacher to give to you, you must be willing to be generous yourself. It is only when the generosity of the teacher meets that of the disciple that communication can really happen. The willingness to give is more than just a sign of receptivity. It *is* receptivity. When you give something valuable, you give up your attachment to it and show your confidence in the teacher. The fact that you get the teaching once you've paid up does not mean that you've paid *for* it. The payment is the manifestation of the openness you need if you are to receive the teaching. The willingness to give everything shows that you are fearless, and that you have complete faith in the teacher. It is also a discarding of old ideas about what is important and what is not.

Of course, it is better to think in terms of paying for the Dharma than not to give at all. A misunderstanding may be cleared up in the course of time, but if you never start giving up your attachments, you will never start receiving the Dharma. Giving is a spiritual practice in itself, and that practice is all the guru wants to see, whether or not they are the personal recipient of your generosity. Giving is a habit to be cultivated. If you are wealthy, it may be easier to make the gesture of a big public donation than to make a habit of being generous on a day-to-day basis, and you may have to work towards that kind of ongoing generosity slowly. But if you have only two coins and you give both of them, you really are giving up everything, although no one is likely to be very impressed. The quiet generosity of those who possess almost nothing is a treasure in itself.

This reminds me of an occasion during my time in Kalimpong. It was in 1956, when I was invited by the Indian government as one of fifty-seven 'distinguished Buddhists from border areas' to visit Delhi for the 2,500th Buddha *Jayanti* (birthday) celebrations. In the course of our travels we came to Benares, where, in the company of a Tibetan friend, I visited an old Tibetan lama who was living there in order to learn Sanskrit. Apparently the Dalai Lama had asked him to teach, but he had refused. Although he was about fifty, which is old for a Tibetan, he said that he had too much still to learn, and that he had to complete his studies first.

We found him in a small bare room at the top of a Hindu ashram, seated on the floor behind a tin trunk which he was using as a makeshift desk. He was very happy to meet us, and we talked for about an hour and a half. As we rose to go, he said, 'Wait, I must give you something.' He looked around the room – which didn't take long because there was nothing in it – seeming almost desperate to find something that would serve as a gift. Suddenly his face cleared. He took his mala, the string of beads on which the recitation of mantras is counted, broke the cord, and gave me one of the beads. 'Please take this,' he said. 'It is all I have, but I must have said many millions of mantras with it over the years.' This gift, from this poor and humble monk, was worthless in material terms, but in spiritual terms it was immensely valuable. Through this eloquent reminder of his years of practice, he was offering the Dharma, which is the best gift anyone can give or receive.

Returning to Milarepa, he probably doesn't even have a mala. But he does have the Dharma, and consequently he rejects any implication that he has any need or desire for anything that can be bought or sold, given or taken away. But implicit in the young man's choice of gifts, and his manner of giving them, there is still a sense of worldly exchange, an assumption that the treasure of Milarepa's attainment and instruction has its worldly price. As each gift is offered, Milarepa counters it with a fresh restatement of his attainment, which is beyond valuation. The very basis of that attainment is, after all, the letting go of worldly objects.

Milarepa's Song of the Clay Pot and the Unhired Teacher

Milarepa tells the young man that he cannot yet give him the teachings, and explains why.

Listen to me, ingenuous young man!
From my hut's roof in the snow mountain
Flows the quintessence of milk and nectar.
Though it is not made of gold or jewels,
I would not pour it into earthenware.

There is a rich confusion of images here. The 'quintessence of milk and nectar' refers to the dissolving of the yogi's subtle energies into the bliss of the enlightened mind. It also recalls meditation practices in which one imagines a bright, nourishing stream of nectar pouring down on one's head from a visualized archetypal figure above. Milarepa poetically conflates this image with the melting snow dripping from the roof of his hut. But as he develops the image and envisages pouring the milk and nectar, it comes to refer to the teaching distilled from his meditation. Although he cannot claim that his own teaching is very precious – 'it is not made of gold or jewels' – it is the most precious thing he has to offer, and he wants to be very careful where he pours it. Not only must the vessel be receptive – the pot must be the right way up – but it cannot be made of just any old earthenware. In other words, our practice is not to fill ourselves with profound and precious teachings but to make ourselves fit to receive them, to become a strong, unbreakable vessel, even a diamond vessel.

Milarepa next points to the cotton belt around his waist – which is probably the meditation band he wears round his neck and knees to keep his body upright during his hours and days of meditation practice.

Around this waist of mine, the poor man of strong will,
Is tied a cotton belt of fanatic devotion!

135

The absence of pretence and hypocrisy
Is the pattern of my belt.

In symbolizing 'fanatic devotion' (or perhaps 'intense' would be a better translation, for nothing that is truly Buddhist can really be described as fanatic), the belt needs no embellishments. Milarepa's devotion does not draw attention to itself. His practice is held together by simplicity of faith and direct and diligent honesty of purpose. The image is reminiscent of the Biblical phrase 'gird up thy loins' – that is, hitch up your robe ready for work. His devotion is a practical and realistic response to the true nature of things.

Bright wisdom is my knife,
Its sheath, the confidence of the Three Measurements.

As is customary, wisdom is likened to a blade, with its associations of cutting, penetrating, and reflecting. Intellectual understanding, by contrast, is represented here by the image of the sheath. Milarepa's sheath is his confidence in his practice, based on the Three Measurements, which Chang suggests refers to the yogi's judgement of how far his experience matches his understanding of the scriptures, and whether it brings him closer to the Bodhisattva ideal and deepens his insight. His wisdom, however penetrating, is thus always put in the context of his understanding of the scriptures. Like a sheath, his understanding protects his wisdom.

Taking Payment for Teachings

Lest goddesses punish me,
I have never asked for wealth or money
When teaching in the past,
Nor shall I do so now.
Dear boy, you may go home;
I do not want your gifts.

Milarepa is not questioning the importance for the disciple of making offerings before the teachings can be received, but he is mindful of the danger for the teacher of losing sight of the subtlety of the principle involved and demanding cash for teachings. It is a little like the communist principle: 'To each according to his need; from each according to his ability.' There is no cash nexus, no bargain struck. Rather than, 'I give you this, *therefore* you give me that,' the principle is, 'I will try to give you what I can, with no relation to anything you may or may not give to me.' If the guru is a real guru, he will give what he can in any case.

Milarepa is beyond being able to sell his teachings; there is no literal danger of being punished by the 'goddesses' – by which he presumably means the ḍākinīs representing his inspiration – because he is not separate from them. They are not external deities looking on in judgement. But he is saying that his ability to communicate the teachings is linked to his inability to sell them. The goddesses – the ḍākinīs and inspirational muses – are there to be served, not used, and if you try to exploit them for your own ends, they will desert you.

Creativity will find its own uses, its own expression. It has its own momentum, and to try to harness it to a practical purpose is to deny its very nature.

The same principle applies to the powers of inspiration to which people like artists, psychics, and mystics have at least intermittent access. If those powers are not honoured, they can indeed be lost. A creative artist who starts using his or her talent to produce work simply to make money is likely to find that the springs of inspiration will eventually dry up. This certainly happened to fashionable society painters like the nineteenth-century English prodigy, John Millais, who began his career as an artist with real promise and went on to turn out popular sentimental works like *Bubbles*. Likewise, spiritual teachers who are bursting with positive creative energy when they set up their own organization or ashram can find that, if they follow the lure of wealth and celebrity when they start becoming successful, their gift leaves them. Not everyone succumbs to such pressures, of course; for example, some lamas and gurus who could have expected to live out their lives quietly in Tibet have evidently adjusted to the pressures of western culture and withstood its temptations rather better than others.

Unfortunately, once someone finds they can heal people or teach people to meditate, and that they can get paid to do so, the vocation can easily turn into a profession, becoming *essentially* a money-making enterprise rather than being generated by inspiration. You might start off idealistically, but the idealism can fade away quickly if you get caught up in maximizing profits. Whether it is writing or painting, or practising medicine or alternative therapies, or even going into Buddhism and meditation, these days almost the first consideration seems to be how you are to get a rewarding livelihood out of whatever you are inspired to do. But if you embark on yoga classes or therapy simply in order to become a yoga teacher or a therapist, or if you sit down to write a 'best-selling novel', you are never going to feel the breath of the ḍākinīs on the back of your neck as you work.

The essence of spiritual inspiration is that it is free and spontaneous. Spiritual attainments should never be used, even for a good purpose. Even directing one's creativity towards some purely unselfish aim is to abuse it. Creativity will find its own uses, its own expression. It has its own momentum, and to try to harness it to a practical purpose is to deny its very nature. We see it as a good thing to try to put everything to good use, however trivial that use may be, and we feel uneasy if we can't put our finger on what something is *for*. But that uneasiness comes down to not knowing what we ourselves are for.

We are uneasy with the thought that we are not here *for* anything. But the truth of the matter is that we are the glorious end-product of millions of years of evolution, and we need find no further justification for ourselves. One of the less appealing legacies of Christianity is its encouragement of an unnecessarily abject view of ourselves. Charles Wesley, one of the founders of

Methodism, liked to remind his congregations that they were mere grovelling worms, but the truth is that, splendid though worms are in their own way, we can safely claim to have left that species behind us by a comfortable margin. Indeed, without being unduly immodest, we can call ourselves the end-product, even the crown, of the evolutionary process. Our human existence is much more significant than we usually like to think. We can have no higher purpose than being ourselves. The only step worth taking from where we find ourselves as human beings is to evolve into Buddhas. We are not here to be useful. We don't have to justify our human status by engaging in some useful occupation. Of course there is nothing wrong with useful occupation, but we should beware of any idea that our purpose on this earth is to fill up our time with useful activities.

The spiritual life is not to be expected to produce material results.

In this context, consider the traditional life of the Buddhist monk. Though he is supported by the laity, there is no pressure on him to make himself useful. The fact that he is a monk is quite enough. All that is expected of him is that he should wear his robe correctly, keep his head shaved, eat his food at the proper time, and that sort of thing. He doesn't even have to meditate. Just living the harmless life of a monk is considered an achievement in itself. This attitude may encourage laziness, and it must be admitted that some monks don't really deserve the respect and support they receive. But the danger is more than offset by the important message that such a radical attitude communicates, which is that the spiritual life is not to be expected to produce material results. In fact, the majority of monks in the East do take up useful occupations like teaching or caring for the sick, but ideally they do this because they are inspired to do it. It is a spontaneous activity, an expression of what they are.

Clergy in the West are impressively active and outgoing by comparison, but this seems to be at the cost of surrendering this principle. Out of concern to justify their existence in terms that the mundane world can appreciate – by engaging in social and charity work, like running youth clubs for teenagers and bingo for pensioners – they may end up neglecting their central function, so that people start to wonder what they are really for, beyond providing a kind of social service.

One can say perhaps that the job of religious full-timers is to demonstrate that the most useful thing you can do is to be. The spiritual life is an end in itself and doesn't have to be justified in worldly terms. In the work and profit-driven culture of the West, we should do more than pay lip service to this ideal; we should do what we can to support at least a few people simply to live a Buddhist life, without any expectation that they should earn their keep in some way, whether by teaching or writing or study or even by working especially hard at their meditation. The only way to experience the value of doing this is to do it. You have actually to experience paying for someone to do nothing in particular. Or, more demanding still, you have to experience being paid to do nothing in particular. Being supported in this way, your contribution then is simply to be happy in whatever you choose to do or not do. You might do things like giving lectures, meditating, or writing; you might do nothing much at all. You might simply be around for people to talk to – and even then your 'job' is to be happy whether anyone talks to you or not.

Our highest aspiration should be to take freely and give freely, acting spontaneously in everything we do.

To do this would be to introduce into our lives a little of the fragrance, the essence, of Sukhāvatī, the Pure Land beloved of Buddhist mythology. You don't have to work there, because clothes and food appear spontaneously; all you need do is sit on a lotus and listen to the Dharma. Ideally, everything we do should have something of this spirit about it. If we work, it should be because we want to, because it makes us happy. Of course, we may sometimes be aware of the spiritual need to push ourselves through barriers of laziness or diffidence. But we should not be working just to fulfil an obligation to put in so many hours in return for pay. Too many people work on the basis of a deepseated feeling of guilt and obligation, and people also exploit and manipulate others on the same basis.

One of the functions of a Buddhist organization should therefore be to provide material support without strings attached for those who are able to commit themselves fully to the spiritual life. It may as yet be difficult to achieve this on a large scale in the West, but one or two models of that way of going about things would at least remind us of that ideal. It would remind us that it is the human being that matters, the human being that is the whole purpose of any truly spiritual movement. Any Buddhist movement runs the risk of allowing its aspirations to sink to the level of purely organizational goals, and once those take hold, it is a small step to start to regard the human beings that make up that movement as little more than the means of realizing those organizational ends. We need always to remind ourselves of our real aim, however inconvenient and impractical it may be to do so. If a human being is a means to anything, it is to his or her development as an individual, and if an individual is a means to anything, it is to Buddhahood.

Imagine the 'job' of doing nothing in particular, not out of laziness but as a practice of embodying the sheer enormity of a reality that exceeds any mundane notion of occupation or utility. Paradoxically, it would be quite challenging. People do not always take cheerfully to being left to their own devices. The devil, as they say, finds work for idle hands to do, and at the very least you're likely to get bored and restless and start to seek distraction. But imagine having someone around who has nothing to rush off and do, who is not tired or busy, who is cheerful, peaceful, yet full of energy, and available to respond to the call of the ḍākinīs in whatever form they might take. Such a 'duty' could be taken up successfully only by someone who was spiritually committed.

After all, how would you employ a Buddha? Does he have to justify his Buddhahood? No. The mere fact that he is a Buddha is enough. By the same token, we can cultivate the vision of Buddhahood by resisting the impulse to make a commodity of ourselves. Our highest aspiration should be to take freely and give freely, acting spontaneously in everything we do, rather than out of a sense of obligation or even responsibility. As far as we can, we should abjure all coercive attempts to make us justify our existence by paying our way and working for our keep.

Chapter 7

Listening for the Teachings

Milarepa's Song of the Yogi's Temple

The young man's offers now become extravagant, even desperate. He proposes building Milarepa a temple, although he introduces the proposal with an almost self-defeating air.

> *You are a real yogi, an ascetic worker,*
> *Disgusted with mundane things*
> *And indifferent to the world....*
> *Although one thing to you is as another,*
> *A permanent home may help your inspiration.*[28]

The young man is not planning to skimp on materials, scale, or design features, and he goes on to conjure up a splendid vision of tall pillars, a large floor decorated with a mandala, a well-adorned pagoda, and a shrine. No doubt most spiritual practitioners would be only too glad to accept free use of a place in which to practise undisturbed. Even the Buddha, while advocating a wandering life for his disciples, accepted offers of land and shelter during the rainy season.

The all-important proviso is that gifts should come with no strings attached. Although truly to give means renouncing all rights in respect to what you have given, someone who gives often has a barely conscious expectation that they are going to get something, however intangible, in return. If you find yourself in the position of being presented with a gift, especially a substantial one, you need to do what you can to make sure that the person who wants to give it is capable of doing so freely, so that there will be no subsequent regrets, resentment, or recriminations. If you get any sense that they have made their offer in a burst of enthusiasm that they are going to regret, you should turn it down.

Milarepa finds a sacred mandala in the world around him wherever he is.

But Milarepa turns this offer down for other reasons. Having chosen a wandering lifestyle, he is determined to avoid even the slightest occasion for the worldly attachment that is likely to accompany any kind of settled situation. His response to the suggestion that a permanent home might be inspiring is scathing.

> *My confused young lad!*
> *Do you not know that this world is transient and unreal?*
> *When you come before the King of the Dead*
> *Your rich man's money is of no avail.*
> *There your wealth can never buy you off;*
> *There you will find no place to swing a strong man's sword,*
> *No place to dance or strut about the stage.*
> *Your flesh will be as dust....*
> *The temple wherein I dwell is the inner unborn Mind;*

Whatever the boy says to try to convince Milarepa that a temple would be useful and convenient, and would promote his spiritual values, from Milarepa's point of view it would be nothing but a compromise and a snare. The very expression 'a permanent home may help your inspiration' gives the game away. To take possession of property in perpetuity, to use a legal phrase, suggests that one is going to get from that property something more than the temporary accommodation that in reality is all we can expect from the world, however much money we have. How can Milarepa take possession of a temple intended to proclaim values that are diametrically opposed to materialism and possessiveness? How can he accept a permanent home in an impermanent universe?

Milarepa reverses the symbolic process. A temple is designed to symbolize in concrete terms various as yet unrealized spiritual ideals, but Milarepa has already realized those ideals and has no need to refer to them symbolically, through external forms. Instead, he refers to the temple of his direct spiritual experience, which is more solid and real than stone and wood.

> I erect the pillars of the Real
> On the foundation of immutability....
> On the ground of the Dhyānic Warmth
> I draw a Mandal of Clear Observation.

The offering of the mandala is one of the foundation yogas of the Tantra. In this practice, the mandala is visualized as a symbolic representation of the whole universe as it is described in traditional Buddhist cosmology. In offering a mandala, you are symbolically offering the whole world, the universe itself – everything mundane. You are saying in effect that you have recognized the true value of the teaching. It is so precious to you that in order to receive it you are willing to give everything you have or could possibly have. When you offer the mandala, your happiness and gratitude for what you have received expresses itself in your desire to offer everything you have, everything you experience, everything you could ever experience, to the Buddhas and Bodhisattvas. Nobody could ever make such an offering literally, of course, but one can do it symbolically, and it is the motivation which is the most important thing. Finally, in case you are carried away by any feelings of elation or inflation, you reflect that all these offerings are ultimately empty. You cannot even hold on to whatever you may hope to gain from your actions.

As well as being a symbolic offering of the world as it seems to us to be, a mandala can also symbolize a vision of the world, a pattern of reality that lies beyond what is apparent in everyday life and thought. One can meditate on a mandala as a visualized circle of forms, with a particular Buddha at the centre and other Buddhas or Bodhisattvas arranged around the central form. This kind of mandala is the archetypal image of concentration, of energies gathering around a central point.

Milarepa's 'Mandal of Clear Observation' – his insight – is inseparable from the 'ground of the Dhyānic Warmth' upon which it is inscribed. What this means is that he is not just concentrating on the mandala as an object of meditation. Having harmonized his cruder elemental or base nature, he has absorbed within himself all the qualities which the Buddhas and Bodhisattvas of the mandala embody and symbolize. It is as though, in his realization of non-duality, he *is* the mandala, and all the Buddhas within it, and all the ḍākinīs and goddesses who come to make offerings to it. They are all aspects of his enlightened experience. This mandala or sacred space is not an inner realm as opposed to an outer or objective realm. Milarepa finds a sacred mandala in the world around him wherever he is, and sees whatever visions come to him as the activity of his own mind. Consequently, he has no fear of error or going astray, and no need of any kind of sacred space, let alone a temple.

Milarepa's Song of the Yogi's Mate
Throwing caution to the wind, the young man now offers Milarepa his sister's hand in marriage. Again, he is aware that Milarepa is hardly likely to look favourably on this idea, and initially he offers her services as a kind of nursemaid before describing her more seductive attractions with his usual hyperbole.

> *She is heiress to a royal tradition.*
> *Do not mistakenly regard her as of common stock;*
> *She is the heart-taker among the crowds,*
> *Radiant as a rainbow, she is more beautiful than angels.*

Milarepa does not mince his words.

Do not talk like a fool. I have already renounced family ties. I am not interested in an ego-clinging woman. The so-called faith of the common people is most unstable and liable to change. I am an old beggar with no family and no relatives. People will laugh at you, if you give her to me. Afterwards, you will regret what you have done. I have no desire to become your brother-in-law.

In turning down the boy's offer, we can take it that Milarepa is not concerned with any spiritual danger to himself that might arise from taking a consort. However, he is happy with the results of having renounced family ties, and he knows that other people, even those who support and admire him, do not have the strength of faith to see a change of lifestyle as only that. If he was to take a wife, they would lose whatever faith they had in the Dharma and their respect for its practitioners, and he would become in their eyes simply an old beggar. Besides, he is not at all interested in making wealthy connections by joining the boy's family, and with just a little mockery he addresses his devotee as 'young lord'. He remarks mildly on the lust and attachment that women generally arouse in men – which, as it happens, is the effect that the 'young lord' has just been attempting to produce upon Milarepa himself – before going on.

A qualified Illumination-Woman is indeed most rare.
To have angelic company on the Bodhi-Path
Is a wonder and a marvel;
Yet you a little have exaggerated.
This is why the Mudrā Practice is so very hard.

Milarepa doesn't rule out the possibility of finding a genuine spiritual consort, but such 'angelic company' is a marvel precisely because it is so rare. The boy's use of the conventional exaggerations of romantic language to describe his sister simply shows how very hard it is to practise the Tantra with a consort; one so easily becomes intoxicated.

Milarepa's song continues in the usual way to extol the joys of the spiritual life in terms of the various characteristics of the offering that have been extolled by the young man. This particular offering gives him the opportunity to present his relationship with the nature of reality in fervent, even passionate terms. There is certainly no nihilism in his evocation of śūnyatā. Śūnyatā is realized on the basis of a full engagement of the emotions, and its realization expresses itself in kindness. Conversely, if you do not love the Dharma passionately, the life of sexual renunciation or *brahmacarya* will be a real struggle. Indeed, it is a struggle that you will lose, one way or another, if you do not find the means to arouse strong feelings within your practice.

> *My wonder woman is the lust-free Śūnyatā.*
> *There is compassion on her face,*
> *And kindness in her smile....*
>
> *She is such a charming witch –*
> *The realization of Truth is her origin!*
> *This is my wife, the yogi's mate.*

The youth seems to imagine that Milarepa is in need of companionship. But in fact, coursing in non-dual two-in-one-ness, Milarepa experiences no delusive separation between 'self' in here and 'world' out there. In this blissful union of unreal opposites, everything is available to him. It is the delusive view that one is separate from others that lies at the root of fear and loneliness and the yearning for companions.

Pleasure on the Path of Renunciation

In Buddhism, the abandonment of worldly attachment is regarded as a prerequisite for spiritual development, and for this reason there are many practices designed to help us break out of the ways in which we are attached to objects of the senses. The recollection of the loathsomeness of food, for example, is meant to help us overcome our attachment to the pleasures of eating. In similar fashion, the recollection of the impurity of the thirty-two bodily substances – hair, fat, phlegm, pus, and all the rest of it – is supposed to help us to overcome sexual craving. And the recollection of death helps us to see that all the things we set our hearts on will eventually cease to be.

These examples of the Buddha's teaching seem to suggest that the path to Enlightenment is a process of cutting ourselves off from the mundane, leaving the world behind, disengaging from the impure. The sober recollection of the unpleasant qualities of worldly things is a traditional means of focusing the mind on that which is beyond the world. It is an approach to practice that is to be found throughout the Pali canon, and it is said to appeal to a particular kind of Buddhist practitioner: the 'doctrine follower', the disciple whose immediate response to Buddhism is predominantly intellectual rather than emotional. Rather than being encouraged by the thought of attaining the unmitigated bliss of the unconditioned, the doctrine follower is spurred on by the knowledge that all objects of the senses are inherently impermanent and must be given up at death. This type of practitioner tends to see the goal of his or her practice as attaining freedom from the disappointments and hardships of conditioned existence and the sufferings of repeated rebirths. Milarepa himself was famously driven in his practice by the fear of future suffering. Having committed so many evil deeds, there was only one possible option open to him: if he didn't gain Enlightenment in this lifetime, he would go straight to hell when he died. His situation was so urgent that only the most intense spiritual practice would be of any use to him.

The danger of that motivation for those of lesser spiritual capacity than Milarepa is that the spiritual life becomes associated only with fear and revulsion. While such a motivation may provide a necessary spur to practice, in the longer term it will be counter-productive without a correspondingly powerful faith in the positive outcome of that practice. In contradistinction to the doctrine follower, therefore, we find the 'faith follower'. Rather than recoiling from the evils of the world, the faith follower feels drawn to the joy and beauty of Enlightenment. Such a person does not feel inspired by the thought of their precarious and unhappy lot in this world, and it would be useless to talk to them about the unpleasantness of conditioned existence. They need to hear about the positive qualities of the unconditioned.

Human beings are ruled to a great extent by pleasure, and we can't function well without it.

Milarepa lives not just an ascetic life but a life dedicated to joy. He is as much a faith follower as a doctrine follower, seeing that the spiritual life is rewarding in its own right, and that nirvāṇa is as attractive and fascinating as saṁsāra is unpleasant and disappointing. We can be positively drawn even to the ineffable emptiness of śūnyatā. And after all, there is pleasure in conditioned existence alongside the pain, and not all of that pleasure ties us to the wheel of repeated rebirth. As well as *kāma-chanda*, desire for worldly pleasures, we also experience *dhamma-chanda*, the desire for the pleasures of the Buddhist path.

Human beings are ruled to a great extent by pleasure, and we can't function well without it; it has a tonic effect that is important for our overall health. If you haven't enjoyed anything for a long time, if you haven't experienced some thoroughgoing happiness and delight recently, you will tend to feel listless and drained of energy. So if you give up the 'pleasurable things' of this life, you will have to replace them somehow. If you don't replace them with pleasures that will draw you towards a higher purpose, your energy will get stuck and may even force its way out in disagreeable ways. Unless you enjoy what you're doing, you can't do it in a very positive spirit for long.

At the same time, if we are eventually to appreciate the limitless pleasure of nirvāṇa, we have to develop our sensitivity and discernment by cultivating a more refined enjoyment of the objects of the senses, crude as these may be when compared to the bliss of the transcendental. To begin with, we need to bring our higher aspirations to bear upon our habitual sources of pleasure, and see where they can be refined. Innocent and harmless pleasures like those of nature, music, art, and even food and drink enjoyed in good company are to be relished.

It is usually in childhood that our capacity for delight in simple pleasures of our own making is most evident. As we get older it seems to fade away, and we find we are unable to enjoy things in the way a child does. We no longer play or absorb ourselves unselfconsciously in some innocent activity, and what we call our pleasures become dull routines, almost a matter of duty rather than spontaneous enjoyment. Of course, children also get upset very easily, and experience unhappiness and even misery to a degree that adults usually manage to avoid. We should aim to experience the spontaneity and capacity for happiness of a child while bringing an adult's perspective to setbacks and small catastrophes.

When it comes to Dharma practice, it is important to take delight in our study, our meditation, our practice of ethics, and, like Milarepa in the tiger's cave, even our renunciation and the difficulties we encounter. The key to this is practice, which means a gradual but steady and determined shifting of perspective in the way we live, not just passively accepting whatever happens to drift into our lives but engaging with life more actively. We need to take responsibility for our enjoyment, not just relying on external supports but generating well-being from our own concentrated attention, experienced through the practice of meditation. We can also learn to share our pleasures, and to put them into the perspective of a hierarchy of values.

**The easiest way to block your progress
towards Buddhahood is to be picky.**

The important thing is to learn to find pleasure in a way that is in harmony with your higher aspirations or ideals. Otherwise, like everyone else, you are going to be caught up in what passes for pleasure in the ordinary world – in other words, an endless cycle of superficial pleasures and nagging frustrations, petty likes and dislikes, habitual and unconsidered preferences. If Buddhahood is the state of non-duality at the highest level, attachment to worldly pleasures is the complete opposite: a product of the reactive or dualistic mind at the lowest level which constantly reinforces our need to define ourselves according to our likes and dislikes. The quickest and easiest way to gain Buddhahood in one lifetime is thus not to make much of your likes and dislikes and thereby to free yourself from attachment to them. Conversely, the easiest way to block your progress towards Buddhahood is to be picky: 'I like this but I don't like that. I'll do this but I won't do that. I'll have coffee but I won't have tea.'

Having likes and dislikes is not the problem. The problem is insisting on them, making them absolute rules that are not to be transgressed. It is this that strengthens the dualistic mind. There is nothing wrong with preferring coffee, but if it upsets you to be given tea instead, and particularly if you feel that you have to make a fuss about it, then clearly you are tightening the bonds of duality around your mind. Our most obvious likes and dislikes are connected with food and drink and they are usually left over from childhood. It is fair enough for a child – a developing individual trying to establish a healthy, separate ego – to insist on personal preferences, but as we mature we should ideally outgrow all this, though unfortunately we tend not to. Our daily lives become enmeshed in a constant succession of petty likes and dislikes which make up a kind of network of reactivity, and this fixes our sense of ourselves and grows stronger every time we allow our preferences to dictate our state of mind.

But the creative mind slices through this neat web of personal predilections and antipathies. Recognizing that pleasures are inherently impermanent, it responds accordingly, never attaching so much importance to likes and dislikes that it is thrown into a state of vexation when they are disregarded. As Śāntideva says in the *Bodhicaryāvatāra*, 'What essence has remained mine from things I once enjoyed, now perished, for which my infatuation led me to ignore the advice of my teachers?'[29] Seen in this light, the objects we crave are illusory, and so are the subjective bodily senses that perceive them.

Of course, preferences and tastes are not all equally subjective. Some are matters of principle – not drinking alcohol or eating meat, for example – though if these really are about principle, your state of mind will not be unduly affected when they are not catered for. Aesthetic likes and dislikes may also have a degree of objectivity, although a discerning taste is not stuck in fixed preferences but is capable of changing and responding to new experiences. The aesthetic criterion also applies to one's tastes in food and drink; some people's palates are clearly more cultivated than others.

With both artistic taste and culinary taste, liking or disliking is different from aesthetic discernment, the one being subjective while the other is a response to objective degrees of value. Unfortunately, most of us proceed most of the time on the basis of purely subjective likes and dislikes, not attempting any more objective evaluation of our tastes, and this is inimical to the development of the creative mind and the spiritual life generally. We do so, moreover, with the support of a commonly held but mistaken view that denies the objective component of taste and holds that it is always a purely personal matter. According to this view, one person's taste in music, say, is no better than anyone else's; it's just different.

To continue with this example, it is true that any assessment of music's spiritual quality is subjective in the sense that it is related to a particular kind of sensitivity. But music is not just a series of pleasant – or unpleasant – sensations; it also has a mental or emotional and spiritual content. In my view there is an objective hierarchy of degrees of aesthetic development, and therefore of spiritual sensitivity. This is not to advocate the enforced appreciation of high art at the expense of other forms of culture or to demand uncomprehending worship of the creative icons of the European past. The principle of a hierarchy of value is more important than any specific judgement. It's a question of the degree of development in terms of consciousness, creativity, awareness, responsibility, and all the other qualities that make up human individuality, that a work of art communicates. The better the art, the more fully it communicates these qualities.

From a spiritual point of view, the important thing to acknowledge is not that one person's taste in the arts is better than that of someone else, but that some human beings really are better than others in certain respects. The terms of reference vary greatly. Some individuals are better than others in terms of physical attainment, others excel in terms of mental skills; some are superior in terms of artistry while others are pre-eminent in terms of moral and spiritual development. There is a passage in the Pali canon which makes this point beautifully. The Buddha praises each of his disciples for his special qualities: one of them is best at meditation, while another is especially sensitive in the way he collects alms, another stands out for his ability to explain the Dharma, and so on.[30]

To sum up, likes and dislikes have an element of objective validity, and in as much as pleasure is essential to the spiritual life, we can say that refining our tastes is important. On the other hand, any tastes and habits that we allow to become a burden to others, and that we cannot happily put aside when we need to, do not deserve any respect. But the main point is that enjoyment is not a luxury, something peripheral to the main business of practising the Dharma; it is not an element to introduce if there's time. It is central to the whole exercise. Only joy will keep us going in the spiritual life. You can only practise the Dharma if you have the energy, the spark, the zest for it. You need to be able to relish it for what it is – a feast for the famished heart and mind.

If you do not love the Dharma passionately, even if you are a doctrine follower, you cannot live the life of renunciation authentically. It may take some effort before you enjoy your Dharma life, but enjoyment has to be on the agenda somewhere. There is a Hindi proverb: 'Bitter in the mouth but sweet in the stomach.' The Dharma is like that for some people. It may taste rather bitter at first, but you taste the real sweetness of it as you start to digest and assimilate it. In the end, the methods of doctrine and faith converge in the same goal, a complementary union of insight and bliss.

Milarepa's Song of Self-Respect

The boy finally wants to offer Milarepa a pair of trousers with which to protect his modesty. As before, he begins by showing his clear grasp of Tantric theory, and his understanding of Milarepa's nature, by admitting that Milarepa has nothing left to hide, being free from all ideas of disgrace and shame. However, he follows this with an argument that challenges Milarepa's chosen path.

> We worldly men are shamed by indecent exposure.
> Even the perfect Buddha, the fully enlightened Being,
> Discreetly follows worldly customs.

Following this preamble, the young man runs through what is for him a fairly cursory description of his trousers – which he says have been tailored by his uncle – before making an offering of them. But, leaving fashions in Tibetan trousers aside, what is behind the offering is the suggestion that Milarepa should abandon his eremitical Tantric lifestyle for one that accommodates conventional social propriety. The boy's critical attitude towards Milarepa's lifestyle is all too common. Many people, perhaps especially those whose own spiritual practice is rather desultory, have decided views with regard to the way of life that should be followed by more serious practitioners. It is as if they believe that the practice of the Dharma should be regulated according to mundane standards of propriety.

The question is: of what should we be truly ashamed?

Milarepa replies by challenging the boy to explain what he finds so strange about his penis being visible, hanging there as nature intended. He points out that he came from his mother's womb naked, and that death will not spare his clothes any more than it will spare his body. He then begins a brief disquisition on the difference between mundane discretion or shame and spiritual dignity or self-respect. The question is: of what should we be truly ashamed?

That is merely the nature-born male organ;
I cannot understand this so-called 'shame' of yours...

Look at sinful, evil, and meaningless deeds;
You are not ashamed of them.

In offering up his weapons, the youth has renounced the 'all important combat' that has been so firmly a part of his identity as a member of the clan or group, but he is clearly holding on to some group values, and here he shows it in his conflation of self-respect with respectability. This is very common. I remember that when I was a small child, most children were not allowed to run about and play when they were dressed in their Sunday best. They were made to sit at home so that they would stay neat and tidy. This was nothing to do with religion; it was all about social niceties. Even during my youth, if a man didn't wear a tie or a hat, he was considered not to be fully dressed, while wearing a coloured shirt was an act of flagrant recklessness. Those particular signs of respectability have changed, but the concern to display the appropriate marks of submission to group norms is still very apparent. In an age of consumerism, respectability is less a matter of a rigid dress code and more about a carefully maintained range of purchases and recreational activities that will ensure peer acceptance. You need to have the right sort of job and live in the right part of town, go on holiday to the right ski resort, drive the right kind of car, and even follow the right religion.

The perception of things as all-important when they are nothing of the kind is reinforced by vulnerability to group disapproval, and also by lack of imagination, an inability to contemplate stepping outside the range of possibilities that society thinks acceptable. Unfortunately, Buddhists have all too often succumbed to this kind of failure of nerve and vision. When you get a narrow and rigid monasticism, when the monastic rules and even the way you dress and shave your head have turned into a kind of Buddhist respectability, or when it becomes all-important to spend the right number of years studying Buddhist philosophy in the right monastic universities, then what is really all-important is to re-emphasize what is really all-important. It was for this reason that some Tantric yogis originally set out to flout convention, to challenge what other people considered important, even within the Buddhist world.

It is easy to forget that the Buddhist message is a subversive one.

When I first came back to England in the early 1960s, after some twenty years in Asia, it was impressed upon me as all-important that Buddhism should be respectable. I soon realized that what the people who were trying to influence me meant by this was that Buddhism should be made as acceptable as possible to the values of the English middle classes. But if Buddhists agree to such a thing, Buddhism ceases to be Buddhism. The same may be said for the versions of Buddhism that are peddled to the consumer society these days, and the way that Buddhism is profiled to appeal to different niche markets, to fit in with whatever that society considers to be all important. It may well find acceptance in this way, but it ceases to be Buddhism.

Of course, if you want to communicate the Dharma to a lot of people, you cannot afford to alienate them by causing offence, especially by breaking their taboos. At the same time, you need to be careful not to lose sight of what you are trying to communicate. It is easy to forget that the Buddhist message is a subversive one, that its values run counter to mundane or worldly norms, and that your commitment to its ethical principles may lead you on occasion to offend conventional notions of morality. If the Buddha 'discreetly follows worldly customs', he does so only in so far as these did not compromise the ideals of the Dharma and the integrity of the lifestyle he had chosen through which to express those ideals.

It is normal to be ashamed of anything that excludes one from the group, and social inclusion is fundamentally predicated on the respect given to taboos, whether one observes them or breaks them. Milarepa speaks from a position that is not in opposition to social convention, but simply beyond it. That is to say, it is not a position at all. He avoids any fixed position, whether of conformity or individualism. In other words he is not a conformist or an individualist, but an individual. He does not define himself in relation to the group, whether by joining it or by setting himself apart from it.

Metta and the practice of ethics gently soak in to transform the deepest fibres of one's being.

A true individual is someone who has developed self-awareness, through one discipline or another, and on that basis a confidence and self-respect that does not depend upon convention or fashion. If you are a true individual, your sense of identity and purpose in life does not rely on your social identity – whether you are a citizen, family member, worker, rebel, or iconoclast. As a mature human being, your self-awareness transcends human social groups of all kinds. Your defining relationship is an inner relationship with the deeper reality of things, the truth behind appearances. One might even say that the true individual is one through whom that deeper reality of things functions and is present in the world. If you are a true individual you can stand on your own two feet and at the same time maintain a harmony with the way things really are.

Milarepa is an individual in the true sense because he is free of the power of social conventions. He doesn't need to conform to other people's expectations of how a spiritual practitioner should look; it doesn't matter to him how he is seen. We tend to be most ashamed of matters over which we have no control, like our social background or what we look like. Milarepa, by contrast, is ashamed only of 'sinful, evil, and meaningless deeds'. The things that preoccupy the vast majority of people are quite simply of no concern to him at all; and conversely, he sees how important it is to feel real shame about deeds and activities about which most people would feel no compunction.

Milarepa concludes by describing how he maintains his self-respect.

My fine wool is the Heart-for-Bodhi
With which I spin the thread of Four Initiations;
The cloth I weave is the liberation Path of Samādhi;
The dye I use is made of virtues and good-wishes.

All the initiations of the Tantric path are spun from the same stuff: the bodhicitta, the will to Enlightenment for the sake of all beings. Weaving the thread of the teachings to which one is introduced into cloth is a good metaphor for spiritual practice, suggesting a harmonious and steady labour resulting in a strong fabric. As for the practice of ethics and mettā, it is appropriate that these are the dye in Milarepa's account of the production of what he calls his 'dignified and altruistic trousers'. Mettā and the practice of ethics gently soak in to transform the deepest fibres of one's being.

Milarepa's Song of Fearless Honesty

Finally realizing that he isn't going to be able to secure a link with Milarepa by offering gifts on the spot, the young man wants to know where he can find him again, hoping to be able to invite him to his house. Milarepa tells him that at harvest time he goes to Din Ri, then after the threshing to Nya Non, and in winter he retires to a remote retreat. The youth tries to discourage Milarepa from taking his chosen route, saying of Din Ri that it is a place of the damned, where flour is like gold and the people are mean and impoverished by famine. As for Nya Non, it is a paradise for bandits and murderers, inhabited by packs of lepers, and littered

159

with cremation grounds and cemeteries. He is no more complimentary about the regions beyond. The border with Nepal is high and cold, with snow and blizzards, while Nepal itself cannot be recommended on account of heat and disease and 'dangerous rope bridges'. Further south one cannot make oneself understood, and the trees are stiff like corpses. He ends by begging that Milarepa will 'visit my country for a fortnight'.

The young man is obviously trying to appear solicitous for Milarepa's welfare, warning him against dangers and inviting him to his own part of the world, with the clear implication that he will see to it that Milarepa is well looked after while he is there. What Milarepa hears, however, is his complacent condescension. It is as though the young man is really saying, 'Here am I, a young man of noble family graciously inviting this poor yogi to my home; he ought to be pleased and grateful.'

Milarepa is quick to put him in his place. He is no doubt already familiar with this patronizing attitude, as are most Buddhist monks in the East today. It is usually the rich man of the village who tends to harbour the presumption that the monks are indebted to him as one of their more generous supporters. He assumes that they are under an obligation to him for helping to rebuild their vihara, or supplying them with robes, or providing them with a feast on regular occasions through the year. It is an understandable assumption, but the monks are usually quick to detect it, and equally quick gently to take their generous patron down a peg or two.

> *You arrogant young man with strong desires,...*
> *It is hard to meet an immaculate man of merit,...*
>
> *I am a yogi who thinks and says whate'er he likes,*
> *But I have never caused malicious gossip....*
>
> *I am an abandoned yogi, who eats for food*
> *The inner Samādhi of Non-discernment....*
> *Cheerful and comfortable am I in times of famine.*

Though the paths are perilous and dreadful,
My prayer to the Gracious One will never fail me....
My inseparable companion is the Bodhi-Mind;...

Since I have no possessions, I have no enemy.
Cheerful and at ease I meet the bandits.

Milarepa rebuts the young man's very terms of reference. He flies in the face of all common-sense perceptions of self, home, security, happiness, and even good and evil. It must come as quite a shock to the well-meaning boy. Milarepa exposes the direct link between craving and hatred, attachment and fear, thereby turning his would-be patron's assumptions inside out.

As soon as we find safety in a place, a group, or even a self, we fear all the more any threat from what we perceive as not self but 'other'.

The young man's fears for Milarepa's welfare are in fact a measure of his own desires. What he offers as protection and security is no such thing. It is not for Milarepa to go for protection to wealthy patrons. It is for them to go for refuge to what he embodies. The youth begs Milarepa to avoid hardships, and Milarepa responds by pointing out to him that the hardships are for the young man himself to face. With his strong desires it is going to be hard for him to locate men of virtue, because men of virtue are not going to choose the easy life towards which those strong desires incline him. The yogi chooses hardship because it enables him to see how much of his experience is not 'out there' but his response to his perception of what is happening. A comfortable life does not provide this possibility of freedom for the mind.

So far as the young man is concerned, his warnings about the dangers of Din Ri and the inhabitants of Nya Non represent good, well-meant common-sense advice. But Milarepa sees them merely as calumny. Fear and condemnation of alien places and peoples goes with a blind attachment to our own community. To take people as we find them would be a threat to our sense of identity. As soon as we find safety in a place, a group, or even a self, we fear all the more any threat from what we perceive as not self but 'other'. As long as we cling to a self, we will always have to deal with fear. What the youth offers as protection and security is therefore no such thing. The young man's fears for Milarepa are his own fears. Milarepa is able to take people as he finds them because he has renounced his group identity in favour of the freedom of absolute emptiness. That is all the protection he needs, and no stranger can ever be a threat to him.

This goes even for bandits. We get a sense of the relaxed nature of Milarepa's relations with bandits from an incident in his biography which concerns a nocturnal visit to his cave from a robber. As Milarepa hears the robber stealthily rooting around, he calls out, 'I don't think you'll be able to find anything there in the dark. I've never found anything even in daylight!' At this, the robber cannot help laughing, and goes on his way.[31] Milarepa has nothing to fear from the intruder, after all. He has nothing worth stealing, and he is as unconcerned about getting anything from him in the way of apology or revenge as he is about clinging to his few possessions.

Accompanying almost any conversation we have is a rather different conversation going on in our heads.

The youth is false and misleading in his speech, not because he means to be, but because his very experience of himself and of the world is false. If he is to practise truthful speech, he may need to be more circumspect and keep his prejudices to himself, even if this means being less candid. Milarepa, on the other hand, can speak his mind without fear that his speech will betray negative emotion. It is not that he is shameless, but that he has no more need for shame. His thoughts are not subject to craving and hatred, so he does not need to guard them. It is one thing to be guarded in your speech; to be guarded in your thoughts requires another level of mindfulness. Milarepa no longer has to be careful even about what he is thinking, so he can be completely open.

I was once teaching a class at our very first Buddhist centre, called Sakura – this must have been in the late sixties – when one of our regular friends arrived looking quite shaken. He said that on the way there, as he was walking along the street, he had cast a casual glance into a passing baby-carriage. As he did so, the baby turned towards him and fixed him with a look that was utterly unnerving in its directness and honesty. The impact of simple, straightforward truthfulness – delivered without premeditation or artifice – was in an obscure way quite terrifying, he said; and he realized that adults rarely looked at one another in that way, that they have lost that direct gaze.

In childhood, honesty comes first, and prevarication is learned as part of the process of socialization, as a way of adjusting to the needs and expectations of others. As a very small child, you don't have to be told that truthfulness is a virtue; you have a natural, effortless directness. But after a while you become aware that other people have perceptions different from yours, and that you can therefore hide what you know from them. The question for the rest of your life is how much use you make of this discovery.

It is a rare individual who can stay honest, straightforward, and open in adult life; most of us live with a kind of background dishonesty. Our words are almost constantly at some degree of variance with our thoughts; accompanying almost any conversation we have is a rather different conversation going on in our heads, in which our unvoiced feelings, reactions, and desires seethe and multiply. Clearly we do this partly to avoid maligning or insulting those around us, but the price we pay is living with this almost constant – and therefore virtually unconscious – gap between our words and our thoughts.

Milarepa singles out the quality of open-hearted candour in the people of Nya Non, so colourfully maligned by the young man. They may be rough, but they are entirely without artifice.

Though Nya Non may be of bad repute,
The people there are candid and ingenuous.

As in the days of old, they are straightforward and outspoken.
Easy-going and carefree,
They eat and drink without pretension;
They keep things as they are,
And groves and forests flourish.

In the eyes of a sophisticated young nobleman they may be uncultured, uneducated, even savage and backward. But Milarepa is able to see the same qualities much more positively, because he has nothing to fear from them. He has nothing worth stealing, and he is unconcerned about getting anything from anybody. So what he sees are people without airs and graces, who enjoy a good time and don't go chasing after novelty.

The boy's dire warnings about bandit country and its unsavoury inhabitants and awful dangers remind me of the reactions of some people when they heard that we were proposing to establish a Buddhist centre in Bethnal Green, in the East End of London. 'You won't survive in such a tough neighbourhood,' they said. 'Bethnal Green is gangland territory; the local roughs won't take kindly to a bunch of effete Buddhists arriving in their midst.' But in the event, those who came to build the Buddhist centre there found that the local people, while perhaps being rather rough and ready, were also old-fashioned, straightforward, and unpretentious.

As for me, I take no interest in worldly wealth,
Nor am I attached to food and drink.
Contented, I care not for loitering and amusement.
When, therefore, I meditate, my Samādhi deepens.

This is why I go to Nya Non.
Having mastered the art of Dumo's Fire,
I have no fear of cold or heat;
Cheerful and in comfort I meet the falling snow.

Today I see no reason to delay my journey,
But I shall not go to your country;
Proud and haughty patrons are distasteful to me.
How can I ingratiate myself with those I do not know?

Milarepa makes the important point that you cannot become friends with people who are proud and haughty, because in putting on such airs they are refusing to let themselves be known as they really are, and can have no hope of being receptive to others. Whether or not they are aware of it, their pride is a mask. An implicit connection is made here between lack of pride and openness to the Dharma.

Milarepa's way of life provides a clear prescription for deepening meditation. He has found from his own experience that if you put aside your desires – for worldly attainments, for sensual pleasures, and for distractions – your samādhi deepens. It is as simple as that. Furthermore, he is not troubled by heat or cold. It is with a little kindly irony that at the end of the song he addresses the boy as 'my dear, contented youth'.

My dear, contented youth, it is time for you to go.
May your health be good and your life long.

Milarepa's intention is to make it clear to the young man that he has to make up his mind. Which is he going to choose, worldly attachments or the guru? He can't hold on to both.

The Youth's Song of Joyful Despair

At this, the young man finally gives up all his cajoling and bragging and tendering of gifts. He has done all he can, and he has still failed to convince Milarepa of his faith. And he has begun to see how his own mind has been working. He has been priding himself upon being the serious object of attention of a great, wonder-working yogi. In his desperation, he draws out his knife and turns the point towards his heart.

> *Proud and happy I was, conceit arose within me;*
> *I thought that I was a well-gifted person,*

This sort of inflation often happens to spiritual practitioners, especially beginners, when they become too elated by their early successes. As a result of some genuine experience within meditation, or perhaps an access of faith such as the boy has had, you start to fantasize about your spiritual prospects. You think, 'Well, it looks as though I have some real aptitude for this that others don't have. My prospects for becoming enlightened are looking good.'

When things are going well and you are pleased with your progress, it is easy to become not just pleased, but pleased with yourself. You lose your mindfulness and get carried away, falling under the sway of what the Greeks called hubris, the sort of overweening pride that makes you forget your limitations and with them the decencies and duties of life. For the ancient Greeks, this was a deadly sin, to think that you are untouchable, to fancy that you have the virtues of the gods and forget that you are a mortal human being.

The young man is of course right in thinking that he is special. Indeed, though he doesn't yet know it, he is one of the eight destined heart-disciples of Milarepa. The trouble is that until now he has thought that being such a disciple is a privileged or prestigious position. He is right to realize that he is not subject to habitual negative mental states and that his motivation is pure. His mistake has been to see this as proof of his spiritual grade or rank.

The young man's next observation seems quite extraordinary, in view of the fact that he is so overcome with dejection that he is preparing to commit suicide.

> *Since the day that I was born,*
> *I have never been so happy as today.*

To feel and express two contrary emotions at the same time, though it sounds contradictory, is an entirely coherent and authentic response, as most of us know from our own experience. It is possible to feel utterly broken, to feel that one's grasp on reality has gone completely, and at the same time to feel supremely happy, even rapturous. Though Milarepa has apparently rejected him as a disciple and is not going to give him any teaching, the young man is ecstatically happy to have met someone in whom he can have faith. It is not even as though he feels he has derived any kind of clarity or understanding from the encounter. He has given all he can of himself and has been rejected anyway. His humiliation is absolute. But he has faith – faith in the intuitive awareness that Milarepa speaks from a position far deeper than anything he has ever experienced himself. This at once undermines and unsettles his sense of identity while also offering a glimpse of a far more profoundly satisfying truth. This is the source of his happiness. His meeting with Milarepa has introduced something radically new into his consciousness – the first glimmering of awareness of the essentially unconditioned nature of reality. The natural consequence of that faith is joy.

> I feel that I am most ignorant and pitiful....
> With a feeling of frustration, I have lost my way.
> I am beginning to believe I have no capacity for Dharma!

In fact, in losing his false confidence in his capacity for understanding and practising the Dharma, he has developed a real capacity for doing so. Understanding just how ignorant he really is, and seeing that he is no match for the situation, his decision to commit suicide is made in a very positive spirit. His situation is, he feels, as good as it is ever going to get. He has had his chance; he has met an enlightened teacher, although he was evidently not up to the challenge of being his disciple.

> 'Tis better for me now to die,
> To die before such an accomplished saint,
> When my heart is full of Dharma.

Up till now, he has tried to tell Milarepa what Milarepa himself needs and what he should do. But now, at last, he leaves it up to Milarepa to make up his own mind. He realizes that all his firmly held ideas count for nothing with someone who is in touch with reality. He surrenders.

> *After hearing such a sorry tale from this poor lad,*
> *With your omniscient mind, you know what should be said.*

A Meeting Across Lifetimes

Milarepa is now convinced by the prophecy of the goddess in his dream. Concluding that there must have been a mutual vow between himself and the young man in a previous life, he completely changes his attitude towards him. Previously he has been dismissive; now he offers praise. Thus far he has been ruthlessly deflating the young man's pretensions (or so it appears – there is really nothing ruthless about Milarepa). Now his harshness has reduced the young man's egotism. The time has come for encouragement, kindness, and appreciation of his good qualities.

This change of approach, and its timing, is obviously important. If gurus are always encouraging and sympathetic, their students start imagining that the spiritual life is easy. On the other hand, if the guru is relentlessly critical, the same students can become so discouraged that they give up. It is generally best to err on the side of encouragement (if only to reduce the risk of students becoming suicidal), though as a guru one should consider one's own temperament and attempt to compensate for its natural propensities.

The balance of qualities making up the ideal type of personality for a teacher is exemplified in Milarepa's own guru, Marpa, who is a classic example of what Carl Jung termed an extraverted thinking type. He was a scholar, but he did more than just translate texts from Sanskrit into Tibetan. He earned his appellation 'the Translator' by his great feat of bringing Buddhist texts and teachings from India to Tibet in the course of three long and perilous journeys. He was as far from the model of the withdrawn and retiring scholar, what Jung terms the introverted thinking type, as one can imagine.

Marpa is an example of someone who is both very learned and a great teacher, but not all scholars can do both. Someone who is an introverted thinking type may become a teacher on account of the depth of his knowledge and understanding of a subject, but he may be totally unsuited to teaching. A person of this type tends to get bound up with his own thoughts, and is correspondingly remote from the objective world. Such people make bad teachers because they are too interested in their own ideas, getting absorbed in the material for its own sake and developing that interest at the expense of the needs of the people they are supposed to be teaching. Jung mentions a famous chemist who admitted in his biography that he consistently failed to answer students' questions because they would spark off trains of thought in his own mind that he could not force himself to ignore. Engrossed in his own thinking, he would forget about the question that initiated it and would wave the student away, saying, 'I'll let you know next week.' The students would be left in the dark, not knowing how to proceed with their work, and they would receive in due course a long and abstruse note that took their problem as a starting point but had no constructive bearing on it.

It may seem as though there is nothing you can do about who you are, but if the Dharma is about anything it is about our inherent capacity to change our inherent conditioning.

By contrast, if, like Marpa, you are of the extraverted thinking type, you will be sufficiently aware of the students' needs and why they are asking their questions to give them at least a provisional answer. Instead of losing yourself in your own reflections, you will allow your students to get on with *their* thinking. If you are yourself somewhat introverted and find yourself in the position of teaching, you need to be careful to apply yourself to the actual questions and the real needs of the person in front of you. You will then at least be *acting* like an extraverted thinking type, and this will have the effect of gradually altering your conditioning. One's personality is not set in stone. It may seem as though there is nothing you can do about who you are, but if the Dharma is about anything it is about our inherent capacity to change our inherent conditioning.

> *It seems our hopes in bygone lives arranged the meeting;*
> *It was our destiny to meet before the Silver Spring.*
> *You must be one whose Karma is unstained,*

As the fruit of good karma, i.e. ethically skilful action, the young man's spiritual aspiration is an aspect of his *karma vipāka* which, being positive, is known as *puṇya* or merit. Negative karma, on the other hand, is unskilful action which bears fruit as negative vipāka. When we speak of our karma catching up with us, we mean that our immoral or unskilful behaviour has borne fruit, *vipāka*. Sometimes one can be aware of these karmic effects from previous unskilful actions as they arise in one's day-to-day experience. You may have made some kind of good and creative resolution, but some combination of factors – perhaps habitual tendencies or external circumstances that you have set up through your actions – prevents you doing as you intended.

There is nothing mysterious or mystical about the law of karma. The principle behind it is that all actions of body, speech, and mind have an effect, not that everything that happens is the result of karma. It is only when all other avenues of explanation have been explored that we should begin to look to karma for the root cause of anything. This is what we have seen Milarepa do in this episode. While he took the dream vision of the green girl seriously and was on the lookout for what it might prophesy, he did not jump to conclusions. He tested the young man to the very limit, and only then did he consider that there must be a mutual vow between them.

The idea of a mutual vow refers to the kind of very positive karma associated with being able to give some kind of conscious direction to one's rebirth. For example, it is certainly feasible to aspire to rekindle a special connection with another person in a future life. It is a general Indian understanding of the workings of karma that one can make a vow or resolution to sustain a link made in one life through to a succeeding life. As a disciple, you could vow to be reunited in future lives with your teacher or with a spiritual companion, a fellow disciple, even a number of spiritual friends. The idea of a band of individuals being spiritually connected down through the ages, lifetime after lifetime, is both resonant and romantic.

Of course, the link that people want to continue in this way is often romantic in a more prosaic sense, and one might be tempted to use as an example the Pali legends which suggest a connection over lifetimes between the Buddha-to-be and his wife, Yaśodharā. This spiritualizing of what is essentially a social and romantic contract is perhaps best seen as part of the process of idealizing everything about the Buddha's life, even before he became enlightened, and all his previous lives as well. The essential point, as far as Buddhism is concerned, is that the connection should be spiritual, not a mundane link based on sense desire.

It is also traditional to vow to be reborn into a future life that doesn't have the limitations of one's present existence. Of course, this is rather a different way of thinking about life than the one favoured by our own society, in which emphasis is placed on the capacities of all of us, whatever our circumstances. In many ways it is a very good thing to seek equal opportunities for all, but we all owe it to ourselves to be honest about the limitations we need to overcome if we are to make spiritual progress.

If you say, 'I refuse to accept that my particular situation is a limitation, and to see it that way is just to take a view of my circumstances that has been imposed upon me by ancient prejudices,' you might feel better, but that doesn't necessarily mean that no limitation exists. For example, you might hold that it doesn't matter whether you are rich or poor, and in a way that is true, but it must be admitted that it is a disadvantage to be poor in a society that places value on material wealth, and that the struggle of dealing with that disadvantage can make practising the Dharma more difficult.

Sometimes we acknowledge our limitations but disclaim responsibility for them by saying that they have been foisted on us by external forces. If you are prone to a bad temper, you might throw up your hands and say, 'I admit it, but there's nothing I can about it. My grandfather had a bad temper, my father was also thoroughly unpleasant, and I am merely the victim of the trait he has passed down to me.' From a spiritual point of view, this attitude is not at all conducive to progress. All you are saying really is that you don't want to be bothered with the realities of the spiritual life. If your conditioning puts you at any kind of disadvantage, you need first to recognize the fact, secondly to put aside the question of who might be ultimately responsible, and thirdly to do something to go beyond that conditioning. You have to acknowledge that when you get angry, you yourself are flying into a rage, not some other person. You have to take responsibility for who you really are.

It is a disadvantage to live in a country in which you do not have the opportunity to become a Buddhist monk in the traditional sense and live the wandering life supported by the lay people. We have to recognize that. The West has advantages too, of course, but there is no point in saying that our opportunities to practise the Dharma are just as good as those of people in traditional Buddhist countries, with their temples, Buddhist universities, and a well-established sangha. In certain respects we are at a disadvantage and we owe it to ourselves to recognize that. Likewise, if a woman has certain disadvantages because of her gender – whether those disadvantages are inherent or imposed – let her recognize that. And if a man suffers disadvantages due to his being a man, then let him recognize those limitations and set about going beyond them.

The real issue about making vows or aspirations for future lives is trying to see honestly which circumstances of your life are truly advantageous from a spiritual point of view and which are not. Instead of pretending to yourself that your situation is just as good as any other, you may need to acknowledge that you have drifted into an unsatisfactory situation that you now take for granted, and that, if you really wanted to, you could move forward from it in this life, never mind a future one. On the other hand, you may need to accept that some limitations cannot be changed here and now, and accept that they are limitations. None of us has to identify fully with whatever circumstances we are born with or have had imposed upon us. According to the Dharma, whatever limitations we face can be transcended, but we are more likely to transcend them if we recognize them as limitations to start with.

This is precisely what the young man has done in his song of joyful desperation. Up to now he has not been able to acknowledge the bankruptcy of his views. Having done so, he can at last begin to make progress, and Milarepa can begin to teach him.

Milarepa's Song of Precepts

Milarepa now gives his new disciple a set of basic precepts upon which to found his practice. His first precepts challenge the young man's very sense of identity.

> Know that kinsmen are the devil-planned hindrances of
> Dharma;
> Think not of them as real, but quench your craving for them.

The term 'devil' as a translation of 'Māra' is in a way too strong, suggesting – at least to people brought up in the Christian tradition – an awesome and omnipresent power of evil. Theologically speaking, no such absolute and ubiquitous principle of evil, corresponding to the absolute and ubiquitous principle of good in the figure of God, is accepted within the Christian tradition. But from an emotional point of view, this is how the devil tends to be perceived. Buddhism, by contrast, emphasizes conditionality, cause and effect, rather than the simple conflict of good and evil.

Māra, the 'devil' of the Buddhist tradition, is just a hindrance, a silly, blundering, psychic nuisance or trickster who is easily seen through with even a modicum of extra awareness and mindfulness, and who disappears the instant he is detected.

It is in this sense that Milarepa describes kinsmen as 'devil-planned hindrances of Dharma'. Kinsmen are singled out to head the list of emotional ties that the boy has to break because in any relatively primitive and unorganized society, with no centralized government and no administration or police force, you have to rely on your kinsmen. You stick by them and they stick by you, and you may on occasion have to fight together against outsiders, whether invaders or bandits. So one's kinsmen are much more than the members of a modern nuclear family. They are a whole clan or tribe. The Mafia is perhaps the most notorious modern-day example of such a close-knit social grouping. To belong to such a group involves you in an often complex network of responsibilities and reciprocal duties, with a strong sense of loyalty and solidarity binding you together in a group and against others.

For a young man there is therefore no question of not fighting to protect the group when it is attacked or threatened. Likewise, a young woman might feel she was going against her own nature if she were not to look after the group's sick and elderly. It is expected of you, and you expect it of yourself. But if you are to grow towards Enlightenment, all your actions should be in pursuit of self-determination, not collective duty. You have to take full responsibility for your actions of body, speech, and mind. While this might mean continuing to fulfil your duties in the family and the wider community, you do this through personal choice, not group pressure, however subtle or self-imposed. When Milarepa enjoins the young man not to think of such a group as real, he is not denying the fact of kinship but warning him against identifying too exclusively with the duties incumbent upon him as a member of a group.

This young man is, moreover, a nobleman, and the higher you go up the social scale, the more important become the ties of blood and family. The strong group mentality arising out of this status-enhanced identification with the clan is a particular hindrance to the practice of the Dharma, and this is what Māra represents in this context. As long as your identity consists primarily in your membership of a particular group, and your principal loyalty is to that group, your practice of the Dharma is going to be limited.

For this reason it is common in many religious traditions to take on a new name when you commit yourself to the spiritual life. The idea is to put your old identity with its attachments behind you, and take on a more spiritually productive one. In the Buddha's day there was no change of name upon ordination, but in Sri Lanka, China, Japan, Tibet, and Thailand new monks all take up a Buddhist name – though in Thailand some monks retain their lay name after ordination and simply prefix it with the title 'Reverend'. In Tibet, lay names are also usually Dharma names, Tibet having been a Buddhist country for centuries. A child might be called Dorje, for example, this being the Tibetan translation of the Sanskrit *vajra*. However, although the vajra is an important Buddhist symbol, the name 'Dorje' is so common that people do not immediately think of the Dharma when they hear it. As we find out later on, the young man in our story is called Dharma Wonshu, but this name is unlikely to have had any particular spiritual significance for him, at least until now.

Similarly, one does not associate the name John with the Evangelist; but when England was being converted to Christianity, one's Christian or baptismal name did have a spiritual significance, while one's surname registered one's place in the world. Of course, some Christians today do feel the true significance of their names. And new members of the Order I founded, the Western Buddhist Order, are given new names, usually in Sanskrit or Pali, to recognize that their going for refuge to Buddha, Dharma, and Sangha is what ultimately defines them.

Money and dainties are the devil's envoys;...
Association with them is pernicious.
Renounce them and all other things that bind you.

Delight in pleasures is the devil's rope;
Think, then, of death to conquer your desires.

We don't like to have to remember that one day we will have to leave behind all that we enjoy, but this fact is the only aspect of what we possess and enjoy of which we can be absolutely sure. Many people follow the injunction of the poet to 'Gather ye rosebuds while ye may,' imagining that the only sensible option in the face of impermanence is to grasp frantically at life's pleasures. But the poem by Robert Herrick from which this famous line comes is about taking your opportunities while they are there, which is slightly different from being waylaid by the 'devil's envoys' and finding yourself in thrall to them. Pleasure in itself is a good thing, and Milarepa is the first to proclaim the joys of life. But if something is so pleasurable that you are unable to be mindful while you are enjoying it, it binds you and will certainly lead to suffering.

Young companions are the tempting devil's snare;
Knowing they are delusive, watch them carefully.

One's native land is the dungeon of the devil;

Attachment to one's kith and kin, and to those with whom one shares a broader identity, whether national or linguistic, can also be bound up with attachment to a geographical location. Hence 'one's native land is the dungeon of the devil'. To make sense of this pronouncement, we could think of the dungeon as a locality with which we are comfortably familiar rather than a whole country or nation, which may be too large and varied for us to be very much attached to it.

Milarepa extends this admonition to any sense of group identity, even that arising out of the companionship of friends. He especially has in mind the friends the young man was on his way to meet. His point is not that friends who aren't interested in the spiritual life are 'evil'; it is more that one can unwittingly allow the assumptions of one's constant companions to seep into one's consciousness. Their ideas and attitudes rub off on you, and it becomes difficult to avoid conforming to their expectations. Without noticing what is happening, you can start, little by little, thinking as they think, behaving as they behave. And if their ideas and attitudes are conventional and materialistic, if they don't appreciate or understand the spiritual dimension of life, the perspectives and ideals that fuel your spiritual practice will tend to fade away when you are with them. It is in this sense that their companionship is delusive.

Milarepa is saying, in effect, that if you are not yet a Bodhisattva, worldly people will have a greater effect upon you than you will have on them.

This is plain, straightforward advice that can be taken quite literally to refer to one's immediate friends and companions, but it also has a more general application. Milarepa is saying, in effect, that if you are not yet a Bodhisattva, worldly people will have a greater effect on you than you will have on them. This seems to be a golden rule for people trying to live a spiritual life. If you can, avoid living apart from other Dharma practitioners for too long, or at least avoid settling in too comfortably with people who do not share your ideals, however amiable they may be in other respects. Your dealings should be friendly and concerned, but they should have a clear cut-off point. When you are observing a particularly strict or intense form of practice, you have to be especially careful about whom you associate with. If you want to get on with your practice, you have to protect it and the conditions on which it is based. This might seem antisocial, but in the spiritual life one has above all to be practical. In any case, when one considers what passes for a social life in the case of a great many people, this policy is less antisocial than it might seem. The reality of modern social life – all those dinner parties and evenings in the pub – is that it is doesn't really involve very much in the way of friendly and enjoyable communication.

A common misapprehension among religious practitioners of all kinds is to imagine that in order to communicate with people you have to be able to speak their language, catch their cultural references, be in touch with the latest trends and jargon, and go along with whatever activities and diversions are currently popular. This is certainly not my experience. When I came back from India to England in 1964, I was completely out of touch with everything that had happened between the war years and the early sixties. Televisions and supermarkets, mods and rockers, night clubs and pop music, were all quite new to me, while other things, like steam trains, were rapidly disappearing.

> After all, if you are not sure you quite believe in
> what you are talking about, why should
> anyone else take it seriously?

In any human exchange, references to the transient features of the cultural landscape are useful only for establishing the most superficial initial contact, and if you wish to communicate yourself more deeply to others, you will need to be able to fall back on something more solid. It is your sincerity and commitment that should come across, and you will only be undermining this by trying to be relevant or up-to-date. People who are themselves blown by the winds of fashion can still respect the integrity of someone who does not appear to be subject to such vagaries. There was a time, for example, when magistrates used to affect ignorance of pop stars and other manias of the day whenever these were mentioned in court proceedings. They would interrupt the questioning of witnesses to say crustily, according to one urban legend, 'And what, pray, are the Beatles?' to which the barrister would reply, 'The Beatles, m'Lud, is the name of a popular singing group.' At that time the public was genuinely impressed by this evidence, as it seemed, of a sort of judicial remoteness. The magistrate's appearance of being above the ups and downs of fashion seemed to be a reassuring sign that even-handed Justice would be done. (Things are rather different now, of course.) But, as spiritual practitioners, we needn't hide our ignorance of the latest fashions, or slavishly try to keep up with them for the sake of being able to talk to other people. Communication shouldn't depend on the cultural flotsam that happens to be passing at the time. It should be based on the human qualities that are common to all of us, whatever our generation. People respond to clear-cut principles, lived out and expressed with conviction, and to a person who knows clearly what they stand for. After all, if you are not sure you quite believe in what you are talking about, why should anyone else take it seriously?

Milarepa has not finished with Māra, and concludes with an exhortation not to waste time.

Put all aside and strive for Dharma.
Only by instant action can you succeed!

By 'instant action' Milarepa means that whatever you need to do, you must make it your spiritual practice. If you think to yourself that you will 'do some practice' when you have finished doing whatever you are doing now, then – even if you do get round to 'doing some practice' – it will not be true practice. Whether you are meditating, reflecting, studying, talking to someone, or working, or just being mindful while you are doing chores, even when you are simply doing nothing and enjoying the view, you should put all thoughts of anything else aside and do what you are doing wholeheartedly.

In time your body of illusion will decay.

Here we find a poetic conflation of two strands of reflection on impermanence: illusion and decay. It is when we see objects change that we conclude that the 'objects' observed are ultimately illusory. One's 'body of illusion' is of course illusory only in the sense that it is not a fixed, unchanging entity. It is illusory *because* it is in process of decay. We can say that the body we perceive to be in the process of change is illusory because there is nothing in it that is not part of that process. Change is all there is. There is nothing that changes.

> *The darting bird of mind will fly up anyway;*
> *'Tis better now to wing your way to Heaven!*

The 'darting bird' refers to the Tibetan belief that at death your consciousness passes out through the top of your head. Get on with it now, is Milarepa's advice; let it rise up in meditation. Here we are reminded that meditation is a preparation for death, and that death is a state of enforced meditation. Milarepa is always concerned as a teacher to instil a sense of urgency in his disciples, bringing the consciousness of death into the present moment and thus bringing the present moment to life, clarifying everything.

This is very helpful for the doctrine follower, but a faith follower may prefer to contemplate impermanence from another angle. Once you see something as illusory in the way I have described, there is no need to reflect that it will decay. Instead, you can begin to experience the freedom that comes when worldly attachments begin to fall away. Instead of considering the uncertain time of your death, you can remind yourself that if you commit yourself wholeheartedly to your practice, you do not know when Insight, and even Enlightenment itself, might arise.

At the very least, things would be much better here and now if you could only bring awareness of impermanence and conditionality into the present moment. By the same token, if you notice you are relaxing the effort to be mindful, just think of the wonderful opportunity you are letting slip. In worrying about how much money you have left in the bank or becoming irritated at being given the 'wrong' kind of breakfast cereal, are you missing the possibility of Enlightenment here and now?

The song ends with Milarepa accepting the young man as his disciple and for the first time calling him 'my son'. Even though as a yogi he is accustomed to maintaining an even mind through all the ups and downs of life, he says he feels a particular joy at this juncture.

> *My son! This is the start of your journey on the Bodhi-Path.*
> *Even I, the Yogi, rejoice at your success.*
> *You too, young man, should be glad and joyful!*

Chapter 8

Laying Down Your Doubts

Beauty on the Spiritual Path

Bubbling over with happiness and inspiration at being accepted as a disciple, and vowing to return, the young man bows to his new teacher and circumambulates him many times before going on his way. Four months later he returns in the company of his nephew and offers Milarepa a piece of white jade, while his nephew offers half an ounce of gold. But Milarepa tells them to take their offerings to the translator Bhari, who is building a stupa at Drin, and to ask him to give them some preliminary initiations.

It might seem strange that Milarepa should send his heart-disciple to another teacher, but we have to remember the young man's character. He is a young nobleman who until very recently took great pride in his possessions, which were of the finest quality. Although thoroughly sincere in his devotion to Milarepa, he is still at a comparatively low level of consciousness, and his mind is still attuned to the world of sensuous desire. If we compare him with Milarepa, the solitary yogi who has no possessions, not even a robe to cover his naked body, we see that there is an enormous gulf between them.

Milarepa could have given the young men the pith instructions himself, initiating them into the highest yoga there and then. But that would have been all he had to offer. He has no ritual implements, no lamps and images, no shrine or offerings. His shrewd assessment is that this prosperous young man, with his appreciation of fine things and his healthy temperament, is going to find the highest teachings of the Tantra rather colourless, bleak, dry, and remote. So he sends him and his nephew to Bhari Lotsawa (which means Bhari the Translator). He was a well-known figure among the Tibetan Buddhists of those days, renowned as a great teacher and yogi, but with a very different lifestyle from that of the ascetic Milarepa. As far as we can tell, he lives not in a cave but in a temple or monastery, surrounded by a large number of disciples, and with plenty going on around him.

I have myself witnessed the way in which some Tibetan lamas still function, with hundreds of disciples gathered together for round-the-clock ceremonies – the wail of conch shells piercing through the chanting, and butter lamps illuminating awe-inspiring images through billowing clouds of incense – and it is very impressive and elevating. Even if it does not represent the very deepest level of spiritual practice and experience, it is a profound and crucial intermediate stage.

> What we are trying to do in all our practice,
> whether of ethics, meditation, or ritual,
> is to refine consciousness.

Milarepa has weighed up the spiritual needs of his new disciple and decided that he will benefit from sharing a monastic situation with many other practitioners. Even though he may have been impelled towards the Dharma by a powerful degree of initial visionary insight, the young man still needs to establish a positive foundation by learning to enjoy his practice of the Dharma at a fairly ordinary level. He needs to be inspired by rich, colourful devotional ceremonies and initiations and fascinating teachings; he needs to handle delicately designed ritual implements and meditate on beautifully painted thangkas.

One of the qualities that makes Tantric ritual so effective is its strong aesthetic appeal. It appeals to the senses while replacing the kinds of things that naturally tend to arouse our interest with objects of more refined beauty, through which our emotional energies are directed towards objects of perception which transcend the senses altogether. Milarepa knows that for his young disciple, purifying and refining his sensuality in this way is a necessary intermediate stage.

What we are trying to do in all our practice, whether of ethics, meditation, or ritual, is to refine consciousness, to draw it away from grasping, attraction, and aversion, and make it subtle enough to begin to appreciate reality itself, which is neither pleasant nor unpleasant. The idea is to try to cultivate a sense of uplift, a feeling of joy in the contemplation of beauty appreciated for its own sake rather than as an object of possession.

In this, of course, the arts can play a part. By exposing ourselves to works of art, we allow them to lead our relatively unrefined, even gross, feelings and reactions in the direction of greater awareness and delicacy of feeling. Thus beauty becomes an intermediary between unreality and reality, an agent of transformation, whether in the form of the arts or through the aesthetic aspects of Tantric rituals and visualizations. This is why in the *Symposium* Plato refers to Eros as a daemon or intermediary, neither man nor god but a demigod, linking earth and heaven. You cannot pass from earth to heaven – from being human to being a god – directly. It is a process, represented by the daemon, of being attracted and inspired towards making progress. Particularly at the beginning of the spiritual life, there must be something for the lower emotions and the senses to latch on to, some enjoyment, some beauty – otherwise they will simply go back to their old objects. We tend to imagine that the objects of our senses are what give us pleasure, but in fact it is the engaging of our energies that is the real source of that pleasure. And the corollary of this is that if we are to engage our energies in the spiritual life, this must be a pleasurable exercise. We cannot transfer the engagement of our energies from one object to another by force of will; they have to be coaxed. This is the value of religious art – that it leads one's energies, one's feelings and emotions, quite naturally and gently upwards. And the lack of it perhaps accounts for the dry, joyless, or even lifeless impression given by the more extreme puritan sects that abjure all ornament.

Some people don't need the arts or colourful ritual to transform their emotional energies, but most of us do, unless we live in very beautiful natural surroundings, which may have the same effect. I certainly felt this when I lived in Kalimpong. The whole landscape was jewel-like in the brilliance of its colours. The sky was bright blue, the clouds were pure white, and the sunrise on the snow peaks displayed a shifting spectacle of colours – pinks, violets, greens, and golds – like a Pre-Raphaelite painting. There was something about the place and the landscape that inspired awe. Perhaps because the town had no history, one felt the presence of nature looming over it, and the mundane world didn't seem to hold sway there. In Tibet itself, due to the high altitude, the air is even clearer, and the colour of natural objects stands out vividly, even though sometimes one can see nothing but the dark brown vastness of the mountains and the intense blue of the sky, without even so much as a flower or a tree to soften the view. Such beauty, however austere, transforms the mind.

The beautiful is that which from moment to moment is always new.

If you can redirect the sense-oriented emotions onto objects of beauty or wild nature, it becomes much easier to engage them with even more subtle objects of perception, such as those experienced in meditation. If you can go from sense desire to appreciative, contemplative delight, you know you can go further and leave behind even that enjoyment for something more beautiful still. The trouble is that we take the beauty around us for granted. It doesn't provoke wonder, gratitude, or worship, because we don't live from day to day, so we don't discover things anew. It's the same old sun and moon, the same old people, the same old world. But if you look with a fresh, new mind, you will experience everything as if for the first time. According to an ancient Indian definition, the beautiful is that which from moment to moment is always new. That is to say, it removes the mind from the world in which things grow old. It is fresh at every successive moment – except that the moment is not connected with the previous moment or the succeeding one. It is timeless, because every moment is unique. There is no question of tiring of such beauty. And the same can happen in one's relations with people. If you see someone aright, if you see them objectively in the contemplative sense, and appreciate and delight in them for what they are, you will never find them boring.

Conversion

We are not told how long the young men spend with Bhari Lotsawa. It could be months, perhaps a year or two, or even longer. We are told that while they are with him they are given the initiation of Dem Chog, which is quite elaborate and would have taken weeks or even months to complete. Our young man then returns to Milarepa, remaining with him for five years. He is initiated into the six yogas of Nāropa and the mahāmudrā, and then Milarepa finally imparts to him his own 'pith instructions' and gives him the name Repa Shiwa Aui, which means 'cotton-clad light of peace'.

The contrast between the young man's former persona and his new dedication to a life of renunciation could hardly be more marked. We are told he was a great sensualist before, but that he now completely renounces the world. In fact, he exemplifies a classic spiritual phenomenon. It is often the kind of person who is most full-bloodedly involved with worldly life who most full-bloodedly enters the spiritual life. The great sinner becomes the great saint. St Augustine of Hippo is the Christian example that comes most immediately to mind, though he was rather different by temperament from the young man in our story. When he was young, Augustine was certainly a sensualist, but he was a tormented, dissatisfied, and guilt-ridden one; and when he became a saint he was still quite guilt-ridden and tormented. It seems that even when he was at his most worldly he had reservations about worldly life, and that he had reservations throughout his spiritual life as well; whichever direction he took, there was always an element of strain and unease.

By contrast, the young man in our story seems thoroughly to have enjoyed his life. He has enjoyed his horse, his saddle, his boots, and all the rest, and without any sense of guilt he has happily given them up in order to plunge headlong into the spiritual life. His is an untroubled progression from the healthy, happy human being towards a state of being that is more than healthy, more than happy, and even – in a sense – more than human.

The real motive force for Milarepa's spiritual life was his thoroughgoing wickedness as a young man.

If it is not altogether appropriate to compare St Augustine with such a minor figure as Repa Shiwa Aui, a comparison with Milarepa is instructive. The great Tibetan yogi is most commonly likened to St Francis, on account of his complete renunciation of all worldly things combined with his kindly and imaginative appreciation of the world around him. However, the real motive force for Milarepa's spiritual life was his thoroughgoing wickedness as a young man, and in this sense he rather resembles St Augustine. On their conversion, each made a complete moral turnaround – although Milarepa was a different sort of sinner and, consequently, a different sort of saint. St Augustine was 'guilty' of little more than sensuality, yet he never seems to have achieved peace of mind. Milarepa, on the other hand, having repented heartily of his murders and sorcery, and accepted a great deal of hardship in order to purge himself, was then apparently free of any residue of guilt. The difference between these two seems to expose the inherent problems of a spiritual life conducted within the context of Christianity, certain aspects of whose doctrine, considered from a Buddhist point of view, would seem to be inimical to a healthy spiritual life. The words 'sensuality' and 'sensualist' both carry an element of moral condemnation in English – a language soaked in the values of

Christianity – a condemnation that is entirely absent from Buddhism.

Vows

Finally, the young man takes certain vows: not to wear leather shoes or more than one piece of cotton clothing, never to return to his native land, and never to secure for himself more food than he can consume in two days. Taking vows or undertaking obligations of a spiritual nature – for example, that you will perform a practice three times a day – is customary at the time of Tantric initiation, and is naturally a part of spiritual conversion. Within the Buddhist tradition great importance is attached to the strict observance of these solemn pledges. Taking a vow you know you can honour builds your confidence in your spiritual capacity, and through that you grow.

By the same token, breaking a solemn vow is held to be extremely damaging karma. It is for this reason that it is best to take a vow that specifies a definite period of time. If you take a vow for life, you can't be sure that you will be able to keep it until the moment of your death, and the result may be an underlying sense of self-doubt rather than self-confidence. Moreover, if you break the vow, your confidence may be undermined, you might experience a lingering sense of guilt, and – at worst – you might not feel able to commit to anything again.

The great vows of the cosmic Bodhisattvas, found in Mahāyāna sūtras such as the *Avataṁsaka Sūtra*, the *Vimalakīrti Nirdeśa*, and the *Lotus Sūtra*, are rather different. They can hardly be taken for a limited period of time because they specifically involve not setting limits on one's altruistic aspiration. The motivation behind the Bodhisattva vows is to bring about the arising of the bodhicitta, which has nothing to do with time, indeed it defies description in terms of time or place. In an advanced Bodhisattva, the bodhicitta will already have arisen anyway, so the vow is more symbolic than literal.

At his own level, presumably short of the arising of the bodhicitta, the young man's vows likewise represent an achievement in terms of depth of understanding and strength of determination. Intense spiritual practice requires a powerful commitment to persist through the challenges it inevitably throws up, if one is to make any real progress. To take a vow, the disciple's commitment must be beyond question, and this requires a high degree of self-knowledge and integration. It is this stability that Repa Shiwa Aui's time with Bhari Lotsawa gave him.

Dropping All Talk of Enlightenment

After all his wonderful Tantric initiations, Repa Shiwa Aui is now brought down to earth with some straightforward, almost Theravādin-style, practical instruction. It's certainly a far cry from the colourful Tantric ritual of Bhari Lotsawa. It is as though, for all their profound meaning, for all that they adorn the essential structure of the Dharma so beautifully, those rituals are the externals, the glittering surface of the Dharma. Most ordinary Tibetans are clearly uplifted and inspired by these elaborate and profound ceremonies without feeling that they are incompatible with a life that lacks much in the way of spiritual commitment. But Milarepa is getting to the bare bones of the teaching now, the solid framework which is the basis of all the inspiring ceremonies.

As we have seen, the master-disciple relationship is intensely personal, a fully developed human being speaking to the mature spiritual aspiration of one who is less developed, so the teaching that arises from it is directly relevant to the particular circumstances and individual needs of the disciple. From his own practice and realization, Milarepa has extracted a personalized application of the Dharma which he gives to Shiwa Aui in the form of a number of precepts.

The song of instruction that follows is straightforward, simple, and direct in its presentation and structure. There is nothing complicated or intellectually abstruse about it. Its significance lies in its transformative power, now that the young man is in a position to take in the instructions fully and thus to be able to put them fully into effect.

Dear son, if you want to consummate your meditation,
Restrain yourself from bigotry and empty talk;
I think not of the noble glories of the past;[32]

Milarepa's first admonition concerns speech. This is where we waste so much of our energy and time, where we lose our mindfulness, and also where we express and thus reinforce our fixed views, our blind spots, our narrow, one-sided, and limited opinions. Through speech we preen ourselves, bask in our achievements or in the reflected glory of our social status, and play up to others' perceptions of us. One imagines that Milarepa has identified this self-important young man as particularly liable to be drawn into a discussion of the noble glories of the past.

More importantly, this first point is about taking the Dharma seriously, not just talking about it emptily. This is a less obvious point than it might seem. I know from my own experience that it is possible to give a wonderfully well-received talk about the importance of giving and generosity, and simple acts of kindness and self-sacrifice, and to see that the audience is thoroughly inspired by this compassionate vision. One may follow the talk with a rousing puja which everyone joins in, evoking and espousing one spiritual aspiration after another. But then try asking for volunteers to help wash up the cups and stack the chairs, and you can find that the enthusiasm stops flowing as if someone had turned off a tap. On the occasion I have in mind, of perhaps fifty-odd people who had evidently liked the idea of the Bodhisattva ideal well enough to sit through a whole evening devoted to it, not a soul stirred in response to a request for ten minutes' help with the washing-up. In short, even when we appreciate the Dharma enough to talk about it, even when we feel truly inspired, we are not necessarily receptive to it.

The Danish existentialist philosopher Kierkegaard famously wrote that the whole of organized Christianity is based on one great assumption: that God is a fool.[33] He gave as an example his observation that every Sunday people go to church and listen dutifully to the preacher telling them to love their neighbour and so on while they know that he doesn't expect them to take him seriously, and he knows that they know this. They all assume that they can fool God in this way, that God will accept this foolishness as something real, as real Christians practising real Christianity. It is a big farce, and one can only feel sorry for clergymen who have to stand up in the pulpit week after week and speak earnestly about matters to which they give only limited credence themselves, and which anyway leave no discernible impression on their dwindling congregations. It must be literally soul-destroying.

Of course, no religion is free of this kind of self-delusion. The danger is that it becomes accepted, even institutionalized. When Buddhist teachers concern themselves exclusively with the social and institutional functions of 'respectable' religion – births, deaths, and marriages – it spells the end for the transmission of a radical spiritual perspective worthy of the name. The danger for any spiritual movement is that its institutions, its practices, even its language and terms of reference, become ends in themselves rather than means towards the transcendence of all mundane preoccupations.

Stay in the valley to which no men come;
Keep from bad companions, and yourself examine;

'An unexamined life is not worth living,' said Socrates, and Milarepa would no doubt have agreed. His disciple is warned to keep out of the way of society in general and unsuitable companions in particular, and to examine himself. Clearly, the two injunctions are connected: the unexamined life is usually the indiscriminately sociable life. Going to the local bar, for example, remains a popular way of avoiding experiencing one's mental states. But at this level of practice, the influence of 'bad companions' can come from the unlikeliest of quarters. The very spiritual community that exists to serve and support spiritual practice can simply support complacency, or perhaps a lack of care. In the end, you have to be able to be alone.

Yearn not to become a Guru;
Be humble and practise diligently;
Never hope quickly to attain Enlightenment,
But meditate until you die.

It might seem strange for a Buddhist to be told not to hope to attain Enlightenment quickly – even more so for a Tantric practitioner; the Tantra is, after all, meant to offer a quick route to Enlightenment. This advice is intended to help its recipient with a particular problem: that we can end up concerning ourselves so much with the end product – or what seems to be the end product – that we lose our appetite for the process of getting there. We make the mistake of separating the end from the means, when the goal is in fact implicit in the path.

For instance, if you are trying to write a book or paint a picture, it is fatal to the creative process just to want to get the thing finished and done with. Even if you feel under pressure to finish it, you still have to create some space in which to be devoted to and immersed in the process for its own sake. It is the same for the practising Buddhist. To practise properly, you have to be so immersed in your meditation, so devoted to your practice, that you are not really bothered about gaining Enlightenment. Even though you know that meditation leads to Enlightenment, you find the process itself so satisfying that you don't mind being in it indefinitely. You just want to meditate. It is something you are going to do until you die. You are in no hurry to get somewhere else. You don't hope to attain Enlightenment quickly, because it's such fun getting there.

This explains the emphasis in the spiritual life on mindfulness, on recollecting and fully appreciating what you are doing at the present moment. Of course you have a goal, but your awareness of it should occupy you only to the extent that it gives purpose or direction to what you are doing here and now. It's the same with any task; at some point you will have to complete it, but you won't do that satisfactorily unless you forget about completing it and concentrate on what you are doing. It's a matter of identifying yourself with the process rather than the achievement. Don't be too eager for recognition and acknowledgement of your commitment and experience. Be happy getting on with your practice. When your inherent momentum simply carries you forward, that is the time to shoulder new responsibilities or take on new commitments. Don't think too much about becoming a Buddha; just get on with trying to be a Bodhisattva.

And with regard to whatever you do achieve, Milarepa reminds his aristocratic new disciple, be humble. If you make a lot of noise about your skilful action, its skilfulness is of course vitiated. The ego will never be satisfied with performing a skilful action for the sake of it. It wants to claim a kind of commission, recognition, a pat on the back. Looking for praise reveals a lack of confidence in what you have done, and this comes down to a lack of confidence in yourself. If you cannot feel you have done something right until someone else recognizes what you have done, your actions will never feel adequate. The consequences of such lack of confidence can be serious. You will perhaps find yourself doing something not because you think it is the right thing to do, but in order to get approval. And skilful actions performed for approval pave the way for unskilful actions.

> *Forgetting words and studies,*
> *Practise the Key-Instructions.*
> *If you would benefit yourself,*
> *Renounce talk and words;*
> *Concentrate on your devotions.*

The emphasis here is on personal devotion, the 'Key-Instructions' being personal precepts for practice rather than universally relevant teachings for general discussion. These admonitions are of significance for Buddhists in the West because we have so many books to read – on Zen, on Mahāyāna, even on the mahāmudrā – and so little time, it seems, for actual practice. If any Westerner practises even a hundredth part of what they read, they are probably doing pretty well. This is of course a situation that runs entirely counter to tradition.

Suppose we put aside all we had learned from books and gave an account of the Dharma based entirely on our own experience. What could we say that wasn't hearsay? At some point we may consciously have practised a precept or two – but all of them? We could talk a little about our efforts in meditation, about our experience of puja, of being on retreat, about friendship, even, if we had actually experienced spiritual fellowship as opposed to just hanging out with our Buddhist friends. Most of us would be hard put to give detailed descriptions of Buddhas and Bodhisattvas, because we wouldn't ever have seen any of them. As for śūnyatā, virtually all of us would draw a blank there, and the same would go for perfect wisdom. But even the most elementary and fundamental truths of Buddhism – like 'Hatred does not cease by hatred; hatred ceases only by love'[34] – are, for a good many of us, untested maxims. How many of us have found out through our own experience that this is the way hatred ceases? How much Dharma do we really know for ourselves?

Reverence can only be offered to what you do not understand.

It seems that it is human nature that once someone has learned one thing, however superficially, they want to move on to something different, something more advanced, even something more esoteric. They see a book that promises to impart secret teachings that have never before been divulged to anyone but a small band of trusted disciples, and they think, 'This is just the thing for me.' Anyone, they think, can understand the basic stuff; *they* want something that will take them further, deeper, beyond the ken of ordinary folk. The Tibetans as I knew them in Kalimpong were just the same as Western people in this respect. If word went round that a great lama had arrived in town with some very special teachings, some secret and advanced initiations, they would flock to hear him. A discourse on the five precepts, on the other hand, would never draw a crowd because they'd heard it all before. Of course, it was true enough that they knew the precepts backwards, but as for practising them, that was quite another matter.

There is nothing wrong with a wide-eyed fascination with the world of human knowledge, nothing wrong with the healthy curiosity of the child who just wants to find out things for their own sake and is forever asking questions. Clearly we don't want to lose that kind of fresh inquiring mind. But here Milarepa is deprecating the appropriation of knowledge as a means of re-inforcing the ego. This kind of acquisition is no different from acquiring material possessions, except that it may offer even greater social and cultural respectability.

Such an acquisitive attitude to the teachings is bound up with a purely intellectual approach to them, together with an idea that one is equal to what one understands intellectually, that if one understands the words one has mastered the meaning. But as the great English poet Samuel Taylor Coleridge said, you cannot reverence what you understand, and this is certainly true when it comes to the Dharma. If you think you've mastered the Dharma, how can you reverence it? Reverence can only be offered to what you do not understand, to what you are able to acknowledge you haven't mastered. The Dharma is by definition something very far beyond where you are, and if you have no reverence for it, you cannot possibly get any closer to it in terms of your actual experience. This is the great danger of theoretical understanding: that the basic egotism behind it will cut you off from real experience of the Dharma.

You don't need a lot of initiations or shelves groaning with Dharma books and Sanskrit dictionaries to make your practice effective. Just reflect on what it really means to go for refuge to the Buddha, the Dharma, and the Sangha, and do your best to live in accordance with that. Perform the puja and try to absorb and really feel what you are chanting and saying. Reflect on the five or ten precepts and use them as the touchstone to see how your practice could be improved. Cultivate spiritual friends.

Meditate regularly. Just one or two practices are enough: the mindfulness of breathing to develop clarity, and the mettā bhāvanā for positive emotion. Perhaps you could reflect on the Noble Eightfold Path, and specifically on how to put it into practice. You might have a string of mala beads and one or two pictures, plus a few books, including one or two anthologies of sayings of the Buddha, and a few favourite lectures on tape or disk. That is all you really need by way of intellectual equipment to take you as far as you want to go. If your practice does not keep pace with your theoretical understanding, if what you read is not being put into action, all that reading is probably hindering your practice. Milarepa goes on to explain that 'in the teaching of Marpa's Line' – the Kagyu or 'Whispered' Lineage – special emphasis is placed on actual practice as opposed to any kind of verbal proliferation.

Milarepa's Song of Dangers and Fallacies

Listen to those high-flown words, and pompous talk;
Look at those charlatans, madly engaged in fervent argument.

Milarepa goes on to make a blistering attack on the plausible charlatans of the spiritual community, and the self-delusion and conceit that creep into any tradition that is over-reliant on conceptual argument. He begins by castigating the scholastic monks of his time and their hobby of public disputation. This was very popular in India during the latter days of Indian Buddhism, and subsequently in Tibet. The tradition of public debate continues to this day in the Gelug school of Tibetan Buddhism, although it is rather frowned on by the Nyingmapas and rejected completely by the Kagyupas, as Milarepa rejects it here.

But the dangers of intellectual conceit are not confined to Tibet. In the West the academic world, even the Buddhist academic world, may present a cool, cultivated façade, but behind it – just as in any sphere of human life – seethe all the passions of the ego, especially envy, jealousy, and malice. The memoirs of academics

make sober reading in this respect. As far as the study of Buddhism is concerned, this civilized kind of conceit manifests especially with regard to the more esoteric or advanced aspects of
Buddhism – anything that is presented as being too difficult or
demanding for most people, and as requiring special training or
study. It is easy to imagine that you are a real authority on the
subject because you can talk knowledgeably about it, and to
assume because of all your subtle understanding that you are a
cut above ordinary Buddhists, who seem to you to practise without knowing what they are doing or what Buddhism is really
about. A practitioner who starts to study the scriptures and finds
they have some academic talent should be careful not to let this
talent turn their head. Once you enter that world, it is hard to
avoid being drawn into its petty vanities and disputes.

Milarepa is not objecting to the constructive exchange of ideas
and views. He does not object even to the adoption of definite
positions. What he warns against is the adoption of *fixed* positions to be tenaciously defended, and the use of arguments to
crush one's interlocutor, to thrust one's point of view on them in
an overbearing manner. Even if you are right – even if your position is based on a degree of personal experience and even insight
– there is no excuse for insisting that you are right, and belabour-
ing someone with your view in the face of their refusal to accept
it. If there is any truth in your position, it will come across in the
openness of your communication, not by fighting tooth and nail.
Whatever insight or realization you have will be conveyed in the
quality of your communication, not the force of your argument.

It is natural to want sometimes to shake someone out of their
complacent false position. You certainly don't want to spread a
superficial agreement over your differences, and it may be skilful
to want to open their eyes to a perspective to which they offer initial resistance. The question is how to do this. There is an Indian
story that suggests an answer. It is about a lad from the city who
is walking through flooded rice fields on one of the narrow
raised footpaths that criss-cross the cultivated land. He comes
across a calf blocking his way and tries to push it to one side, but

it won't budge. However hard he pushes, the calf pushes obstinately back. After a while, a girl comes out of a nearby shelter, looks him up and down, and says, 'You look like an educated man, but you don't seem to have much in the way of common sense.' And so saying, she puts her finger in the calf's mouth and leads it gently away, the calf happily sucking on her finger as it follows after her.

You can influence people more by listening to what they are trying to say, seeing why they want to be where they are and gently drawing them towards your vision of things, than by meeting their views head on and just browbeating them. As Buddhists, the basis of our communication with others should be just that – communication, not point-scoring or verbal kung fu. The most important thing is to be open to the other person. Once they see that it is the truth you are looking for, not victory, they may well begin to listen to what you have to say. Try to experience them as living, feeling, thinking human beings, not just a mouthpiece for a set of views with which you may or may not agree. If your approach is genuine, if you have a real desire to find the truth of the matter, you may even find that you are not quite as well informed as you thought you were.

> In talk they seem intent to frighten you;
> In sleep, they slumber, pompous men;
> They walk like haughty Mongols.
> Dangers and obstacles encompass them.

Milarepa paints a vivid picture of those who argue – whether on behalf of right view or not doesn't matter – without the basic desire really to communicate. Despite all the noise of their fervent wrangling they are asleep. They are unaware, spiritually completely unconscious, even as they are relishing their mastery of the Dharma. They think they are engaged in discussing the finer points of doctrine, but that isn't what is happening at all. Although they don't know it, they are just like rutting animals competing for dominance. If you want to have a contest of wills, that is quite healthy at its own level, but if you imagine that in doing so you are discussing the Dharma, you are in trouble.

If you listen carefully you can usually hear if there is an ego pushing behind someone's words. When you realize that this is what is happening, you have to be careful not to be drawn into the game they want to play, and be clear in your own mind that your aim is different from theirs. Your aim is not to win the argument but to communicate the truth as you see it. If you fail to establish communication, you have lost right from the start, however watertight your argument might be. If you come up against an ego-propelled argument, you are better off withdrawing from that particular topic and re-establishing friendly communication about something else.

It is not reasonable to expect people to be reasonable.

When you listen very carefully for the ego that is inflaming an argument, you will sometimes find that ego to be your own. You can be as urbane as you like, but if your ego is tied up with your argument, you will not really be open to the other person and you will therefore fail to communicate with them. It is not the form of words you use that counts so much as the spirit informing them. If you have a clear and orderly mind, you will want to put your point across in the form of a logical argument, and you may even feel the need to press your argument vigorously, but you can be vigorous without being crushing.

Another source of conflict to look out for is any expectation that other people should be rational. It is not reasonable to expect people to be reasonable, and you should never be surprised when they are not. If it upsets you to be met with an unreasonable reaction to a rational argument, you yourself are being unreasonable. It is inevitable that people will be unreasonable even when they are trying to be rational. Of course they will react emotionally – what else does one expect? Why be hurt and taken aback? People aren't rational, and in some ways it is good that they are not – good that they aren't *narrowly* rational, at least. In the long run we need to have access to other, non-rational aspects of ourselves, and to do that we may need to put up with each other's unreasonableness from time to time.

Disputes will therefore occur regularly, even in the spiritual community. Sometimes they may even seem like profound disagreements as to the nature of the commitment that you share. However, the problem is usually a misunderstanding, and this in turn often comes down to a difference in temperament, which is what needs to be addressed. For example, those with a more extrovert temperament tend to interpret their commitment in terms that involve the assumption of a need for structure and organization. Those with a more introverted disposition, by contrast, tend to the opposite view, feeling that their commitment is leading them in the direction of being unstructured, even unorganized. Some apparently profound disagreements can arise out of such contrary perspectives, but they would be much less damaging if those opposing perspectives could be recognized as coming from differing psychological propensities.

The Three Kingdoms and Six Realms are jeopardized
By desires forever leading sentient beings into danger.

The three kingdoms are the three planes of mundane existence: the *kāmaloka*, the world of sensuous desire, the *rūpaloka*, the world of pure or archetypal form, and the *arūpaloka*, the formless world. The six realms are those of the gods, jealous gods, hell beings, hungry ghosts, animals, and humans, as depicted on the Tibetan Wheel of Life. So Milarepa is saying that the whole of conditioned existence, even in its most pure and elevated aspects, is subject to the danger of desire.

If the desire is to overcome one's opponents in debate about the Dharma, the danger is all the greater. It is always dangerous to allow your mindfulness to evaporate in the fervour of wanting to be right and to prove the other person wrong. But if you are making the Dharma the occasion for your unmindfulness, you are making the route to liberation into yet another mundane trap and that will leave you really stuck. There is nothing more dangerous than pseudo-Dharma. If you cling to your idea of right view as if it were a fixed thing that you can fight for and win, you are making a fundamental mistake.

Dangerous Paths

Milarepa goes on to elaborate on the kinds of danger to which his new disciple is likely to be exposed.

> *There are seven dangers you should watch:*
> *Falling into the blissful Hīnayāna peace;...*

In the traditional Mahāyāna view, the blissful Hīnayāna peace was the 'incomplete' nirvāṇa of what it called the Hīnayāna, the 'lesser method', following which the disciple aimed to become an arhant – that is, to gain nirvāṇa for himself or herself alone. The Bodhisattva ideal of the Mahāyāna schools – the vow to save all beings from the sufferings of conditioned existence – was meant to stir a deeper spiritual ambition. In certain Mahāyāna sūtras, especially the *Lotus Sūtra*, the term 'arhant' refers to someone bent on nirvāṇa only for themselves, with the implication that they are unwilling to take the last great altruistic step of commitment to the Bodhisattva ideal – to become not just an arhant but a Buddha. However, the Buddha himself made no explicit distinction between the attainment of an arhant and that of a Buddha; the rather more narrow and restricted use of the term arhant developed only later in the Mahāyāna tradition.

The term 'Hīnayāna' is best understood not as part of the lexicon of sectarian polemic but as referring to the kind of limited ideal of personal salvation or emancipation that may be espoused by any practitioner of any school. As far as Milarepa is concerned, the Vajrayāna represents, by contrast with this limited model, the most practical, direct, experiential approach to the Dharma, especially through meditation. This is the way of practice, the way of experience, the way of actual self-transformation. In this context, the 'blissful Hīnayāna peace' can be understood as providing a counterpoint of limited spiritual ambition against which to emphasize the dynamic and other-regarding quality of the Mahāyāna goal.

The blissful Hīnayāna peace is that of a subtle, pseudo-spiritual ego; it is Enlightenment envisaged as being 'for me' and as closing the door on other people and their problems. It is pseudo-spiritual individualism in all its forms, whether or not it speaks the language of compassion. Milarepa is pointing out that transcendental experience gained on the basis of the merit accumulated through effective practice is not enough. When some sort of spiritual experience comes out of the blue, you might be tempted to think, 'Well, that's it, I'm there, I've reached the goal,' but Milarepa says, 'Not so. You still have to keep working at your practice, even then.' You may have had the vision, but you still have to work at transforming yourself in accordance with that vision. As long as even the subtlest ego persists, there can be no true state of Enlightenment.

This pseudo-spiritual individualism is the first of Milarepa's seven dangers. As far as we are concerned, it is our tendency to approach our practice from the point of view of our own interests. The next danger occurs on a much cruder level of consciousness.

Using your Buddhist knowledge to get food;...

Milarepa is concerned that Shiwa Aui and his cousin could end up like so many priests, debasing Buddhism from a purely spiritual teaching – a universal truth and a training for the individual – into an ethnic religion, a means of giving people what they want in return for a livelihood. They might have had a real experience of the Dharma, and their perception of things might have undergone a genuine shift, but they haven't yet attained any firm realization. The breakthrough into a new way of perceiving that they have experienced, real and valuable though it may be, is not enough to safeguard them against this danger once they go back to practise in the midst of the world. They will have to be mindful of the spiritual lie of the land. It is all too likely that they will find themselves inclined to feather their nests and ingratiate themselves with the villagers for the sake of their patronage.

This is a common error. You attain some genuine spiritual experience, but then your ego intervenes to appropriate the fruits of your practice and attainment for selfish ends. A degeneration of the ideal with which an individual may have embarked on their spiritual career happens in all religions. Indeed, it can happen in any career in which one is motivated by devotion to some ideal of truth or serving others. In the end you may stop giving yourself to that ideal, your only real concern having become to make money and to be respected as a professional middle-class person.

By Milarepa's time, the Dharma had been the religion of Tibet for some four hundred years, but it need not take that long for a quiet corruption to establish itself. The rot can set in almost immediately, as is evident from the records of events towards the end of the Buddha's own lifetime, which suggest that by no means all his followers even then were truly striving earnestly for the goal.

As the Dharma has spread into different cultures it has tended, unlike Christianity, to merge with pre-existing spiritual traditions rather than simply replace them, converting the whole culture rather than drawing converts out of it. This inevitably meant there was a danger that the spiritual ideals of the Dharma might be contaminated by the more mundane considerations of the ethnic rituals with which it merged. In Tibet, as in India, the Dharma sprang up amidst a rich variety of magical rites that were originally employed in pre-Buddhist cultures for mundane purposes, like destroying enemies, making money, arousing love, and so on. The Tantra took them over and turned them to spiritual use by giving them a symbolic meaning. You would perform the ritual not in order to gain something from it for yourself or your 'client', but in order to meditate on its symbolic significance. The rite of destruction, for example, was used in this contemplative way as a means to destroy one's egotism and defilements.

But the sublimation process can easily slip into reverse; the vivid ethnic use of these rites can seem a lot more compelling than the subtleties of their Dharmic symbolism.

Thus the initiate could easily be drawn into exploiting the rites and practices commercially, by performing them as magical rites in return for a fee. As a village priest in Tibet or India, you could set up in business in this way, offering to fulfil the worldly ambitions and desires of local people through magical rites. You ceased to be a living embodiment of the Buddha's teaching and became instead little more than a fortune-teller, or even a beggar. 'Using your Buddhist knowledge to get food' is to see the Dharma as a thing that can be exchanged for worldly advantage.

You should not turn the holy Dharma into a consecrated meal ticket.

It is often said that ordinary Indian people are deeply religious and spiritually minded. However, this is true only if you conflate religiosity, or a belief in the efficacy of magical means of securing material or egotistic objectives, with the truly spiritual life. In the case of the average Tibetan too, at least in old Tibet, any Tantric initiation was taken as a general blessing to help one gain prosperity and well-being. It is only a short step from accepting this perception of the rite to accepting money for it.

So how does the authentic spiritual community sustain itself? The economic principle of the sangha may be summarized in terms that set it apart from the principles of modern capitalist society. Each member gives according to his or her ability and takes according to his or her needs. In Buddhist cultures, the monk is given what he needs by the lay community in the way of food and clothing. For the lay people this is *dāna*, giving for its own sake, as a virtue in itself. As far as the monk is concerned, he is happy to give whatever he can, but not by way of exchange. He gives teaching, but he doesn't turn it on like a tap. Ideally he teaches simply by communicating himself as best he can. If there is teaching in that communication, that is fine, and if there isn't much on a particular occasion with a particular person, that is fine as well.

In the 1950s, when the Buddhist conversion movement in India was just beginning, I came across one or two cases of people who had been ordained as monks after a fashion and were going round administering the Refuges and converting people for a price. This is the kind of thing that Milarepa is warning against. One is turning something that is meant to diminish the ego into something that reinforces it, and this is particularly unskilful. It is one thing to take the mundane path rather than the spiritual path, but to turn the spiritual path into the mundane path leaves you with no way out of your corruption.

So Milarepa warns against using the Dharma as a means of support, that is, against being a professional Buddhist. The principle here is that you should not teach the Dharma in *exchange* for something else. You should not turn the holy Dharma into a consecrated meal ticket. It has to be given freely, to be communicated as something beyond price. Making your communication of the Dharma your livelihood inevitably tends to turn the teaching into a commodity.

Inflating yourself with pride of priesthood;…

By priesthood is meant technical monastic ordination within the Tibetan tradition, which Milarepa insists is not an achievement that in itself sets you above other Buddhists. Ordination is essentially about going to the Buddha, the Dharma, and the Sangha for your refuge; it is about taking the Buddha and his teaching and his enlightened disciples as your point of reference in everything you say, think, and do. Public ordination is a recognition of this commitment on the part of the Buddhist community, and an expression of their confidence in your ability to carry it out. In this sense, we might concede that those who have been ordained are quite special individuals, and even in certain respects on a higher level than others. But therein lies a danger. Ordination can become a matter of pride and personal satisfaction, of status.

When an ecclesiastical ceremony is taken as entitling you to deference and respect, then it has nothing to do with going for refuge, and everything to do with ego. The danger of such 'pride of priesthood' is real throughout the Buddhist world, especially in cultures where Buddhism is tied in to the wider social establishment and where spiritual status is denoted by ecclesiastical rank. The danger comes when the monks themselves take this socio-spiritual hierarchy literally; when they do so, they join the professional classes, rather in the manner of a nineteenth-century English vicar taking tea with the gentry and offering platitudes to the parish poor. It is always possible to adopt a particular lifestyle out of hypocrisy, hoping to acquire the reputation that goes with being a serious practitioner without the trouble of really committing yourself to practice. Of course it is also possible to live the kind of simple existence associated with the spiritual life while having no aspiration whatsoever.

There is no Buddhist priesthood in the strict sense of the word. However, in all Buddhist countries there are those who have received ordination as monks and there are also individuals who have committed themselves wholeheartedly to the practice of the Dharma without any formal rite of ordination. In the Kagyu tradition, of which Milarepa is part, the renunciation of worldly attachments and the wholehearted commitment to Dharma is strong, but nonetheless the Kagyupas do not bother about monastic ordination. The same is true among the Nyingmapas, although followers of both schools often lead very ascetic lives.

But regardless of one's chosen lifestyle, whether one is living as a monk, a hermit, or a householder, saṁsāra is always present, and always operational. It is always there because saṁsāra is nothing more or less than our own reactive mind. We bring it with us wherever we are. It never lets up; it never takes a holiday, even if we do. Our habitual grasping for worldly things is like a gravitational pull; if we are not vigilant, it will quite easily overcome the much more remote force impelling us towards Enlightenment.

Hugh Latimer, the sixteenth-century English martyr who in the end was burned at the stake by Queen Mary, once gave a famous sermon in which he made much the same point in a rather striking fashion. He warned idle bishops that the Devil was the busiest bishop in the land, always active in his diocese, never taking a holiday or even stopping to rest.[35] And Māra is no different in this respect. He is much readier to let us go off on retreat than he is to let go of our minds once we are there. It might seem that all we have to do to be at peace is get away from our distractions – but this is not so. In his enthusiasm, Shiwa Aui may go to live far up in the mountains, but Māra will have no trouble finding him there and prattling to him of the entertainments of the town: the singing, the dancing, the fairs and the festivals, the processions and the celebrations, the drinking parties, all the fun and frolic of eleventh-century Tibetan social life. And if he fails to get through to him with that kind of message, he will try to fill him with 'pride of priesthood'.

Falling into yogic-madness;...

Many different kinds of practice fall under the general heading of the Tantra, and some of these, especially those concerned with the arousal and channelling of subtle energies – for example, through *pranāyāma* or breath control – can be psychically destabilizing. Without the guidance of an experienced teacher, the psychophysical energies that such a practice is designed to stir up can run out of control. They can 'heat the brain,' as it is said, so that you become psychologically unbalanced.

This would seem to be the yogic madness Milarepa is referring to here, a state of psychic disturbance brought about by uncontrolled vital energies being released in yoga and meditation practice. Understood in this way, the ignorance that lies behind this danger is not so much a case of subtle ego-clinging as a lack of understanding of the practices. There is also the possibility that Milarepa is referring not to a real madness triggered by one's practice but merely to zaniness. Even in Milarepa's time, wild

and wacky behaviour, more self-indulgent than truly spontaneous, was sometimes adopted by people who wanted to impress
others with their 'crazy wisdom'. As with the 'charlatans, madly
engaged in fervent argument', a studied spiritual unconvention-
ality is usually a mask for a superficial understanding and practice of the Dharma.

Indulging in empty speeches;...

The danger here lies in airing one's knowledge, especially
knowledge that is not based on personal experience, in order to
impress. It is the tendency to pronounce your opinions and
views on the Dharma not for the sake of whoever might be listening but simply to hear your own voice authoritatively holding
forth. The danger is not just vanity, but misusing the Dharma. If
you are airing your own views rather than making it clear what
the Dharma has to say, your communication is just an empty
noise, however impressive your command of rhetoric. That is to
say, your ḍākinī will desert you. The ḍākinī, remember, is the
third Tantric refuge, representing spiritual inspiration as it
becomes available to you. When you are in touch with the
ḍākinīs, you will find forces of inspiration welling up within you
– but of course what can well up can also dry up. Let yourself
become arrogant or glib, and the forces of inspiration will slip
away. You will be so busy listening to the sound of your own
voice that you won't be able to hear the voice of the ḍākinī
within.

You need to know where your inspiration
comes from and make sure that you keep
the channels to that source open.

Anyone who has ever given a talk on the Dharma will have
experienced this from time to time. After a while you become
aware that the spirit in which you prepared your material or in
which you began to teach has left you, and that what you are

saying is coming out in a rather dead, mechanical way. You no longer feel in touch with it. Nothing is coming up from within; the ḍākinīs have taken flight. When this happens, you need to allow time for the forces of inspiration to well up again. The ḍākinīs are easily disturbed, and to stay in contact with them you have to listen very carefully. Theirs is a subtle and refined form of energy, and you can't take it for granted. In other words, you need to know where your inspiration comes from and make sure that you keep the channels to that source open.

Falling into the trap of nothingness.

Milarepa balances his caution against falling into the blissful Hīnayāna peace with a warning about a danger inherent in the perfection of wisdom teachings of the Mahāyāna. This danger is that the central concept of śūnyatā or emptiness can easily be misunderstood. The unwary student is likely to interpret it nihilistically, thinking of nirvāṇa as the cessation of the conditioned and nothing beyond that, a state of nothingness. But śūnyatā is not nothingness. All things are empty, but this does not mean they do not exist; it means they are empty of anything fixed or permanent.

It is true that nothing has any unchanging essence. Everything, including you, is in constant flux. Things may be said to exist only in dependence on conditions. So everything is composite, conditioned, and nothing that the conceptualizing mind tries to pin down exists in quite the way the mind thinks it does. But the way the mind does perceive things is still useful, indeed necessary, in helping us communicate and understand things on a mundane level. Indeed, we cannot make any progress on the spiritual path without the distinctions the mind makes – without, for example, being able to make a distinction between saṃsāra and nirvāṇa. Ultimately we may have to realize the emptiness of that distinction, and that nothing at all exists as a separate entity. But it is better, as Nāgārjuna puts it, to cling to a self-view as big as Mount Meru than to get caught up in a wrong view of śūnyatā. The idea of śūnyatā is strong medicine, but it becomes strong poison if it is taken the wrong way. On the other hand, if we apprehend śūnyatā correctly, even if our understanding is limited, we will be able to appreciate our experience even as we let go of it, and act for the welfare of others without thinking of the distinction of self and other as ultimately valid – that is, without making a big fuss about it.

Thus, ignorance is the cause of fallacies and dangers.

The seventh danger is the cause of the preceding ones. It is ignorance, the mistake of believing you are a fixed entity, a self or soul, that you are marked out as special and separate from other living beings. Ignorance permeates the whole of saṁsāra, and is the root of all hindrances and obstacles to the spiritual life.

Milarepa is referring here not just to general ignorance of the mundane world, but specifically to ignorance in the sense of misunderstanding the Dharma, losing touch with the real significance of Tantric practice. Ignorance of this kind is immensely dangerous, and leads even the most sincere practitioner astray. Because the Dharma is the way to emancipation, if you use it for mundane ends while imagining you are practising correctly, you really are in trouble. The Dharma has to be approached warily, with respect. As the Buddha himself said, getting it wrong is like grabbing a snake in the wrong way: you are going to get bitten.[36]

The teaching of the Whispered Lineage is the Ḍākinīs' breath.

The ḍākinīs represent untrammelled energies whose natural medium is the openness of reality, and their breath is inspiration; appropriately, the English word 'inspiration' literally means the drawing in of breath. So the ḍākinīs' breath is the very inspiration of inspiration itself. The Whispered Lineage is pure inspiration. It is not the inspiration you get from books, from thinking, from intellectual understanding; it is not the inspiration that comes from the Freudian – or even the Jungian – unconscious. It comes straight out of the open space of reality itself, straight from the enlightened mind. You could say that the Dharma itself is the ḍākinīs' breath, the Buddha's breath. And if the Dharma doesn't inspire you, then it isn't the Dharma – at least not for you at this time. It may perhaps inspire you later, but that inspiration has to be there for the Dharma to operate as the Dharma. You may lead a good life without inspiration, but you won't get far with your spiritual life.

Milarepa is asserting that it is not enough to take your stand on books or accepted teachings or tradition, or on conventional religious life, with its ordination, its monasticism, its robes, Tantric rites, and ceremonies. No – there must be that pure inspiration from the experience of reality itself. This is the only valid basis for a spiritual tradition or school of practice. This is what the Kagyu school stands for: actual practice as opposed to any kind of verbal proliferation. To put it in an extreme way, if you can't feel the ḍākinīs' breath on your shoulder, whatever you do spiritually speaking is just hypocritical posturing. So a good motto to carry with you through the spiritual life is: don't forget the breath of the ḍākinīs.

Never doubt this truth.

The chief protection from the seven dangers comes from one's relationship with the lineage, which stretches all the way back to the Buddha. In particular it comes from one's relationship with the guru as the embodiment of the Buddha in this life. It is faith, in other words, rather than wisdom, that will be your lifeline when your Tantric practice begins to go off course. Effective Tantric practice relies, above all, on energy, on positivity and inspiration, and the chief enemy at this level is the insidious fetter of doubt, whether it is doubt in oneself or in the practices.

We have already seen how crucial this personal transmission of the Dharma is, especially in the Tantra, and even more especially in the Kagyu tradition, the Whispered Lineage. A slightly cynical, worldly impulse will very easily throw into doubt the idea that this Tibetan Buddhist school is the ḍākinīs' breath. Shiwa Aui is inspired enough at the moment, but when his inspiration deserts him, he will need to know to guard his faith. Now is the time when he must be mindful of the conditioned nature of his inspiration, and be alert enough to anticipate occasions when it may be lost, and his faith along with it.

This danger is very real. If he does come round to thinking that the lineage is not in fact experientially based, that its conclusions are merely the result of thinking about reality, then Shiwa Aui will lose faith in Milarepa himself. More importantly, he will lose faith in the unique bond that has been created by the whispered transmission. If he were ever to think that the teachings Milarepa had given him were just so much repetition, just book knowledge, a product of conjecture and supposition, his Dharma practice would be in tatters. This is why Milarepa emphasizes the breath of the ḍākinīs, and the fact that his teaching is based on his own experience – based, that is, on reality. Only by safeguarding his faith in the authenticity of Milarepa's teaching will Shiwa Aui be able to make progress in his practice.

> *Shiwa Aui, how can you ever go astray*
> *Since you are near me, the great Cotton-clad One?*

When he says 'since you are near me', Milarepa does not mean that his new disciple should necessarily stay with him physically. Our teachers do not always appear to us in the form in which we originally met them, or indeed in any human form at all, and there is no need to be afraid that in the absence of your teacher you are going to stop learning, or even stop receiving new teachings. You can receive guidance or instruction in all sorts of other ways. It can be from your own mind, from the mental states that reveal themselves to you in your practice of meditation and mindfulness, ethics and reflection. It can be from your study of the Dharma, from the sparks struck by the formulated teachings as your mind applies itself to them. It can be from nature itself; you may find, with Shakespeare's exiled Duke in *As You Like It*,

'Tongues in trees, books in the running brooks, sermons in stones, and good in everything'.[37] Being 'near the teacher' means remaining open to the teaching that is all around you, wherever you are.

It is not healthy to rely on the guru to such an extent that you are closed to the possibility of receiving instruction from other sources. If you do want to surrender yourself entirely and devotedly to your spiritual teacher, at least avoid seeing him or her in too literal and limited a way. You can listen out for your teacher even when he is nowhere near in geographical terms, and hear him speaking to you through all sorts of situations in which he plays no part at all in any literal sense.

> If there is one thing for us to take to heart
> from Milarepa's teaching, it is this:
> more and more of less and less.

Don't turn your faith and devotion into a limiting factor. The aim of education is to enable you to develop your own understanding and capacity to learn. The teaching does not come just from the teacher, it comes from the pupil too, and from the material taught. The qualities needed in oneself as an aspirant, together with the goals to which one aspires, are also teachers, especially in the form of Bodhisattvas. All these different teachers represent the communication of different facets of one reality, and they may equally be regarded as the communication of the guru.

> *Lay down your doubts and meditate.*
> *He who relies on the true Teachings will never go astray.*

Individual doubts may be dealt with by effective argument, but in the end, the doubting mind can never be laid to rest outside of practice. The 'true Teachings' are true in the sense that one can verify them for oneself, and one can obviously have full confidence in following this principle. This explains the emphasis, in the Kagyu tradition, on renunciation and unstinting spiritual practice. If there is one thing for us to take to heart from Milarepa's teaching, it is this: more and more of less and less. Concentrate more and more on those things that are simple, capable of being expressed in a few words, yet of basic importance. Make 'back to the beginning' your watchword. Keep going back to what you think you understand, what is so straightforward that you never think twice about it, and consider it, reflect on it and on how it bears on your experience of life and practice as a Buddhist. Very often we do not realize the extent to which we understand but do not practise. We think we understand a spiritual teaching because we can follow its logic, but to put it into practice, day in and day out, involves a very different kind of knowledge.

What, for example, does something as basic as the first of the five precepts really mean? Is it enough to say that it is an undertaking not to take life? It literally means 'abstain from violence to breathing beings', but what are the implications for us in terms of changing the way we relate to others? This is the way the precepts work; practising them is supposed to change us. Conversely, if you harm others you are committing two breaches of the precept at the same time: you are harming others as well as yourself.

If the first precept seems straightforward, if you think you can more or less forget about it, you are completely misunderstanding the nature of basic practices. They are basic not in the sense that they are something to leave behind, but in the sense that they are to be constantly maintained. Not hurting or harming living beings is a good start, but if you leave it at that, you are going to be applying the precept in a fairly crude and unthinking way. It should be much more creative than a self-imposed restriction on your violent and destructive impulses. It means letting go of hatred and developing respect and friendliness towards people and animals. It also includes the quality of mindfulness in one's relations with others.

More specifically, the first precept is an undertaking not to hinder or trespass on the individuality of another. What, after all, is that 'breathing being'? At the heart of the precept is the awareness that a living being is essentially a growing being, a developing being. This is the *raison d'être* of that being's existence: not only to live but to grow, to evolve. The precept asks you to consider what any living being's process of development consists in, where their energy is moving, and how to avoid getting in the way. If you see that you can assist in this process of development, then the first precept demands that support from you as well. It also involves your duty to your own development. If you hinder another, if you fail in your duty to them, you are also failing in your duty to yourself; you are hindering your own growth and development, blocking your own positive energy.

Why does this precept come first? What makes it the basis of all Buddhist practice? The answer is simple. It is the first principle of ethical and spiritual living because it allows people the space to grow in their own way. D.H. Lawrence said that the first principle of good parenting was to let the child alone – and that this was also the second and third principles. Obviously you have to stop the child falling into the fire or running into the road, but, other than that, a parent's duty is to support a child's growth rather than interfere with it. The same thing goes for the way we respond to other people and support their growth.

> If you can communicate the fact that practising
> the Dharma makes you happier and less selfish,
> that is more than enough.

It can be good to share our experience with someone who wants to talk things through, but sometimes we are too quick to follow this or even replace it with advice and subtle pressure, however friendly. Do we really know what is truly best for someone? Do we really know what constitutes growth and development for them as an individual? It is remarkable how sometimes a person who has only the vaguest idea of the direction their own life is taking can be quite definite in their analysis of the practice of others. So this is the first precept: just stand clear. Of course, don't harm beings in the obvious sense, but also allow them to evolve according to their own individuality. If we leave people unharmed but cannot resist interfering with and checking their growth, our practice of this precept still needs a lot of work.

The first precept alone therefore gives us quite a lot to be getting on with. It is perhaps surprising how little we need to know in order to practise the Dharma, and even to communicate it. It is no use trying to beat the intellectuals at their own game, but people – even intellectuals – will always be convinced by basic honesty and sincerity, by simple clarity of purpose and friendliness of demeanour. Showing that you are trying to practise one precept, and that your heart is in it, may be more impressive than being able to discourse learnedly on all the schools of Buddhist philosophy. If you can communicate the fact that practising the Dharma makes you happier and less selfish, that is more than enough.

Think not, my son, of meaningless word-knowledge
But concentrate on your devotions.
Then you will soon attain the great Accomplishment.

Meaningless word-knowledge is conceptual understanding that is not put to the test of experience. Faith based on book learning is always vulnerable to being challenged and negated by more book learning, but this is the wrong way round. The purpose of learning is to support the faith and inspiration that comes from actual practice. We should not of course forget that Milarepa's teacher, and the founder of the Kagyu lineage, Marpa, is celebrated for his book knowledge. Not for nothing is he known as Marpa the Translator; he spent much of his time making long trips to India, where he gained initiations and collected Tantric texts, bringing this wealth of literary material back to Tibet. However, Milarepa warns Shiwa Aui that theories, views, and reflections are only a guide to the truth. The experience of the truth is found in practice.

Shiwa Aui's Song of Renunciation

Milarepa's vehement warnings against the dangers of book learning are evidently heeded. We are told that from this time Shiwa Aui gives up his search for intellectual knowledge and concentrates on his devotions, to the neglect of his diet and appearance. It would seem that Milarepa has seen Shiwa Aui in the early years of his discipleship poring over texts, getting to know them and fiercely debating over the finer points of Buddhist logic. Perhaps he has expressed ambitions to become a scholar of Buddhism. Anyway, his worldly ambition clearly lingered in this form beyond his initial conversion. But now he cuts a wretched figure. As a result of his total devotion to practice he has, like Milarepa, become an emaciated and ragged-robed yogi. One day an old friend comes across him and commiserates with him over his fall from being 'a gay spark from a rich family' to his present sorry condition. In reply, Shiwa Aui sings a song that indicates how far he has come.

> Oh my Father Guru, the Jetsun, the real Buddha,
> The Field-of-Offering for my parents!

Just as a field is where you sow seeds and harvest the crop, a holy person is traditionally regarded in Buddhism as a 'field of merit' where the offerings you plant will ripen into *puṇya* or merit. Shiwa Aui's parents have, so to speak, made an offering of their son to Milarepa. The offering being so valuable and Milarepa being such a holy person, the merit that will accrue to them in future will be correspondingly abundant. Far from being the wretched failure of a rich family, as his friend is suggesting, Shiwa Aui has brought an immeasurable source of wealth to his parents. Having pointed out that he has provided well for his family's prosperity, Shiwa Aui goes on to declare his independence, indicating exactly why he is much better off without his family.

> *Brothers, sisters, and all (relatives) give rise to Saṁsāra:*
> *But I have now renounced them.*
> *The Jetsun is my sole companion and comrade in the Dharma.*
> *Alone he is my source for the Buddha's Teaching;*
> *With him, the real Buddha, I remain in solitude.*
>
> *A group of three or four leads but to empty talk,...*
>
> *Books and commentaries bring one nought but pride,*
> *But the authentic Buddha gives*
> *The one-sentence Pith-Instruction.*

Gone now is any regard for outer appearances, for his bookish, garrulous, socializing and clannish old self. Gone is any regard for worldly accumulation or the sense of group identity bound up with it. His family ties him to the samsaric realm of likes and dislikes, of empty habit and empty talk, whereas his guru offers him true communication with a true individual.

Here we find the characteristic emphasis of the Kagyu, which is to avoid too much study, group discussion, and even ritual or anything like highly organized religious practice. Instead, you have just two people living in close proximity – the enlightened teacher and the faithful disciple – with this simple but direct communication between them: 'the one-sentence Pith-Instruction', the most intensive teaching one can receive.

> *The more one has, the more one craves.*
> *So I forsake my home and renounce my native land.*
>
> *The country with no boundary-posts is the place near Buddha*
> *Wherein the faithful one can practise virtuous deeds.*
>
> *Associates and servants cause more anxiety and craving,*
> *So I renounce them for all time.*

According to the rules of conduct originally established by the Buddha, monks should not live near a frontier if they could avoid it, because of the border disputes that made such regions dangerous and disturbing. This is the most obvious sense in which the 'country with no boundary posts is the place near Buddha'. Shiwa Aui refers to this obscure rule of the *Vinaya* to highlight the deeper issue represented by boundaries: the more you possess, the more you have to defend; and the more you identify with those possessions, the more entrenched becomes your view of yourself, and the more fixed the boundary between self and other.

Shiwa Aui is not afraid to state the obvious fact that getting what we want does not provide a lasting solution to any of our problems. It is the wanting itself that is the real problem, the erroneous view that we can 'fix' reality by reorganizing the world of people and things to suit our aims and preferences. In Shiwa Aui's case, he has learned that even his most valued possessions, his family, his entourage, and all the privileges and protection that derive from being a member of a clan, cannot protect him from impermanence and death.

After this, Shiwa Aui served Milarepa until he died, and he eventually became enlightened himself. By contrast, it seems that his nephew, Sang Jye Jhab, turned out 'foolish and powerful', presiding over a small temple near Nya Non, and 'the Jetsun was slightly displeased with him'. One can imagine how this unsatisfactory disciple would have set himself up as the disciple of the great Milarepa, and lived off the offerings of the laity by performing weddings and funerals, baby-namings and crop-blessings. We can imagine him perhaps in the end becoming a married yogi with lots of disciples, and tending his little garden. Milarepa was not of course troubled within himself over this spiritual capitulation, just a little disappointed.

A Final Teaching
The meeting between Milarepa and this young nobleman at Silver Spring has archetypal qualities. It began with a normal,

happy, healthy young man with a fine family, wealth, and education, riding out to have a good time with his friends. He meets a yogi, a strange, shamelessly naked figure lying by the roadside. He doesn't much like the look of him, but he is jerked out of his initial contempt by something that doesn't make sense to him. Faith arises, faith which the yogi Milarepa tests until the young man is reduced to despair. But his joy in his faith remains, and Milarepa finally accepts him, teaches him, and trains him. The young man spends a lot of time with Milarepa, and eventually gains Enlightenment. No doubt there were many ups and downs during the five years of the young man's apprenticeship about which we are not told, but the main outlines of his story are clear and straightforward.

The Dharma can only be given, not bought.

Its main theme is the impotence of a bargaining attitude with regard to the Dharma. The Dharma cannot be bought. The young man makes his series of offerings in a spirit of real devotion but also with a degree of egoism. Above all, he assumes that what he possesses, his 'valuables', have some kind of absolute value, and that they must count for something even in exchange for the Dharma. The unspoken assumption is that if he makes these offerings, Milarepa will feel obliged to offer him some of his own valuables in return. However subtly the young man dresses this bartering for the Dharma as 'offerings', his imperfect motivation cannot be hidden from Milarepa, and the offerings are therefore rejected as unacceptable.

Because the Dharma can only be given, not bought, in a sense the young man is trying to take the not-given (to use the words of the second precept). He wants to keep hold of his ego, to get hold of the Dharma for himself, but as long as that ego is there he is not going to be able to receive the Dharma. This will, this grabbing, this ego, has to be broken down. He has to realize his complete spiritual impotence. Only then, when he starts doubting whether he has any capacity for the Dharma at all, does faith arise, and he can move forward.

In the end, the young man has to offer *himself*, and when he does this, when he no longer keeps anything of himself in reserve, there is no one left behind to expect something in exchange. When he says, 'You know what should be said,' there is no further presumption that he can tell Milarepa anything he needs to know. He knows he cannot buy Milarepa. This is when Milarepa starts to give him encouragement and teachings.

The moral of the story seems to be that you get results only after you have put all your energy into something, failed, and given up, or given in. Having tried over and over again to achieve something (in fact, to grab at it), you are eventually forced to accept defeat, to recognize that you are powerless, that your egotistic will can achieve nothing in this situation. Then something within you shifts. To take a superficial example, you might enjoy arguing, and you might try to argue various points of view with someone; but as you try one argument after another, in the end you may just have to accept that the other person has a keener intellect than yours. Only having tried your utmost do you realize your intellectual inadequacy, at least as regards reasoned argument. Whether in this or in some other way, it is good for us to try very hard, fail, and accept what that means.

At a much higher level, the Zen koan works on the same principle. You are presented with a puzzle of some kind: 'What is the sound of one hand clapping?' or 'How do you get a goose out of a bottle without breaking the bottle or injuring the goose?' You turn a riddle like this over and over in your mind, trying to work it out, thinking about it so intently that it dominates your every waking moment. You think and think and think, perhaps for years on end, until finally your reasoning powers let go their grip and your rational mind gives up – really gives up. It isn't that your mind is at a loss while it casts about for another approach, or that it simply loses interest; you experience the total impotence of the thinking mind, and that is your breakthrough, your flash of Insight with a capital 'I'. The ego has to exhaust itself against some impenetrable object.

This object may be a person, as in the case of Milarepa, or a problem, as in the case of the koan, or some situation in ordinary life, like having a strongly held view demolished by argument, or being turned down by the lover you'd set your heart on, or failing to get the qualification you'd set your sights on. Whatever it is, you find yourself unable to step forward or back. You are right up against it, and in the end you can only surrender – and this is very good for you in terms of stripping bare your egoistic will.

The whole process is much more radical when you confront not just a situation involving other unenlightened individuals, but someone like Milarepa. Someone who is enlightened knows exactly what they are doing, they can see your unenlightened egoistic will all the way down to its roots, and they are determined to root out every last fibre of it. They will close every loophole and leave you with nowhere to go, no leg to stand on, no straw to clutch. They will bring you to rock-bottom, even to despair. Only then, when you are thoroughly purged of your egoistic pride, will you get a single word of encouragement. And that is how you become a heart disciple.

Notes and References

1 Unless otherwise stated, quotations in chapters 1 and 2 are taken from Garma C.C. Chang (trans.), *The Hundred Thousand Songs of Milarepa*, Shambhala Publications, 1999, pp.1–7.

2 *Majjhima Nikāya* 10.

3 *Makhadeva Jātaka*, Jātaka 1.9.

4 *Lalitavistara* 481–2.

5 *Dīgha Nikāya* 16.1.28.

6 *Udāna* 4.4.

7 *Mahāsaccaka Sutta, Majjhima Nikāya* 36.31.

8 *Nivāpa Sutta, Majjhima Nikāya* 25.

9 Unless otherwise stated, quotations in this chapter are taken from Edward Conze (ed.), *Buddhist Texts Through the Ages*, Philosophical Library, 1954, p.258 and pp.266–7.

10 Sangharakshita (trans.), *Dhammapada*, Windhorse Publications, 2001, verse 200.

11 *Ariyapariyesanā Sutta, Majjhima Nikāya* 26.20.

12 Unless otherwise stated, quotations in this chapter are taken from Chang, op. cit., pp.161–3.

13 *Saṃyutta Nikāya* v.283, in Bhikkhu Bodhi (trans.), *The Connected Discourses of the Buddha*, Wisdom Publications, 2000, p.1741.

14 *Bodhicaryāvatāra*, 5.13.

15 Unless otherwise stated, quotations in this chapter are taken from Chang, op. cit., pp.164–70.

16 *Sāmaññaphala Sutta, Dīgha Nikāya* 2.82.

17 See page 201.

18 There are various renditions of this phrase. See, for example, Lu
    K'uan Yü, *Ch'an and Zen Teaching*, Samual Weiser, 1993, vol.1, p.31.
19 *Dhammapada* verse 203.
20 *Dhammapadaṭṭhakathā* iv.150–1.
21 *Dhammapada* verse 204.
22 W.Y. Evans-Wentz (ed.), Oxford University Press, 1928, p.96.
23 William Blake, in his preface to *Milton*.
24 *Pātimokkha*, Suddhapācittiyā 50.
25 Unless otherwise stated, quotations in this chapter are taken from
    Chang, op. cit., pp.171–2.
26 *Bhagavad-Gīta*, vii.2.
27 Lobsang P. Lhalungpa (trans.), *The Life of Milarepa*, Penguin Books,
    1995, p.48.
28 Unless otherwise stated, quotations in this chapter are taken from
    Chang, op. cit., pp.172–83.
29 Śāntideva, *Bodhicaryāvatāra*, Windhorse Publications, 2002, chapter 2,
    verse 61.
30 *Etadaggavagga*, *Aṅguttara Nikāya* i.14.
31 Lhalungpa, op.cit., pp.120–1.
32 Unless otherwise stated, quotations in this chapter are taken from
    Garma C.C. Chang, op. cit. pp.184–6.
33 *The Moment*, fourth instalment, 1855.
34 *Dhammapada* verse 5.
35 'The Sermon of the Plowers', 18 January 1548.
36 *Alagaddūpama Sutta*, *Majjhima Nikāya* 22.
37 *As You Like It*, act 2, scene 1.

Further Reading

Clarke, Sir Humphrey, *The Message of Milarepa*, John Murray, 1958

Evans-Wentz, W.Y., (editor), *Tibet's Great Yogī Milarepa*, Oxford University Press, 1928

Guenther, Herbert V. (trans.), *Jewel Ornament of Liberation*, Shambhala Publications, 2001

Guenther, Herbert V. (trans.), *The Life and Teaching of Naropa*, Shambhala Publications, 1995

Heruka, Tsang Nyön, *The Life of Marpa the Translator*, Shambhala Publications, 1986

Lhalungpa, Lobsang P. (trans.), *The Life of Milarepa*, Penguin Books, 1995

Powers, John, *Introduction to Tibetan Buddhism*, Snow Lion Publications, 1995

Sangharakshita, *Creative Symbols of Tantric Buddhism*, Windhorse Publications, 2002

Index

A

ability 137
academia 197
adi-Buddha 107
adornment 82ff
alcohol 153
anger 87
animals 24
anubhāva 112
appreciation 168
approval 127
argument 199
arhant 202
arrogance 209
art 151, 153, 185
arūpaloka 201
aspiration 142
Atīśa 1
atmosphere 22ff, 43
attachment 8, 152,
    see also ego-clinging
attainment 124, 126, 138
Augustine of Hippo
    187
avadhūtī 86

B

bandit 162
bardo 32, 72, 94
beauty 45, 150, 185f
belt 130
Benares 134
Bethnal Green 164
Bhagavad-Gīta 124
Bhari 183, 187
bindu 85, 104
Blake, William 88
Bodhicaryāvatāra 90, 152
bodhicitta 117, 159, 189
Bodhisattva 177, 194,
    202
bodhyaṅgas 57, 103
body 52, 83
boots 89ff
Brahmā Sahampati 63
brahmacarya 148
brahma-vihāras 118
breath 85
    ḍākinīs' 138, 211ff
Buddha 10, 19, 25, 32,
    63, 75f, 98
    female 65

C

calf 198
ceremony 184
chakra 86, 104
change 170
chanting 89
Chen, Yogi 22, 84
cheno 112
children 23, 151, 163
chinlap 112
Christianity 138, 173,
    187f, 191, 204
coat 101ff
Coleridge, S.T. 196
comfort 161
communication 63, 111,
    191, 200, 209, 214
companionship 14, 38,
    176, see also sangha
compassion 34, 55
competition 16
complacency 198
conceit 92, 166, 197
concepts 74
conditionality 173
conditioning 170ff

Index

confidence 189, 194
conformity 38, 158, 177
consort 147
conversion 206
corruption 204, 206
craving 28
creativity 138
custom 157

D
ḍākinī 65, 137, 209, 211
dāna 115, 205
dangers 164
    seven 203ff
death 32, 72, 97, 149,
    179f
debate 197
deer parable 36
deity 43, *see also* spirits
Dem Chog 73
demon 10, 21ff, 25
desire 150, 165, 201, 220
devaloka 25
devil 173, 208
devotion 12ff
dhamma-chanda 150
Dhammapada 54, 103,
    110
Dhardo Rimpoche 125
Dharma Wonshu 69ff,
    175, *and passim*
dharmakāya 98ff
dhyāna 32, 81, 92,
    see also meditation
Diamond Sūtra 124
disciples 66, 111

distractions *see*
    hindrances
doctrine follower 149
Dorje Lamo 126
Dorje-Chang 107
doubt 212ff
dream 64, 72, 94

E
eagle 31
economics 205
ego 8, 92, 128, 200, 222
ego-clinging 11, 93
emotion 200, *see also*
    mettā, negativity
encouragement 168
energy 82, 83–9, 101ff,
    154, 185, 212, 222
enjoyment 185, *see also*
    happiness, joy
Enlightenment 64, 96,
    103, 117, 152, 193, 203
environment 21ff, 186
equanimity 51, 58
escape 36
ethics 89, 95, 115, 157
evil 173
evolution 138
expectation 139

F
faith 167, 214
faith follower 149
fashion 156ff
fault-finding 128
fear 48ff, 56, 162

fearlessness 52
fetter 9
folklore 22
food 148, 153
forest 23f
friendliness 118, 215, 217
friendship 15, 196, 176

G
gang culture 116
Gelug school 197
gender 172
generosity 115, 205
gifts 78ff, 134, 143,
    see also offerings
    belt 130
    boots 89ff
    coat 101ff
    hat 105
    horse 79ff
    jacket 93ff
    jade 108
    knife 130
    mandala 145
    marriage 146
    temple 143ff
    trousers 155ff
Glastonbury 23
goal 47
going for refuge 39, 196
grace 112
gratitude 106
guilt 187
guru 13, 68, 75, 107, 111,
    125–42, 212, 214, 219
guru yoga 12, 105

H

habit 150
happiness 140, *see also*
  enjoyment, joy
hardship 161
hat 105
heat 53, 102
Herrick, Robert 176
hierarchy 17, 153, 207
Hīnayāna 202
hindrances 9, 49, 211
honesty 163, 217
horse 79ff
humility 194

I

ideal 121
identity 175
ignorance 211
imagination 100
impermanence 176,
  179, 210
indecision 125
India 24
individualism 203
influence 112
initiation 73
inner yogas 85
insight 11, 12, 75, 77, 100,
  112, 125
inspiration 4, 37, 65,
  137, 138, 209ff
isolation 59

J

jacket 93ff
jade 108

Jātaka 12
jewel 53, *see also*
  adornment
jewel parable 47
Johnson, Samuel 15
joy 50, 150, 154, 167,
  see also happiness
judgement 128f
Jung, Carl 168

K

Kagyu school 13, 111,
  207, 212, 219
Kalimpong 2, 10, 22,
  114, 125, 186
kāma-chanda 150
kāmaloka 201
karma 9, 66ff, 96, 170,
  189
karma vipāka 170
Khamba 113
Kierkegaard, Soren 191
kindness 168
knife 130
knowledge 123, 218
koan 222
Krishna 124

L

lama 114, *see also* guru
Latimer, Hugh 208
laughter 48
Lawrence, D.H. 216
laziness 139, 141
leadership 17
limitation 171
lineage 105, 212

loneliness 15, 53, 57,
  see also solitude
Lotus Sūtra 47, 202
love *see* friendship,
  mettā, romance

M

madness 208
mahāmudrā 8, 68, 73
Mahāparinibbāna Sutta
  25
mandala 145
Mañjughoṣa 119
Mañjuśrī 18
Māra 19, 173, 208
Marpa 12, 18, 67ff, 72,
  127, 168, 217
marriage 146
median nerve 82, 86
meditation 32, 193, 197
  brahma-vihāras 90,
    118
  and desire 165,
  and energy 103, 121,
    151, 208
  and fear 48ff
  and place 23, 43
  its effects 81, 84
  and rapture 54, 92,
    103
  see also mindfulness
men 17, 172
merit 117, 170, 218
metaphor 121,
  see also parables
mettā 118
mettā bhavānā 90

Index

Milarepa as green 2
Millais, John 137
mindfulness 8, 34, 179, 193, 215
miracle 71, *see also* sorcery, supernormal power
money 130, 137ff, *see also* wealth
monkey 57
morality *see* ethics
motivation 149
music 2ff, 151, 153

N
nāḍī 85
Nāgārjuna 210
nakedness 11, 124, 155
name 175
Nāropa 72
nature 25, *see also* animals, trees
negativity 87, 89
nettles 2
nihilism 210
nirmāṇakāya 76, 99ff
nirvāṇa *see* Enlightenment
novelty 126

O
obedience 127
offerings 79ff, 143ff, 221, *see also* gifts
old age 12, *see also* youth

openness 199
ordination 206

P
Padmaloka 23
Padmasambhava 25
parables
    deer 36
    jewel 47
    snake 211
parenting 216
patronage 204
payment 130, 137ff
perception 210
perfection of wisdom 210
perseverance 222
Plato 185
playwords 74
pleasure 150ff, 176, 185
possessions 220f
power 34, 127
    psychic 70
praise 154, 194
prajñā 55, 73
prāṇa 85, *see also* energy
pranāyāma 208
precepts 173, 196, 215ff
preta 28
pride 93, 166, 223
prīti 54, 103
psychic power 70
puṇya 117, 170, 218

R
rapture 54, 103
rationality 200
reality 46
rebirth 97, 171
receptivity 133
refuge 20, 39, 196
religion 192, 204, *see also* Christianity
renunciation 39, 90, 113, 148, 154, 207, 215
repression 88
respectability 156
retreat 36, 81
ritual 184, 204
river 69
robber 162
romance 171
rose-apple tree 32
rules 157
rūpaloka 201
Ryōkan 121

S
sacrifice *see* renunciation
Sakura 163
samādhi 121, *see also* meditation
sambhogakāya 98ff
saṃsāra 96, 117, 150, 207, 211
saṃvara 73
Sang Jye Jhab 220
sangha 13ff, 37, 38, 172, 205

Śāntideva 90, 152
Sāriputta 26, 106
Satipaṭṭhāna Sutta 8
security 162
self 211, *see also* ego
self-view 9
sensuality 188
sex 148f, 172
Shakespeare, W. 213
shame 158, 162
Shiwa Aui 187ff *and*
   passim
śīla *see* ethics
simplicity 215
six yogas 72
snake parable 211
Socrates 192
solitude 45,
   see also loneliness
songs of Milarepa 2ff
sorcery 67,
   see also miracle
speech 191, *see also*
   communication
spirits 22ff, *see also* deity
spirit fox 97
spiritual community
   see sangha
spontaneity 142
storm 7ff
struggle 34
suffering 50
śūnyatā 45, 83, 210
supernormal power
   125, *see also* miracle

T
Tantra 72, 83ff, 89, 93,
   102, 131, 193, 204, 208
teacher *see* guru
teaching 63, 110, 138,
   191, 194ff, 205, 209
temple 143ff
Tibet 1
   language 3
   people 69
tiger 56
tiger's cave 44
trees 23f, 32
trikāya 98ff
trousers 155ff
truth 199,
   see also reality
truthfulness 162,
   see also speech
Tsongkhapa 56
tumo 53, 72, 102
two-in-one 55

U
Udāna 4

V
vajra 107
vajrācārya 13
Vajradhara 107
vajra-gīta 4
vajra-guru 13, 68,
   see also guru
Vajrayāna 83ff, 100
vanity 209

vegetarianism 153
violence 115, 215ff
vīrya 121
visualization 12, 14, 72,
   100, 102
void 45, 83, 210
vow 171, 189ff

W
walking on water 70
warrior 119ff
wealth 108, 110, 172,
   see also money
weapons 113ff
Wesley, Charles 138
Western Buddhist
   Order 175
wisdom 55, 73
women 44, 65, 172
work 123, 140

Y
yab-yum 73
Yaśodharā 171
yidam 100
yoga 12, 72, 85, 105
Yogācāra school 46, 73,
   98
Yolmo 43
youth 31,
   see also old age
yuganaddha 55

Z
Zen 12, 47, 97

The windhorse symbolizes the energy of the Enlightened mind carrying the truth of the Buddha's teachings to all corners of the world. On its back the windhorse bears three jewels: a brilliant gold jewel represents the Buddha, the ideal of Enlightenment, a sparkling blue jewel represents the teachings of the Buddha, the Dharma, and a glowing red jewel, the community of the Buddha's enlightened followers, the Sangha. Windhorse Publications, through the medium of books, similarly takes these three jewels out to the world.

Windhorse Publications is a Buddhist publishing house, staffed by practising Buddhists. We place great emphasis on producing books of high quality, accessible and relevant to those interested in Buddhism at whatever level. Drawing on the whole range of the Buddhist tradition, our books include translations of traditional texts, commentaries, books that make links with Western culture and ways of life, biographies of Buddhists, and works on meditation.

As a charitable institution we welcome donations to help us continue our work. We also welcome manuscripts on aspects of Buddhism or meditation. For orders and catalogues log on to www.windhorsepublications.com or contact:

Windhorse Publications   Consortium   Windhorse Books
11 Park Road   1045 Westgate Drive   PO Box 574
Birmingham   St Paul MN 55114   Newtown NSW 2042
B13 8AB   USA   Australia
UK

Windhorse Publications is an arm of the Friends of the Western Buddhist Order, which has more than sixty centres on four continents. Through these centres, members of the Western Buddhist Order offer regular programmes of events for the general public and for more experienced students. These include meditation classes, public talks, study on Buddhist themes and texts, and bodywork classes such as t'ai chi, yoga, and massage. The FWBO also runs several retreat centres and the Karuna Trust, a fundraising charity that supports social welfare projects in the slums and villages of India.

Many FWBO centres have residential spiritual communities and ethical businesses associated with them. Arts activities are encouraged too, as is the development of strong bonds of friendship between people who share the same ideals. In this way the FWBO is developing a unique approach to Buddhism, not simply as a set of techniques, but as a creatively directed way of life for people living in the modern world.

If you would like more information about the FWBO please visit the website at www.fwbo.org or write to:

London Buddhist Centre
51 Roman Road
London
E2 0HU
UK

Aryaloka
14 Heartwood Circle
Newmarket NH 03857
USA

Sydney Buddhist Centre
24 Enmore Road
Sydney NSW 2042
Australia

ALSO FROM WINDHORSE PUBLICATIONS

LIVING WITH KINDNESS:

THE BUDDHA'S TEACHING ON METTA
by Sangharakshita

'Just as a mother would protect her only child at the risk of her own life – let thoughts of boundless love pervade the whole world.' Karaniya Metta Sutta

Kindness is one of the most basic qualities we can possess, and one of the most powerful. In Buddhism it is called metta – an opening of the heart to all that we meet. This book takes us step by step through the Buddha's words in the *Karaniya Metta Sutta* to consider its meaning, its ethical foundations, and its cultivation, culmination, and realization. Excellent for beginners and an insightful refresher for those looking for another way to engage with metta.

> 'Will help both Buddhists and people of other faiths to come to a deeper understanding of the true significance of kindness as a way of life and a way of meditation.' *Pure Land Notes*

160 pages
ISBN 1 899579 64 8
£9.99/$14.95/€14.95

LIVING WITH AWARENESS:

A GUIDE TO THE SATIPATTHANA SUTTA
by Sangharakshita

Paying attention to how things look, sound, and feel makes them more enjoyable; it is as simple (and as difficult) as that.

Mindfulness and the breath – this deceptively simple yet profound teaching in the *Satipatthana Sutta* is the basis of much insight meditation practice today. By looking at aspects of our daily life, such as Remembering, Looking, Dying, and Reflecting, Sangharakshita shows how broad an application the practice of mindfulness can have – and how our experience can be enriched by its presence.

200 pages
ISBN 1 899579 38 9
£11.99/$17.95/€17.95

MEDITATION:

THE BUDDHIST WAY OF TRANQUILLITY AND INSIGHT
by Kamalashila

A clear and comprehensive handbook of Buddhist meditation for both beginners and the more experienced – what meditation is and where it might take us. This book covers all you need to know on how to establish a meditation practice, as well as helpful advice and greater detail for those wishing to deepen their experience of meditation. Complete with photographs, charts, and diagrams.

> 'This is a truly practical guide to read, enjoy and use. A great addition to the meditator's bookshelf.'   *Yoga and Health*

304 pages, b/w photos, charts
ISBN 1 899579 05 2
£13.99/$21.95/€21.95

WILDMIND:

A STEP-BY-STEP GUIDE TO MEDITATION
by Bodhipaksa

Buddhist meditation teacher Bodhipaksa shows us how we can use simple meditation practices to realize the potential of our minds and hearts, freeing ourselves from restrictive habits and fears and developing a more loving heart and a clearer mind. Drawn from the very successful online meditation website, www.wildmind.org, it is written in short sections to encourage reflection and for practices to 'sink in'.

> 'one of the most comprehensive and accessible books on the subject'
> *Good Reading*

256 pages, b/w photos
ISBN 1 899579 55 9
£11.99/$18.95/€18.95

MEETING THE BUDDHAS:

A GUIDE TO THE BUDDHAS, BODHISATTVAS, AND TANTRIC DEITIES
by Vessantara

This best-selling book invites us on a vivid and inspiring journey to the magical heart of Buddhist visualization and devotional practices. With Vessantara as our experienced guide, we are introduced to the main Buddhas, Bodhisattvas, and Tantric deities we may be fortunate to meet in that miraculous realm. This unique 'encyclopedia' of the Buddhas and Bodhisattvas in the Indo-Tibetan tradition is an incomparable – and inspiring – resource.

'Attentive reading could become a devotional act in itself.'
The Bloomsbury Review

376 pages, 36 b/w illustrations, 27 colour plates
ISBN 0 904766 53 5
£16.99/$27.95/€27.95

FEMALE DEITIES IN BUDDHISM:

A CONCISE GUIDE
by Vessantara

Female deities in Buddhism take many forms to inspire, beguile, rouse, and protect us. Respected Western Buddhist teacher Vessantara invites us to learn more about ourselves as women and men by reflecting on these enlightened beings. Within us lie the seeds of love, wisdom, and freedom that these figures symbolize in their fullness.

'My thanks to Vessantara for a treasure trove of fascinating information, explanation, and anecdote on the feminine divine. This is an invaluable introductory source book.' **Sandy Boucher**

'Deep and profound, yet easy to read' *Pure Land Notes*

144 pages, 8 colour plates
ISBN 1 899579 53 2
£8.99/$12.95/€12.95

EXPLORING KARMA & REBIRTH

by Nagapriya

Every Buddhist should read it. **David Loy**
An excellent introduction **Stephen Batchelor**
Cogent, knowledgeable, and penetrating **Norman Fischer**

Exploring Karma & Rebirth helps us to unravel the complexities of these two important but often misunderstood Buddhist doctrines. Clarifying, examining, and considering them, it offers an imaginative reading of what the teachings could mean for us now. Informative and thought provoking, *Exploring Karma & Rebirth* insists that, above all, to be of enduring value these doctrines must continue to serve the overriding aim of Buddhism: spiritual awakening.

176 pages
ISBN 1 899579 61 3
£8.99/$13.95/€13.95